In this innovative introduction, Robert Layton reviews the ideas that have inspired anthropologists in their studies of societies around the world. *An introduction to theory in anthropology* provides a clear and concise analysis of the theories, and traces the way in which they have been translated into anthropological debates. The opening chapter sets out the classical theoretical issues formulated by Hobbes, Rousseau, Marx and Durkheim. Successive chapters discuss Functionalism, Structuralism, Interaction theories, and Marxist anthropology, while the final chapters address the competing paradigms of Socioecology and Postmodernism. Using detailed case studies, Professor Layton illustrates the way in which various theoretical perspectives have shaped competing, or complementary, accounts of specific human societies.

An introduction to theory in anthropology

An introduction to theory in anthropology

ROBERT LAYTON
University of Durham

CAMBRIDGE
UNIVERSITY PRESS

PUBLISHED BY THE PRESS SYNDICATE OF THE UNIVERSITY OF CAMBRIDGE
The Pitt Building, Trumpington Street, Cambridge CB2 1RP, United Kingdom

CAMBRIDGE UNIVERSITY PRESS
The Edinburgh Building, Cambridge, CB2 2RU, United Kingdom
40 West 20th Street, New York, NY 10011-4211, USA
10 Stamford Road, Oakleigh, Melbourne 3166, Australia

First published 1997
Reprinted 1998 (twice)

Printed in the United Kingdom at the University Press, Cambridge

Typeset in Minion 10½/13pt [CP]

A catalogue record for this book is available from the British Library

Library of Congress Cataloguing in Publication data
Layton, Robert, 1944–
    An introduction to theory in anthropology / Robert Layton.
        p.   cm.
    ISBN 0 521 62018 X (hardcover)
    1. Anthropology–Philosophy.   2. Anthropology–Methodology.
I. Title.
GN33.L37   1997
301'.01–dc21   97-10237 CIP

ISBN 0 521 62018 X hardback
ISBN 0 521 62982 9 paperback

Contents

Figures

Tables

Note on the text

This book is not designed to provide a complete history of anthropological thought. The book has been written with an eye to current debates and it focuses upon the way in which theories have impinged upon anthropology rather than tracing their history in full. The application of each theory is exemplified by showing how they have helped explain social and cultural processes among particular peoples. Where possible, I have tried to show how different theories provide complementary, or competing interpretations of the same ethnographic cases. I consider that the most important theories at present are those of Socioecology and Postmodernism and have been influenced, in selecting earlier theories for discussion, by their contribution to the development of current theoretical debate. Diffusionism is not reviewed and the idea of evolution as progress probably receives less coverage than it deserves. Even in the theoretical fields that are considered, many important writers and works have not been mentioned. Going back to the sources which are discussed, I invariably found that they were far richer in ideas than any secondary source could indicate. The book is intended to orientate readers towards the original texts, rather than to replace them. The publisher's anonymous readers have made many helpful comments and recommendations which improved the final text.

CHAPTER ONE

The idea of a social system

Anthropology is the study of people; social anthropology is the study of human society. Social anthropology can be described as 'comparative sociology', which is the study of the vast range of human societies in order to develop general theories about how societies work. More particularly, social anthropology has often been regarded as the study of 'small-scale' societies, whose relative simplicity makes them easier to study in their entirety. Social anthropology can also be characterised as 'the translation of culture'; making sense of the apparently exotic customs of unfamiliar peoples.

In about 450 BC, the Greek historian Herodotus wrote an account of the events which had ultimately led, a generation earlier, to the Greek defeat of the Persians. Herodotus' idea was that the Persians' defeat was not caused solely by the deeds of great men, nor from the will of the gods. Herodotus explained the Persians' defeat as the outcome of conflict between alien cultures. This justified his documentation of the cultures which surrounded the ancient Greeks and, to substantiate his argument, he provided detailed accounts of contemporary societies very different from his own, tracing the history of their contact with the Persian empire. He has, therefore, been described as the father of anthropology (Gould 1989: 1). Herodotus portrays an ancient world of tantalising cultural diversity, in which familiar values are often put into question by the unexpected or exotic. The Scythians, who lived north of the Black Sea, were invincible because of their nomadic way of life. A people who lacked fortified towns and lived in wagons which they took with them wherever they went, who fought on horseback and depended on cattle rather than fields for their subsistence, could never be defeated. There were no trees in Scythian territory and, whenever they killed a cow, the Scythians made a fire of the bones to cook the meat. As soon as Cyrus invaded Scythian territory, the Scythians moved on. On the only occasion the Persian and Scythian armies confronted each other, the Scythians were diverted by a hare which jumped up from the grass between the armies. The Scythians revealed their contempt for the Persians by galloping off in pursuit of the hare (Herodotus 1954: 286ff.). Another good example of Herodotus' technique is provided by the episode in which Cambyses sends envoys to people whom Herodotus knew as the Ethiopians. The Persian king had sent his agents to spy out the land in preparation for conquest, but instructed them to appear friendly. Hoping to overawe the Ethiopians with their sophistication, the envoys offered the king of Ethiopia various presents, including dyed fabric and wine. To their surprise, he dismissed dyeing as a trick which made things appear other than they were. Although he liked the taste of the wine, the king ridiculed Persian food as 'dung', remarking that they must need the wine to survive into old age on such a diet. The Ethiopians, said the king, lived to the age of 120 by drinking milk and eating boiled meat. Cambyses was enraged when he heard of the king's reply but, not surprisingly, the subsequent Persian invasion was a failure (Herodotus 1954: 211–12).

The Roman historian Tacitus used similar techniques in his account of the German tribes living on the edge of the Roman empire in about AD 100. Tacitus, less patriotic than Herodotus, implicitly opposed the honest, simple lives of the Germans with the decadent indulgence of life in Rome. He also wished to assess the military threat the Germans posed to the Roman empire, which he did by investigating the form of German society. The Germans had wide tracts of cultivable land available and every community allocated fresh plough land to each household, each year. Germanic local democracy was conducted in a very different style to the Roman Senate: 'When the assembled crowd thinks fit they take their seats fully armed . . . If a proposal displeases them, the people shout their dissent; if they approve, they clash their spears.' Silver vessels presented to chiefs and ambassadors when they travelled abroad could be seen in their houses, put to the same everyday uses as earthenware (Tacitus 1985: 104, 110, 123).

Ethnography, or 'writing about peoples' is the descriptive tradition in anthropology. Complete description is impossible. Consciously or otherwise, our ideas and assumptions lead us to notice certain aspects of peoples' social life, but to disregard others. Neither Tacitus nor Herodotus were disinterested in their subject. Both set out to document unfamiliar cultures in order to support an argument, yet archaeological evidence has confirmed some of their statements, such as the elaborate burial customs of the Scythians and the agricultural system and village organisation of the Germanic peoples (Herodotus 1954: 294n.; Hedeager 1992: 205, 230, 250). Theory directs our attention to particular features of social behaviour, and suggests connections between what we observe and hear. The theories of evolution as progress which dominated the social sciences in the nineteenth century encourage a broad gaze across cultural diversity, while interactionist theories promote a close focus upon the details of individual actions. Some theories grow out of others which have come to seem inadequate. Socioecology, for example, supplants Functionalism as a way of explaining the connections between customs. In other cases, theories collide head-on: Marxism explains social life in terms of its material consequences; Structuralism explains it as the outcome of ideas and values. Whether there are general explanatory laws of social life, or whether every society must be understood in its own terms, remains a lively issue in anthropology. Theories are not idle speculation. Wherever they guide practical action, they have political implications. Many of the theories to be outlined here originated in attempts to make sense of the writer's own social condition, and to place it in the context of other, seemingly exotic, ways of living in society.

Framing the modern questions

The problems which have preoccupied recent social anthropology are rather different to those which interested Herodotus and Tacitus. They were first formulated during the Enlightenment. Theories which attempt to resolve these problems were established at the same time. Until the seventeenth and eighteenth centuries, European kings had been believed to rule by Divine Right, and human society was supposed to reproduce, on a lower scale, the Divine society of Heaven. These assumptions were questioned during the Enlightenment (see Watson 1991). Once people considered themselves free to decide for themselves what was, or was not, proper social behaviour according to natural rather than divine law it became possible to ask both how actual societies might be improved, and how present societies had diverged from the natural, or original human condition. Both the European past and more exotic but living, human societies were seen as sources of information that could help answer these questions. The quality of the evidence and the techniques for assessing it were greatly inferior to those found in the work of Herodotus and Tacitus (compare Trigger 1989: 55–60).

During the years leading to the Civil War in England, supporters of Parliament who opposed the king's claim to rule by Divine Right relied on Tacitus' account of ancient Germanic democracy. They argued that these customs had been brought to England by the Anglo-Saxons and historically transmitted to their own time via English common law. Royalists argued to the contrary that current common law had been brought to England by William the Conqueror, extinguishing any liberties that might previously have existed. While most participants in the debate assumed that Germanic society had been historically unique, the Levellers took the argument a step further by contending that ancient Germanic society was the 'original human condition' which revealed the natural rights of man prior to the appropriation of land by a wealthy elite and thus, in a sense, inaugurating a general theory of human society (see Burrow 1981; Hill 1958; MacDougall 1982).

Hobbes (1588–1679), who was at one time tutor to the future King Charles II, experienced the disorder caused by the English Civil War and asked what it was that holds a society together. Contrary to the primitive communalism postulated by the Levellers, Hobbes envisaged the opposite condition to regulated social life as one of random disorder, in which people sought their own self-preservation by trying to control others. Such a condition would be a war of every man against every other man, and life would be 'solitary, poore, nasty, brutish and short' (Hobbes 1970 [1651]: 65). Hobbes imagined that people living in such a condition would therefore be compelled to choose a leader, or sovereign, and surrender sufficient of their personal freedom to the sovereign to give him the power he needed to uphold a social contract. People would only be willing to work for the general good if they could be confident that anyone cheating would be punished by law. Hobbes offered virtually no evidence that his war of each against all had ever existed, although he did remark that 'For the savage people in many places in America, except the government of small families, the concord whereof dependeth on naturall lust, have no government at all;

and live at this day in that brutish manner' (Hobbes 1970 [1651]: 65). Hobbes' main aim was to construct a logical opposition between order and disorder, rather than to identify an actual condition against which contemporary European society could be assessed (Hill 1958: 271).

Rousseau (1712–72), a diplomat and citizen of Geneva during the last years of the feudal *ancien régime*, took a different view again of the original human society. Like the Levellers, Rousseau regarded the European regimes of his time as oppressive. In his essay on *The Social Contract* he wrote, 'Man is born free; and everywhere he is in chains' (Rousseau 1963 [1762]: 3). Admitting that he did not know how people had originally lived, he hypothesised in the *Discourse on the Origin of Inequality* that they must first have existed as isolated individuals in a state of nature, satisfying their meagre wants immediately but rarely, if ever, coming into contact with one another. But humans are not like animals. Animals are nothing more than machines wound up by nature, whereas 'Man' acts through free will. Rousseau guessed that people formed an association when natural sources of food began to be depleted and people turned to agriculture, banding together to defend their tilled land against others who wanted to annexe it. 'All ran head-long to their chains, in the hopes of securing their liberty' (Rousseau 1963 [1755]: 205).

Rousseau relied on descriptions of the contemporary, exotic people of the Caribbean as support for his reconstruction of the original human condition. Just as he imagined the original human to have had few wants, 'satisfying his hunger at the first oak, and slaking his thirst at the first brook' (Rousseau 1963 [1755]: 163), so the eighteenth-century Caribbean will reportedly sell you his bed in the morning, not having anticipated that he would need it again, and ask for it back in the evening (for Rousseau's source, see du Tertre 1992 [1667]: 133). Similarly, 'the Caribbeans, who have as yet least of all deviated from the state of nature' are the most peaceable of people in their love affairs and far from the selfish individuals imagined by Hobbes (Rousseau 1963 [1755]: 187). 'What a sight would the perplexing and envied labours of a European minister of State present to the eyes of a Caribbean!' (Rousseau 1963 [1755]: 220). Even the rich now depend on the service of others but, as long as people wandered freely as individuals, no one could exact obedience or servitude from another. The many desires of Hobbes' savage, such as covetousness, ambition and magnanimity, are in fact the product of society: 'The first man who, having enclosed a piece of ground, bethought himself of saying "this is mine", and found people simple enough to believe him, was the real founder of civil society' (Rousseau 1963 [1755]: 192).

Social systems

The founding fathers of social anthropology were struck by the way in which, during social life, people were influenced by the thoughts and actions of those around them, giving rise to the concept of society as a system of interrelated parts. Although a general theory of systems was not developed until the mid-twentieth century (von Bertalanffy 1951), two qualities of systems were already apparent to eighteenth- and nineteenth-century theorists. A system is made up of a set of components which are interrelated in such a way that the properties of the whole are different to those which the components exhibit in isolation. The whole has a degree of internal coherence and a recognisable boundary so that it tends to persist as a system rather than break down and merge with its environment (cf. Buckley 1967).

For Hobbes, people were constrained by each other's actions because they, or their ancestors, had entered into a social contract. This contract prevented them from acting entirely of their own free will, but benefited everyone. Rousseau similarly regarded society, not as a natural thing but a 'sum of forces (which) can only arise when several persons come together'. If any individual rights remained, this would perpetuate the state of nature. Each associate must give himself up, not to an individual sovereign, but to the collectivity or association by obeying 'the supreme direction of the general will' (Rousseau 1963 [1762]: 12–13). The apparent paradox of a whole greater than the sum of its parts was, for Rousseau, exemplified by the problem of the origin of language. If language originated in the use of arbitrary or conventional signs, how could these be agreed without the prior existence of society? Such signs could only be agreed by common consent (Rousseau 1963 [1755]: 176–7). Yet how could society come into being without the prior existence of concepts such as *property*, or *mutual interest*? Rousseau surmises that such ideas could have been signified with the kind of cries used by rooks or monkeys and that, thereafter, language and society developed together.

Two general approaches to explaining the way in which social systems come into being emerged during the eighteenth and nineteenth centuries. These can be called the interactionist and the organic. Adam

Smith proposed an interactionist theory, according to which the social order emerges from the interaction of individuals pursuing their self-interest. Smith considered that society was brought about by the division of labour. The division of labour was not created by wisdom or foresight, but had its origin in a natural human propensity, 'to truck, barter, and exchange one thing for another' (Smith 1976 [1776]: 25). Smith noted that the propensity to exchange was uniquely human, since no one had ever seen two dogs exchange bones, yet humans depended upon one another in countless ways. It would be useless to rely on others' benevolence. People are more likely to gain what they need by appealing to others' self-interest. 'It is not from the benevolence of the butcher, the brewer, or the baker, that we expect our dinner, but from their regard to their own self-interest' (Smith 1976 [1776]: 27). Since, in the society of his own time and place, most goods were exchanged by trade or barter, Smith imagines the division of labour originating through barter in simple societies:

> In a tribe of hunters or shepherds a particular person makes bows and arrows, for example, with more readiness and dexterity than any other. He frequently exchanges them for cattle or for venison ... he finds at last that he can in this manner get more cattle or venison, than if he himself went into the field to catch them (Smith 1976 [1776]: 27).

Once the division of labour has begun the productive powers of labour are increased, but only to the extent that the division of labour allows. Among the Hottentots of southern Africa, specialists can only partially support themselves from their trade; even an English village carpenter cannot specialise in building carts or cabinets (Smith 1976 [1776]: 32n.). The more that can be obtained by exchange, however, the harder everyone will work to produce a surplus to trade, causing 'in a well-governed society, that universal opulence which extends itself to the lowest ranks of the people' (Smith 1976 [1776]: 22). The differences between a philosopher and a workman are almost entirely the product, rather than the cause, of the division of labour achieved by the market.

Comte (writing during the first half of the nineteenth century) took the opposing view that, far from originating in a contract between free individuals, humans are intrinsically social beings. Society has organs, like the body of an animal, in which the function of the part is determined by its place in the whole. The notion of the 'individual' is a social construct, derived from the role which society assigns to individual action. This has become known as the 'organic analogy'. Herbert Spencer developed the analogy during the middle years of the nineteenth century, regarding social progress as the consequence of the evolution of social systems. Spencer considered that societies develop like animal or plant organisms. In contrast to Darwin's theory of natural selection, in which random variations between individuals in a population have different consequences for survival in a particular environment, Spencer's theory embodied an internal dynamic driving populations towards increasing complexity. Just as the embryo begins as a small clump of undifferentiated cells and develops into a complex system of tissues and organs, so human societies become increasingly differentiated through time (Spencer 1972 [1857]: 39). Since all societies must follow the same developmental sequence, any existing or past society can be classified according to its degree of complexity. Contemporary, but simple societies retain what were once universal levels of organisation. The simplest societies resemble organisms in which the body is segmented into many similar parts but, in the most complex societies, every part plays a unique role. None the less, the policies of government will only succeed if they conform to the wishes of the collectivity (Spencer 1972 [1860]: 55, 64).

The formulation of general theories

Among the authors whose ideas are summarised above, only Smith and Comte elaborated a detailed theory that could be put to the test. The thinkers who most influenced the development of anthropological theory were Durkheim and Marx, who took the ideas of the social contract, evolution as cumulative change, and the generation of social relationships through exchange, and developed them into well-argued bodies of theory. Comte influenced Durkheim and Smith influenced Marx.

Marx (1818–1883)

Marx was active fifty years before Durkheim but his influence on anthropology was less immediate, and his theory of how social systems work is more complex. Marx and Darwin were contemporaries. Marx's book *A Contribution to the Critique of Political Economy* was published in the same year as *The Origin of Species*. Whereas Darwin upset the Church by denying that God had created a fixed number of species at a single moment, Marx upset the political establishment by denying the universal benefits of the capitalist system. Darwin's theory of natural selection was, like Spencer's theory of evolution, consonant with the capitalist market ethic in which competition eliminated the weak or maladapted and favoured the strongest, or best adapted. Rather than implicitly condoning nineteenth-century industrial society, Marx interpreted it as irremediably unjust.

Marx took four ideas from Adam Smith:

1 Social relationships are generated by exchange.
2 A person can produce more than he requires for his own subsistence (Smith 1976 [1776]: 22).
3 The power conferred by the ownership of money is the power to buy other people's labour (Smith 1976 [1776]: 48).
4 While supply and demand may cause the value of a good to fluctuate, its true or natural value is determined by the cost of the labour required to make it (Smith 1976 [1776]: 47).

But, whereas Adam Smith argued that the market produced universal improvement in people's wealth, Marx argued that it created inequalities.

Marx was writing at a time when urban slums housed ten or more people to a room, with perhaps only one bed between three; when children of eight years old were already at work and the working day lasted between ten and fifteen hours. It was clear to Marx that universal opulence had not extended itself to the lowest ranks of the people. Marx recognised that social systems have unique properties which cannot be reduced to individual motivation or, as Hegel had argued, the general development of the human mind. 'In the social production of their existence men inevitably enter into definite relations which are independent of their will ... It is not the consciousness of men that determines their existence, but their social existence that determines their consciousness' (Marx 1971 [1859]: 20–1). Unlike Durkheim, Marx regarded social systems as inherently unstable, rather than normally existing in a stable condition. In the terms of mid-twentieth-century systems theory, Durkheim later identified processes of *negative feedback*, such as punishment for deviance from social norms, which tended to restore equilibrium. Marx aimed to identify processes of *positive feedback*, which would increase the effect of any deviation from stability. Marx found the driving force of social instability in the capacity of human beings to produce, by their own labour, more than they needed to subsist. He recognised that the way in which a social system controlled people's access to the resources they needed was equally fundamental. The concept of property arises from the character of society. Marx echoed Rousseau in his observation that 'an isolated individual could no more possess property in land than he could speak. At most he could live off it as a source of supply like the animals' (Marx 1964: 81–2). The way in which people exchange the goods they produce but do not keep for their own subsistence, their 'surplus production', is also a characteristic of the social system, because each individual needs others to exchange with. Patterns of exchange depend in turn on a division of labour, and different social systems divide their members' labour in different ways. The various forms which the three social traits take, in combination, constitute *modes of production*. Each mode of production has three aspects:

> a distinctive principle determining property;
> a distinctive division of labour;
> a distinctive principle of exchange.

Like Durkheim and other nineteenth-century social theorists, Marx conceived of social evolution as the consequence of an internal social dynamic rather than as adaptation to an environment. Although Marx's evolutionary scheme had several alternative pathways, rather than constituting a single ladder of development, the dynamic processes still tended to drive social change in a particular direction. Even Darwin, in fact, had difficulty grasping the inherent relativity of his model of natural selection and had to write notes to himself that 'I must not talk about higher and lower forms of life' (Trivers 1985: 32).

A fundamental element of Marx's analysis of society was his theory of how the items which are exchanged acquired value. In contrast to the liberal economic theory that the value of goods is determined solely by supply and demand, Marx argued that the basic value of goods is determined by the amount of labour needed to produce them. Supply and demand merely have a secondary effect. If several different items are produced by the same quantity of labour, each will have the same value. Conversely, if the same item can be produced by two techniques which require different amounts of labour, the less laborious technique will displace its alternative, because the same goods can be sold for less. The way in which labour is allocated between alternative techniques of production is thus a social force, 'a productive organism of spontaneous growth' (Marx 1930 [1867]: 84). Marx argued that just as, according to contemporary anthropologists, the deities of religion are external expressions of mental phenomena, so the commodities which are exchanged become concrete expressions of social relationships. When people believe that commodities are worth something in themselves, not recognising that it is the labour put into making them which really has value, commodities have acquired a *fetishistic* character.

The Capitalist Mode of Production

The greater part of Marx's analysis is explicitly directed at explaining the processes which gave rise to capitalist society in the West, and it was in relation to capitalist society that his ideas are best exemplified. In *Capital*, Marx argues that simple economies are characterised by direct exchange between producers. The farmer exchanges his surplus grain for the tools made by the craftsman. One commodity is exchanged for another of equal value and goods are primarily valued in terms of their usefulness:

commodity' → money → commodity"

The germ of capitalism lies in the origin of a new concept of exchange, in which the aim is to make a profit. Marx called this mercantile exchange. The value of a good in exchange comes to dominate over its use value:

money' → commodity → money"

Since no one can subsist on money, this type of exchange only makes sense if the second sum of money is greater than the first. A capitalist is a person who uses capital, at first in the form of money, to carry out transactions to make a profit. How can this be achieved? Initially, in Marx's opinion, there were two ways of making a profit: by lending money and charging interest, or by trading in commodities. These exchanges arose in the 'pores' or 'interstices' of medieval society, within the cities. If the merchant puts no labour into the commodities, however, he cannot increase their value. This seemed to limit the scope for making a profit. The only way capitalist transactions could really gather momentum was to begin trading in a commodity which itself generated value, namely, human labour. This is not possible as long as the people who make goods, the craftsmen, own their own workshops and obtain the raw materials they need directly from producers. The craftsman must be detached from his workshop and made to work in one belonging to the capitalist. Now the capitalist can buy the labour of the craftsman by paying him a subsistence wage and selling the produce of his labour. If a craftsman needs to work six hours to earn his subsistence, but the capitalist makes him work for eight, the extra two hours labour earns the capitalist his profit. With this he can buy more labour, or more equipment for his workshop. It is a case of positive feedback (see Figure 1.1) or, in Marx's words, 'self-expanding value... a monster quick with life' (Marx 1930: 189).

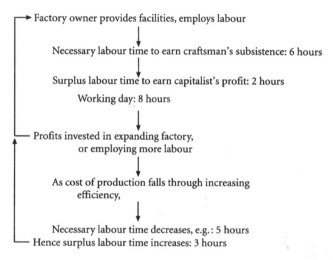

Figure 1.1 Marx's model of positive feedback in capitalist production

Marx emphasised that the social conditions under which trade in commodities could expand sufficiently to make capitalism viable were not universal, but did occur in the medieval social system of Western Europe. Craftsmen were concentrated in the cities, and there was a well-developed communication network. Both had contributed to an elaborate division of labour. Capitalism began with the enlargement of medieval guild workshops. Marx argued that medieval guilds deliberately tried to restrain the transformation of guild-masters into capitalists by limiting the number of craftsmen they could employ but, once a capitalist had established himself in a particular field of production, his methods had inherent advantages: a larger number of workers averages out the differences between their skills; it is cheaper to provide accommodation for each worker; component tasks can be performed simultaneously by different teams; and the workers encourage each other to work harder.

All of these developments took place before mechanisation, but made it possible to manufacture goods more cheaply. Capitalist methods therefore succeeded at the expense of the older organisational methods of the guilds. Whereas, at the beginning, a minority of workers were selling their labour to capitalists simply because through poverty or accident they lacked their own workshops, eventually all labourers had to sell their labour to capitalists. The social system had been transformed, and left them no alternative.

The growth of capitalism might, at this point, have slowed down. Guilds had been destroyed and craft techniques exploited to the full. Capitalists, however, were still trying to make a profit, since this is the rationale for mercantile exchange. There were only two ways they could do so: either by increasing the length of the working day, or by improving production techniques. There are limits to the former. While capitalists and workers may argue about what is the length of a 'natural' working day, this social construct is ultimately limited by the tendency for workers' efficiency to decrease after many hours' labour, or even for them to die more frequently than they can be replaced. The early capitalist mode of production had therefore created a social environment in which technological innovations, should they occur, will rapidly spread through the social system.

The advantage of a machine is that, while it requires labour to manufacture, it will continue to operate for many years without wearing out, and is relatively cheap to maintain. In the long run, it costs less to use machines than to pay skilled craftsmen. Mechanisation is a more effective form of investment for capital. One machine can simultaneously do the work of several people – a spinning jenny operated twelve to eighteen spindles – and machines can be designed to complete tasks quickly and efficiently. The capitalist system thus underwent a second phase of positive feedback. Skilled handiwork was no longer the regulative principle of production. Any resistance from skilled workers was undermined by the employment of the unskilled to operate machinery. Because physical strength was no longer required, once water or steam power has been harnessed to work the machines, women and children could be employed at lower wages than men. The capacity of machines to operate continuously lengthened the working day. Marx did not argue that capitalists are a different species of person, with an inherently different psychology. Rather, certain people were exposed, by virtue of their position in the social system, to different opportunities or constraints.

There is, however, a second and crucial element to Marx's analysis of social process. As the capitalist system starts to run out of anyone's control it develops *internal contradictions*, social forces which cause its own collapse. When James Watt improved the efficacy of the steam engine, he designed it so that the waste steam from the cylinder which drove the piston would suck hot air from the fire through tubes in the boiler, thereby heating the water more quickly. The faster the engine ran, the more it produced fresh steam. Watt had to invent a 'regulator', which would reduce the supply of steam to the piston if the engine ran faster and hence prevent his engine tearing itself apart. Perhaps Marx envisaged capitalism running out of control like a steam engine without a regulator. Capitalists constantly sought to minimise the amount they had to pay in wages, by reducing the number of people they employed and increasing their working hours. Their ability to do so depended on lengthening the working day to the maximum the remaining workers could sustain. The decision as to what constituted a normal working day 'presents itself as a struggle between the aggregate of capitalists, the capitalist class, and the aggregate of workers, the working class' (Marx 1930: 235). The more workers are brought together in larger factories, the more their power to resist their employers increases. They come to perceive what is actually a social process as the outcome of 'an alien will', that of someone who is purposively subjugating them. As jobs become more specialised, the work becomes more dull. Workers become *alienated* from rather than committed to their work. Increasing reliance on machines results in higher unemployment. Marx predicted that the workers would eventually band together to overthrow the capitalists and take control of the productive resources. A final state of equilibrium would be inaugurated in which each received according to their needs and each produced according to their abilities (Marx and Engels 1967 [1848]). Marx failed to realise that Communism would have its own internal contradictions.

Marx and non-Western societies

While Marx never made a detailed application of his theory to non-Western societies, he did sketch out a general approach in his unpublished manuscripts, which have since been published under the title

Pre-Capitalist Economic Formations (Marx 1964). Some of the alternative modes of production he proposed are referred to at various points in *Capital*. Marx followed the tradition of the Levellers and Rousseau in postulating an original human condition, which he termed *primitive communalism*. For Marx, the original condition was already a social one. He specified its characteristics in *The German Ideology* (written in 1845–6), where he described primitive communalism as 'the undeveloped stage of production where a people sustains itself by hunting, fishing, cattle-raising or at most by farming'. Familial kinship forms the basis for all social relations. There is no concept of land ownership and each group temporarily exploits an area of land before moving on to another. Marx recognised that an analysis of social process must have a historical dimension and, in *Capital*, he argued that to study the development of human labour it was necessary to go back to 'the spontaneously developed form which confronts us on the threshold of the history of all civilised races'; a good example of which was the self-sufficient peasant family working the land. While Marx sometimes presents this as the original social condition, at others he regards it as a condition which tends to reappear whenever one mechanism for extracting surplus labour breaks down, and persists until another replaces it (e.g. Marx 1930: 349 and 351n.). Although the division of labour is socially determined, Marx envisaged that in this simplest mode of production it would depend solely on the age and gender of each household member. Each individual is an instrument of the group's productive efforts. Part of the household's produce is reserved for future production and part is consumed immediately to provide the household's subsistence. Trading in commodities is minimal. As relationships between households develop, as the population increases and as war or trade come to characterise inter-community relations, so the social system begins to change. A formerly egalitarian population becomes differentiated into chiefs, commoners and slaves. Depending upon accidents of geography and demography, the social system may evolve along one or another pathway out of primitive communalism. Each may preserve some aspects of its former mode, but will possess a different social division of labour. Wherever one sector of the society holds a monopoly over productive resources, those who work the land will have to supplement the labour time necessary for their own subsistence with surplus labour to benefit the landowners. The consequences will depend on the opportunities for trade which exist in that system.

Marx envisaged three possible routes out of primitive communalism: the *Asiatic, ancient* and *Germanic* modes of production. The Asiatic mode, characteristic of pre-colonial India, Mexico and Peru, is the most stable. The individual is never detached from his community. The village commune remains a self-sustaining unit for agricultural and craft production which contains all the means of its own perpetuation, and the production of a surplus. If the population increases, part of the community splits off and sets up a new village with the same structure as the old one. The demand for each craftsman's and specialist's labour is fixed. Communities of this type may be incorporated into wider political systems ruled by kings who sustain their political organisation by extracting surplus production as tribute, but cities are not diagnostic and tend to develop only where external trade is transacted with other polities. The stability of Asiatic community organisation enables it to outlive the rise and fall of dynasties.

The ancient mode of production, typical of Classical Greece and Rome, is, by contrast, based on the city state and is inherently unstable. The city and its attached territory form an economic unit. Land belongs to the state and only citizens have the right to use it. Anyone who loses the portion of land allocated to them loses their citizenship. Membership of the local state becomes the organising principle for social relations, rather than the kin relationships which regulated primitive communalism (see Figure 1.2).

Two processes tend to undermine the ancient system. Since the system depends on the concept of the citizen as landholder, as the state's population increases, new land must be found for the increasing number of citizens. This causes warfare between neighbouring states and the

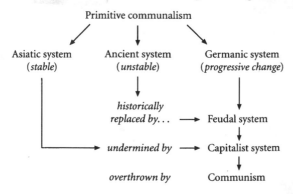

Figure 1.2 Marx's multi-linear model of progressive social evolution

military element of social organisation tends to displace agricultural production. In order to reserve access to land for citizens, the conquered must be reduced to slavery. Eventually slaves outnumber citizens and only a minority of those incorporated into the social system have a vested interest in ensuring its perpetuation. If, secondly, a citizen loses his property he loses his citizenship and is reduced to slavery. Trade and manufacture cause the development of a market through which profit and loss can be made. The costs of losing make citizens suspicious of trade and they tend to exclude craftsmen from citizenship. Ancient systems thus tend to break down and, historically if not inevitably, they tend to be replaced by feudal regimes.

The Germanic system is also unstable but, unlike the ancient system, it is flexible. Marx must have drawn on Tacitus in constructing this mode of production. Instead of breaking down, it tends to undergo a progressive transformation into the feudal mode of production. The Germanic system resembles primitive communalism in relying on the household as an independent unit of production but differs from it in recognising two types of land ownership: private and communal. The need to manage collective resources and defend them from attack gives rise to periodic assemblies, but there are no cities and chiefs are democratically elected. The ability of households to trade in their craft produce provides the germ of social differentiation.

The feudal mode of production has both rural settlements and cities. In the countryside, serfs are subordinate to feudal lords who own the means of production, the land. While both serfdom and slavery originate through conquest in war, serfs have greater independence than slaves (Hobsbawm 1964: 42). Slaves, characteristic of the ancient mode, are entirely dependent on their masters and all they produce is appropriated by their owner, who returns no more than the slaves need to subsist. Serfs, however, farm primarily for themselves and only periodically render labour service on their lord's estate. Serfs have the potential to accumulate a surplus of their own. If the feudal lords were eliminated, villages would continue to function as self-perpetuating units, as they do in the Asiatic system.

Although he recognised the importance of continued access to common land for rural stability (Marx 1930: 794–801), Marx considered that it was within the cities that the destabilisation of the feudal system began. Cities were centres for craft production and trade. Guilds allowed merchants to buy their products, but not the labour of craftsmen.

Certain least-skilled crafts, such as spinning and weaving, were weakly controlled by guilds and it was here that capitalists got a toe-hold in the control of production. Labour displaced from the countryside by the enclosure of common land and dispossession of smallholders could be recruited to work for capitalists. What starts as a spontaneous process becomes consciously sought for and systematically implemented: a new mode of production which the capitalists will strive to maintain, just as the guilds strove to maintain the medieval feudal system. As capitalism extends to the control of international exchange, so the Asiatic systems of America and Asia fall under its domination and are transformed.

Durkheim (1858–1917)

Although Marx published his ideas almost half a century before Durkheim, Durkheim's theory was both simpler and had more to say about the character of non-Western societies. It was immediately influential upon anthropology, whereas Marx's theory was not taken up until the mid-twentieth century.

Like Hobbes, Rousseau and Marx, Durkheim was preoccupied by the problems of his own society. He was influenced both by the general disruption caused by the Industrial Revolution, and the specific events during the Franco-Prussian war when Paris was surrounded by the Prussian army, and the people of Paris revolted against the government by creating the brutally suppressed Commune of 1871. Like Hobbes, Durkheim asked what it was that held society together, but his answers, influenced by the work of Comte, were more sophisticated. Durkheim carried out his own research on suicide rates in France, and relied on the ethnographies that were becoming available to analyse less familiar societies. He set out to establish the ground-rules for a science of society. When Durkheim was a postgraduate student, sociology was held in disrepute (Lukes 1973: 66), but he succeeded in making it scientifically respectable and established a sociology department at the University of Bordeaux (Lukes 1973: 97ff.).

Unlike Spencer, Durkheim contended that the social sciences were a distinct field of study, not a branch of psychology or biology. He emphasised that social life was the product of interaction and that it could be studied scientifically, in order to derive general laws of social behaviour. Durkheim's formulation of the social sciences contributed to a long-lasting split between social and biological anthropology, based on three fundamental differences of approach:

1 Durkheim emphasised that social interaction must be
   understood in systematic terms, not by taking individual
   customs out of their context. This appeared to conflict with
   the axiom of evolutionary biology that, since natural
   selection acts on the individual, the individual is the unit of
   analysis.
2 Durkheim argued that social behaviour is learned, and is
   determined by the body of custom transmitted within the
   social tradition. Evolution, however, was held to act on
   patterns of behaviour which are genetically determined.
3 Durkheim followed Spencer in classifying societies into
   types, according to the complexity of their social structure.
   The transition from one type to another was held to be a
   fairly rapid moment of transition, whereas natural
   selection is a slow, yet continuous process. *gradual or punctuated equilibrium*

Social facts

Durkheim defined social facts as 'ways of acting or thinking with the
peculiar characteristics of exercising a coercive influence on individual
consciousnesses' (Durkheim 1938 [1901]: liii). Society is not the mere
sum of its individual members. The system formed by people's association as members of society is a specific reality with its own characteristics. Durkheim assumed that what he called psychological impulses
were general to humankind as part of our bodily constitution and
could not, therefore, explain the diversity of human societies. He also
challenged Hobbes' and Rousseau's image of a social contract entered
into by previously autonomous individuals. Durkheim argued that
since all known human societies have developed out of earlier societies
there has never been a time when people were able to come together of
their own free will and form a social contract. Social phenomena have
social causes and are not brought about by individuals acting on their
own account. When Durkheim fulfils his obligations as a brother,
husband or citizen and when he discharges his contractual obligations,
he is performing duties which are already defined, externally to himself
(Durkheim is here anticipating the Functionalists' concepts of status
and role, discussed in the following chapter).

The same is true when Durkheim accepts the beliefs and practices of
his religion. The existence of such beliefs and patterns of obligatory
behaviour before the birth of those who currently hold, or practise,

them implies that they exist independently of individuals, and impose themselves upon Durkheim regardless of his personal will. While conforming to the requirements of society its constraints may not be apparent but, once he steps out of line, morality is enforced by public ridicule and the law by formal punishment, either as repression or as restitution (these concepts, too, were developed by the Functionalists into a theory of social control).

Each society and period has its own constraints. Durkheim is not obliged by any natural law to speak French, nor to pay for goods with French currency but, in practice, he has no choice. If he owned a factory he would not be obliged to use industrial technology but, if he resorted to medieval craft techniques his enterprise would soon fail, because others would put him out of business.

Besides the specific constraints imposed by any particular society there are, however, general social currents which lack the organisation of institutions but are still compelling. The waves of enthusiasm, pity or indignation which infect a crowd are a product of interaction between the members of the crowd (no doubt Durkheim was here thinking of the tragedy of the Paris Commune). Because such social currents are not dependent on previously existing institutions, Durkheim supposed that they provided the context within which the earliest forms of society emerged.

Durkheim anticipated the value of participant observation, a technique central to anthropological research. Social facts cannot be studied by armchair introspection. The social scientist must go into the field to discover how a society conceives of its own institutions. The evidence will be found in the external, objective signs provided by patterns of behaviour such as the organisation of the family, contract law, the types of acts deemed to be crimes and the forms of punishment considered appropriate. Durkheim followed Comte in arguing that the character of 'crime' and 'morality' vary according to the type of social system, and the scientist cannot assume that what are considered crimes in his own society are the only possible forms. Rather, he must observe what forms of behaviour are subject to punishment in the society under study.

This led Durkheim to ask, in general terms, what might be considered normal, and what pathological, behaviour in any type of social system. He recognised this could not be determined in advance, simply by declaring that savage customs were immoral. Two ways of measuring 'normal behaviour' were rejected on practical grounds, considering them too difficult to assess. The first was the degree to which a social system was adapted to its environment. Although this might have enabled a *rapprochement* with biological anthropology, Durkheim was proposing to investigate the adaptive qualities of the social system, not that of the behaviour of the individual people who participate in it. Durkheim's second hypothetical criterion was the probability of the system surviving in its present form, which he concluded was difficult to assess within the lifetime of the researcher. In the end Durkheim adopted an empirical position which was essentially tautological: the normal condition for a given type of social system is that condition most generally observed in societies of that type (cf. 'The Romans outnumbered the Greeks because they had more men'). What is normal for a mollusc is not normal for a vertebrate. Durkheim argued that even crime and suicide may be said to have normal rates of occurrence in any type of society and, equally, certain types of punishment may be normal in a particular type of society. Since social phenomena cannot be controlled experimentally, the only scientific method suitable for the social scientist is the comparative method. If one aspect of two social systems is the same, hypotheses concerning the general character of those systems can be tested by asking whether other aspects of the two societies are also similar.

Durkheim's method therefore depended on developing a classification of societies into types. He argued that this should not be done through an exhaustive description of all features of any society, but by identifying what he considered its 'decisive features'. Since all societies are made up of component groups, they can be classified according to the nature and number of their components, and how these components are combined. In order to achieve such a classification, Durkheim relied on the ideas of earlier writers, particularly Herbert Spencer, to derive a fourfold classification of societies, each distinguished by the form of its components (see Table 1.1).

Simple societies were said to be characterised by isolated family groups ('hordes'), who had no contact with one another, while compound societies of type *a* were made up of clans who periodically assembled as a tribe. In societies of compound type *b*, kinship gives way to local organisation while in complex societies an overarching governmental structure develops, which deprives local communities of their political autonomy. Implicit in this typology is an Enlightenment

Table 1.1 *Durkheim's unilinear model of progressive social evolution*

Type	Components
Simple	Hordes
Compound *a*	Clans
Compound *b*	Local communities
Complex	Central government

notion of social evolution, which proceeds in one direction, towards increasing social complexity and sophistication. The revolutionary idea introduced by Darwin and Wallace, that evolution might be wholly lacking in any direction, and that the success of any population can only be judged in relation to its specific environment, had not been appreciated by the nineteenth-century social sciences. For Durkheim, like other nineteenth-century social scientists such as Marx, Comte and Spencer, evolution does not take place in response to selective pressures imposed by the environment, but through an internal social dynamic.

Society as an organic system

Durkheim made frequent use of the 'organic analogy' elaborated by Comte and Spencer to exemplify the systematic qualities of social life. The organic analogy compares society to the body of an animal. Just as cells are constantly being replaced in the body so, it is argued, when people die their places in society are taken by others without affecting the structure of the organism. The function of each organ within the body is the contribution it makes to sustaining the life of the organism and, in social life, the function of each institution is the contribution it makes to the survival of the society. Durkheim used the organic analogy to compare compound societies, which lacked centralised government, to a simple segmentary organism such as a starfish or (less accurately) an earthworm, in which each segment contains all the essential organs and therefore performed identical functions, and a complex society to the human body, in which each organ played a unique function and the whole could not survive the loss of any of its parts.

Durkheim coined the idea of a collective consciousness (*conscience collective*) to describe the shared feelings and impulses which are experienced in their simplest form within an excited crowd. In his book *The Division of Labour* (Durkheim 1933 [1893]) he set out to investigate how the collective consciousness changed as a society was transformed from a compound to a complex state. Implicitly, he took the changes which were taking place in late nineteenth-century France during the Industrial Revolution as his model. Durkheim was disturbed by industrial unrest and by booms and slumps in the economy. He wanted to know how individualism could exist within an industrial society, without the system breaking down into a Hobbesian war of each against all. Although Durkheim set out to answer his question empirically, by looking at the forms of morality in actual societies he did not, at this relatively early stage in his career, use ethnographic studies of non-Western societies (Lukes 1973: 159). Rather, he took the ideal character of compound societies as axiomatic, and asked how French society of his day differed from his model.

Durkheim proposed that the collective consciousness had several aspects, such as the extent to which all participants shared the identical values and the strength these collective values exerted over the individual. He envisaged a mathematical relationship between these various aspects, such that if one varied the others would all vary accordingly (perhaps modelled on Boyle's Law, which specifies how the volume, pressure and temperature of a gas are interrelated). In a compound social system, each unit caters for its own subsistence and therefore performs identical functions. In a complex system, each unit performs complementary functions, and all are dependent on the other units for their survival. Durkheim argued that when a compound society is transformed into a complex one, the collective consciousness changes in such a way that individual consciousnesses become more differentiated, shared values and beliefs advocate the development of individual skills rather than conformity to a single pattern of behaviour, and the state develops to articulate changing values, to direct policy and to enact laws (particularly contract law) which will facilitate the transformation of the social organism.

Durkheim argued that this process could be empirically measured by plotting changes in the character of punishment. In a compound society deviance is punished by a strong reaction generated by the collective consciousness, and norms are reinforced by repressive sanctions. In a complex society, breach of contractual agreements between individuals is punished by restitutive sanctions and repressive sanctions are maintained only for wrongs such as murder which threaten the individual liberty of all.

Since Durkheim insisted that social events have social causes, he was determined to show that the transformation of society did not come about through the actions of individuals, but rather through collective processes. Lukes has pointed out that Durkheim appears to rely on Darwin's theory of natural selection for the argument that the more alike two animal organisms are, the more severely they compete for resources. This competition can only be successfully resolved if the two organisms differentiate from one another (Lukes 1973: 266–7). Durkheim argued by analogy that, as the territorial segments of a compound society expand, so they come into competition for resources and resolve this competition by means of complementary economic specialisations. Thus an initial equilibrium, in which society is compound in form, gives way to a period of transition, which is resolved when equilibrium is restored, but society is now complex in form.

Durkheim regarded the lack of co-ordination between different elements of industrial production, the degrading nature of work and the disputes between workers and factory owners which characterised the height of the Industrial Revolution as pathological conditions symptomatic of a period of transition rather than intrinsic qualities of industrial society. 'At certain points in the organism, certain social functions are not adjusted to one another' (Durkheim 1933 [1893]: 344). Durkheim favoured 'soft' socialist policies, in which government intervened to regulate markets and to create the conditions within which individual skills could be fully realised. He was against the hereditary transmission of property but he was also against trade unions, which he considered merely prolonged social disharmony. He recommended that factories should be organised as benevolent extensions of the family, somewhat in the manner implemented in post-Second World War Japan (Abegglan and Shack 1985; Clark 1979). Despite Durkheim's proclaimed view that what should be considered normal for any type of society is the condition present in the average society of that type, he was obliged to project the 'normal' conditions for industrial society into the future.

Ethnography in the eighteenth and nineteenth centuries

It is probably clear, even from the short passages quoted at the beginning of the chapter that the classical tradition of ethnography (that is, 'writing about peoples') to which Herodotus and Tacitus contributed was far more sophisticated than that of the eighteenth and nineteenth centuries. Adam Smith's image of the primitive arrow-maker is derived from extrapolating the familiar back into the past; Rousseau's original condition is constructed by turning the familiar upside-down. The puzzling behaviour of the Caribbean who sold his bed is, if it has any truth, probably the result of the native's unfamiliarity with the difference between reciprocity and market exchange. Spencer, in a wild collation of differences, lumps the behaviour of English schoolboys with that of 'unsettled tribes' (e.g. Spencer 1972 [1857]: 50).

Herbert Spencer compressed the diversity of human societies into a single, unilinear progression: the so-called 'simple tribes' in which everyone is hunter, fisher and builder of huts, the complex Indian caste, and medieval European guild systems are all reduced to steps on the ascent to nineteenth-century commercial society. While it is undeniable that the earliest human societies were simpler in organisation than many recent ones, and that some recent societies may resemble earlier ones more closely than did the society of nineteenth-century England, Spencer's method of compressing diversity into a unilinear scale and insisting that progress up that scale is inevitable reduces the possibility of exploring alternative explanations for human social diversity to a minimum. Spencer's method does not invite researchers to go out and explore the diversity of human societies. On the contrary, it tempts observers simply to glance at other societies sufficiently to place them in predetermined categories.

The influence of Durkheim and Marx upon anthropology

Durkheim's theory, despite its allegiance to progressive evolution, insists that social behaviour in exotic communities should not be taken for granted, but studied to discover what is 'normal' in societies of particular types. His typology itself proved extremely influential in determining how the diversity of human societies investigated by anthropologists during the colonial era was interpreted. Durkheim's postulate that societies tended inherently to remain in equilibrium through the operation of custom, the allocation of social positions to individuals and the control of deviance, laid down the framework within which the internal structure of small-scale and supposedly stable societies was analysed.

Marx's theory becomes influential in anthropology as anthropologists moved from the study of social structure, inspired by Durkheim, to the study of social process. Marxist theory made it possible to recognise that egalitarianism or hierarchy were the consequence of principles of exchange, the distribution of rights to property and the control of labour. Once anthropologists confronted the impact of colonialism, and stopped attempting to reconstruct small-scale social systems as if they had not been incorporated into colonial regimes, the predatory effects of capitalism could no longer be denied. These developments will be outlined in the following chapters.

CHAPTER TWO

Functionalism

The Functionalists looked inside the units of what Durkheim had termed 'compound societies'. They investigated the internal structure of the social segments, examined the social relationships that held the segments together, and attempted to explain the apparent stability of segmentary societies. Functionalism developed shortly after the colonisation of New Guinea, and East and West Africa by Britain and other European powers, and its research was conducted among colonised peoples. The effect these circumstances had on Functionalist theory has been widely debated (see particularly Kuper 1983: 99–120; Grillo 1985). The Functionalists tried to reconstruct the form the societies they studied had taken prior to colonisation. The British policy of 'indirect rule' depended on identifying traditional patterns of authority. Some Functionalists undeniably attempted to make their research useful to colonial authorities. Whether they were successful, or whether their work was circumscribed by such a goal, is questionable. Malinowski, a leading Functionalist, was open in his criticism of the effect of British colonialism and missionaries upon the well-being of the New Guinea islanders he studied (see, for example, Malinowski 1922: 464–8), and he inspired research into contemporary conditions in East African mining towns. Functionalism is, none the less, vulnerable to the criticism that its theories failed to throw light on the effects of colonialism. This defect was one reason why Marxist theory underwent a revival at the end of the colonial era.

The Functionalists employed three different definitions of function:

1 The first defines 'function' in a quasi-mathematical sense.
   Every custom is interconnected with all others in the
   community, so that each conditions the state of the others.
2 The second, used particularly by Malinowski, is drawn
   from physiology. The function of customs is to satisfy the
   individual's primary biological needs through the medium
   of culture.
3 The third was derived by Radcliffe-Brown from the
   theories of Durkheim. Each custom's function is the part it
   plays in maintaining the integrity of the social system.

Malinowski and Radcliffe-Brown are considered to have established
the Functionalist school in anthropology, although they drew upon
the earlier work of Seligman (1910), Spencer and Gillen (1899), and
others. They reacted against the nineteenth-century idea that living
societies could be ranked according to the stage they had reached in
social evolution and argued that the customs of small-scale societies
could not be explained as survivals from an earlier era but had, rather,
to be explained in terms of their present function. Radcliffe-Brown
himself described Functionalism as an irresponsible label invented by
Malinowski (Radcliffe-Brown 1952: 188) and there are fundamental
differences in the concepts of function they relied upon. The two men
were complementary in their skills. Malinowski was a brilliant fieldworker, who studied the life of the Trobriand islanders over a six-year
period between 1914 and 1920, and wrote a series of ethnographies
showing the interconnections between Trobriand customs. Radcliffe-
Brown was more influential on the development of theory. Unlike
Marx, neither Malinowski nor Radcliffe-Brown considered that
economic relations had primacy over other aspects of social life. In the
absence of written histories or detailed archaeological evidence it was
useless to speculate about the history of small-scale societies.

In the United States, Franz Boas reacted against the evolutionists
(Stocking 1982: 5, 16). He, too, emphasised the importance of studying customs in their social context. 'Primitive people' do not live in a
Rousseauesque state of natural simplicity, but are heirs to a long tradition. 'None of these people is free from conventional proscriptions and
rules' (Boas 1940a [1896]: 663). He advocated a detailed study of customs in relation to the total culture of the tribe practising them, and an
investigation of their distribution among neighbouring peoples (Boas

1940b [1887]: 276). Boas argued that human genetics ('race'), language and culture change at different rates, negating any attempt to link them in stages of development. Unlike the Functionalists, Boas also drew attention to the role of diffusion and intermarriage, concluding that a people's history must be studied to account for the particular configurations of genetic and cultural traits which they possess at any moment. Rather than seek functional connections between customs, Boas adopted the vaguer notion that the *Geist* or spirit of the people gave some unity to their culture. Each people develops borrowed arts and ideas in its own way. Boas pointed out that emotions which seem natural to us are revealed as the products of our culture when we contrast them with the emotional reactions of other peoples (Boas 1940a [1896]: 635–6; cf. Stocking 1982: 71). This notion gave rise to the 'culture and personality' school, exemplified by Ruth Benedict's *Patterns of Culture* (Benedict 1934) and, most famously, by Margaret Mead's *Coming of Age in Samoa* (Mead 1928). George Stocking has put forward the interesting argument that the 'culture and personality' approach gained in appeal when the horrors of the First World War revealed a less civilised side of Western culture. The claims that hard work, controlled sexuality and religious orthodoxy were justified by their civilising effects could be questioned by examining the different morals and ethics of other cultures, and their impact on social life (Stocking 1986: 5).

This book will say nothing more about the culture and personality school. Stocking considers the notion of *Geist* a 'rather loose romantic conception' (Stocking 1982: 8) and argues that a more scientific approach to anthropology in the United States was inaugurated at the time of Radcliffe-Brown's arrival in Chicago in 1931 (Stocking 1982: 18). The book will pick up the threads of American anthropology where it considers those, such as White and Steward, who reacted against Boas' cultural relativism and tried to reintroduce theories that would be generally applicable to different cultures. The continuing centrality of culture as a concept shaping American anthropology will, however, be seen, in later chapters, in work of Goodenough, Sahlins, Geertz and others. Finally, the book will assess what may be seen as Boas' revenge through the medium of the 'Writing Culture' school, which has again challenged the universal validity of Western theorising (Geertz 1988; Clifford and Marcus 1986).

Argonauts of the Western Pacific

In his study of inter-island exchange in the Western Pacific, Malinowski formulated and demonstrated his approach to anthropological field research. No one, he wrote, would dream of reporting research in physics or chemistry without giving a detailed account of the experiments they had carried out, but ethnographic accounts generally did not at that time give details of the actual experiences which led the writer to his conclusions, nor was a distinction drawn between direct observation, statements made by 'the natives' and the author's inferences. Malinowski's aim was to show how different customs were functionally dependent on one another, and to reveal the social and psychological bases on which social institutions were constructed, hoping by those means to develop a new theory of anthropology that would stand beside evolutionism. He set out to show that explanations of customs wholly in terms of their present function were easier to test and therefore more scientific (Malinowski 1922: 515–16). Malinowski undertook to live among the Trobrianders, pitching his tent in their villages on islands off the north-eastern coast of New Guinea. He describes his personal experiences in vivid prose, quotes the islanders' statements at length, and makes it clear where he had drawn general conclusions of his own. Malinowski set out to discard biased and pre-judged opinions, and to base his research on objective hypotheses. He advocated keeping a field diary to note down all the subtle experiences which at first seemed novel, but soon became accepted as part of ordinary routine.

Although Malinowski paints individual portraits – 'To'udawada silently chewing betel nut, with a heavy and bovine dignity, the excitable Koutauya chattering in a high pitched voice with some of his grown-up sons' (Malinowski 1922: 212) – he insists the incidental feelings of individuals had to be distinguished from their thoughts and sentiments as members of a community. In Malinowski's assessment, the 'natives' followed the 'forces and commands of the tribal code' without comprehending them (Malinowski 1922: 11). Evidence had to be collected through case studies, either personally observed, or provided by informants in order to grasp 'the native's point of view'. Tables detailing all aspects of kinship behaviour, exchange and ceremonies were to be compiled in order exhaustively to chart their interconnections, from which general, scientific conclusions could be drawn. To prevent his analysis becoming unwieldy, Malinowski took the exchange network called the *kula*, linking the Trobriands with neighbouring islands, as the central strand of his analysis and explored its ramifications through all aspects of the Trobrianders' way of life. He participated in a *kula* voyage from the Trobriands, via the Amphletts, to Dobu (a voyage of over 120 miles in each direction).

Malinowski found that the *kula* was built upon the exchange of two types of manufactured object: red shell necklaces called *soulava* and white shell bracelets called *mwali*. Only a limited number of men on each island participated in the exchanges, each having a number of partners on the same or other islands. The two types of object travelled in opposite directions, according to strict rules; *soulava* moved clockwise around the islands, *mwali* moved anti-clockwise. No man kept an object for long; the point of holding a necklace or bracelet was to be able to give it away to a partner, in order to perpetuate the relationship. Malinowski contended that no participant was aware of the total structure of the exchange system, which linked thousands of people across an area measuring approximately 200 by 300 miles. Each participant only knew his own partners and those immediately beyond them. None the less, it was an institution central to the social life of the Trobriands and other island groups. Malinowski challenged the notion that 'primitive' people lived in a Rousseauesque isolation, only engaging in trade as a last resort, and for their personal gain. *Kula* expeditions demanded extensive planning and the co-ordination of many people's effort. The vast complex of relationships was constructed by individuals who engaged in purposive action according to social rules, for objects with no utilitarian value. Malinowski compared *kula* valuables to the crown jewels: useless in themselves, yet endowed with cultural value. 'The psychological and sociological forces at work are the same, it is really the same mental attitude which makes us value our heirlooms' (Malinowski 1922: 90–1). The difference lay in the way *kula* valuables circulate from one person to another like sporting trophies, rather than remaining locked and guarded like the crown jewels.

Malinowski repeatedly denied any wish to reconstruct the origins of exchange. He emphasised that the Trobriander was just as subject to social codes as a European, which regulated any 'natural acquisitive tendency' that might have been attributed to the archetypal primitive man living in a state of nature. Trobrianders manufactured artefacts 'not under the spur of necessity... but on the impulse of talent and fancy, with a high enjoyment of their art' (Malinowski 1922: 172). The rules of *kula* exchange prohibited the simultaneous exchange of an armband and a necklace, but also insisted that no one kept a valuable for more than a year or two. When a valuable is presented to one's partner there can be no haggling over whether it is equivalent in value to the one last handed to the giver. Malinowski graphically describes the exaggerated miming of reluctance by the giver to part with such a valuable object, and the studiously passive behaviour of the recipient, who may let a small boy in his household pick up the valuable and carry it to his home (Malinowski 1922: 352). Barter for subsistence goods was given a different name, *gimwali*, and was subject to a different code of conduct. None the less, the function of the *kula* was to enable Trobrianders to satisfy their natural desire to acquire possessions, rather than to thwart it.

Malinowski also took issue with the concept of primitive communalism. The operation of the *kula* depended on the right of individuals to hold, and to give away, the valuable armbands and necklaces. The very concept of giving and receiving depended on a distinction between 'mine' and 'yours'. Where communal labour took place in the construction of seagoing canoes, it had to be recruited by men with the skill and social authority to do so. The magical spells recited at various stages in canoe manufacture had an economic function. They put order and sequence into the various operations and inspired the builders with confidence. Individuals did not merely work for themselves; social forces co-ordinated work by defining who could be called upon to join in canoe construction, and on what grounds. A concept of ownership existed in Trobriand culture, although it was not the same as the European concept of private property. The prefix *toli*, which might be translated as 'owner', also meant 'master', and was given to the man who directed the building of a canoe. He could not be left out of any expedition on which the canoe travelled, and he had the right to hire out the canoe to other users.

Barter operated in conjunction with the *kula*. Different islands possessed different resources and produced different artefacts. A *kula* expedition always set out with its canoes loaded with goods which it was known would be valued at the destination. From a Western perspective, it might seem that the trade in commodities was the primary purpose of the expedition. For the participants, however, it was the exchange of valuables, based on the love of give and take for its own sake. *Kula* partners provided safe-conduct in what otherwise might be hostile and exotic villages. The Amphlett islanders specialised in the production of pottery, but imported stone for making tools, which originated from Woodlark Island and reached them via the Trobriands. Different Trobriand villages specialised in making wooden dishes, lime-pots and baskets, which were also traded for Amphlett pots. In exchange, the Amphlett islanders obtained strips of rattan used as belts and the lashing for canoes, bamboo and barbed spears from Fergusson Island, which they traded with the Trobrianders. Barter takes place after *kula* partners have given or received valuables. *Kula* partners do not engage in these exchanges with one another, but haggle and barter over commodities with other members of their partner's community, thereby avoiding the risk of alienating their partners.

Malinowski's theory

Malinowski was not highly regarded as a theoretician, nor as someone who could offer a set of acceptable general principles by which a range of societies could be described and compared. When he moved from description of Trobriand life to explanation Malinowski's contribution was less impressive. He emphasised that observation of how people actually perform a custom is as important as eliciting the rules people are expected to observe. Malinowski saw the 'native' as a reasonable man, choosing which of his exchange partners he would give with, or from whom he would solicit a *kula* valuable, and thereby manipulating the possibilities inherent in social relations to his advantage. Malinowski considered that culture was founded on the biological needs of individuals, providing a reference point which enabled parallels to be drawn between simple and complex societies. The term *function* is used here in a second sense, namely: 'satisfying (the individual's) primary biological needs through the instrumentalities of culture' (Malinowski 1954: 202).

Malinowski argued that culture 'consists in a more efficient and better founded way [than natural selection] of satisfying the innate biological desires of man' (Malinowski 1947: 33). Yet this could not explain the diversity of human societies, since biological needs are universal to the species. While Malinowski may have chosen to call his book on Trobriand kinship *The Sexual Life of Savages* (1929) as a way of increasing sales, it also expressed his theory that culture functioned to satisfy biological needs. In retrospect, Malinowski might be seen as a precursor of Sociobiology (see chapter 6), but Malinowski did not consider the possibility that different ways of satisfying biological needs might be appropriate in different natural or social environments. It was not until the 1970s that adaptationist theories were developed which could reconcile variability in cultural behaviour with the universal criterion of reproductive success.

In terms of analytical technique one of Malinowski's main contributions was probably the use of case studies. These were also used extensively by his student Firth in the ethnography of Tikopea (Firth 1936), and taken up by the 'Manchester School', exemplified in Gluckman's study of Barotze law (Gluckman 1955), both of which contributed to the understanding of social process. Malinowski's demonstration that the total network of the *kula* was the outcome of exchanges between individual partners showed how social structures are constructed by human action. Although this insight was disregarded by Radcliffe-Brown's Structural Functionalism, it ultimately contributed to the development of exchange theory (see chapter 4).

Radcliffe-Brown

For Radcliffe-Brown, the function of a custom was the contribution it made to the continued life of the 'social organism' (Radcliffe-Brown 1952: 178–9). His primary aim was not to explain the diversity of human societies but rather to discover laws of social behaviour by demonstrating that in societies of a certain type, certain characteristic social relationships would be found. Radcliffe-Brown showed, for example, that in communities where property was inherited by patrilineal descent, a man had a predictably constrained relationship with his father and a predictably relaxed relationship with his mother's brother. The father and his brothers would all be addressed by the same kinship term, 'father', because they all stood in the same jural relationship to the speaker. Radcliffe-Brown called this the principle of 'the unity of the sibling group'. He rejected the idea, advanced by some evolutionists, that the relationship with the mother's brother was a survival from a supposed era when matrilineal descent had preceded patrilineal descent, or that a man called his father's brothers 'father' because in some distant, promiscuous past people had been unaware of their true paternity (Radcliffe-Brown 1952: 24–5). Although Herbert Spencer's theory of social evolution influenced Radcliffe-Brown in his attempts to show how a society might be transformed from one type into another, Durkheim's influence dominates his work. Radcliffe-Brown made the organic analogy central to his theory of Functionalism. He defined functional unity as 'a condition in which all parts of the social system work together with a sufficient degree of harmony or internal consistency (to continue as a system), i.e. without producing persistent conflicts which can neither be resolved or regulated' (Radcliffe-Brown 1952: 181). Radcliffe-Brown recognised that the idea of the functional unity of a social system was a hypothesis and that some degree of opposition or antagonism between groups within society was an essential feature of every social system. Not all customs need necessarily have a positive function and some social systems may display a higher degree of integration than others. He also appreciated that while the structure of an animal organism is directly apparent, social structures cannot be seen, only deduced from the observation of regularities in the actions of the participants. He accepted that, in a social system, one custom or institution may be replaced by a different one without the social system itself breaking down. Societies can change in a way that animal organisms usually cannot.

Despite Radcliffe-Brown's cautions, the organic analogy has intrinsic limitations. The organs of the body function to maintain an equilibrium, whereas societies frequently change. In the words of the Norwegian anthropologist Fredrik Barth, the organic analogy invites a 'morphological' approach to social analysis, in which the actions of individuals are aggregated to discover the norm, which is taken to be a general custom (see chapter 4). The organic analogy further implies that society itself has 'needs' which must be satisfied by the actions of its members, rather than the other way around as is the case in Malinowski's approach.

One of the notorious aspects of the history of Functionalism is that Malinowski's two most influential students, Fortes and Evans-Pritchard, abandoned him for Radcliffe-Brown. But Fortes, in seminar papers late in his life, made it clear that he found Malinowski's instructions for analysing social life impracticable. Malinowski advised Fortes to draw up a large table listing all the customs he had identified among the Tallensi and explore their economic, political and ceremonial aspects in order to trace the interconnections between each custom and every other custom to which it was related. Malinowski had hoped that the *kula* would prove to be the first example of a widespread institution, as totemism was known to be (Malinowski 1922: 514), but the Tallensi lacked a single, unifying exchange network like the *kula* of the Trobriands, and Fortes found it impossible to derive a clear overview of Tallensi social structure from Malinowski's method.

In place of this Radcliffe-Brown offered some simple, general constructs from which testable predictions could be made. The most famous of these constructs is the concept of the unilineal descent group. The legend, as told by Fortes, is that Evans-Pritchard wrote to Fortes while they were both in the field, advising Fortes that when he returned to London he should meet Radcliffe-Brown. When a meeting had been arranged, Fortes arrived to find Evans-Pritchard sitting on the sofa describing Nuer society, while Radcliffe-Brown stood, leaning against the mantelpiece, listening. After a while, Radcliffe-Brown declared, 'That sounds like a unilineal descent system to me. Read Gifford, young man' (see Kuper 1988: 191–2 for another account and assessment of this incident).

Although Malinowski had studied matrilineal descent among the Trobrianders, he considered clans and subclans only briefly, concentrating on the way in which matrilineal descent affected interpersonal relations, such as those between a man and his father, or his mother's brother. This is partly explained by the fluidity of Trobriand descent groups (see Weiner 1976: 38–43). Both Fortes and Evans-Pritchard were able to take the concept of descent advocated by Radcliffe-Brown and apply it to their fieldwork data, demonstrating that the segments of Nuer and Tallensi society consisted of patrilineal descent groups (see chapters 4 and 5 for a brief summary of their analysis). Each descent group was found to be approximately equal in size and politically autonomous. Links between lineages were established by the rule that no one could marry within their own group, and the rule that groups were collectively responsible for the actions of their members against outsiders.

Unlike Malinowski, Radcliffe-Brown did not attach much importance to case studies. Malinowski distinguished between what he termed 'the inponderabilia of actual life', that is, the daily routines, conversations and friendships which could only be observed first hand, through which were 'spun the innumerable threads' of 'the real substance of the social fabric' (Malinowski 1922: 19), and the more formal legal duties, ceremonial obligations and etiquette, the 'definite, crystallised legal frame' of society, about which questions could be asked, yet which were felt less intimately by the people who adhered to them. For

Radcliffe-Brown, 'the actual relations of Tom, Dick and Harry may go down in our field notebooks and may provide illustrations for a general description. But what we need for scientific purposes is an account of the form of the structure' (Radcliffe-Brown 1952: 192). Radcliffe-Brown followed Durkheim in 'reifying' society. His method has been described as 'Structural Functionalism', because it focuses on the structure of social relationships, and attributes functions to institutions in terms of the contribution they make to maintaining that structure.

Key concepts in Functionalist analysis

The basic building blocks of Functionalist social analysis are the concepts of *status* and *role,* most clearly articulated by the American anthropologist Linton (Linton 1936: 113ff.) who was Radcliffe-Brown's contemporary at Chicago, and slightly later by Radcliffe-Brown himself (Radcliffe-Brown 1940a). Malinowski wrote of the 'sociological differentiation of functions' and of 'offices' without using the terms 'role' or 'status'. As formulated by Linton, a person occupies a status when they are attributed the right or the duty to behave and be treated in a certain way during social interaction. When they act as expected of them in that status, they are performing the associated role. According to this theory:

1 A status is a position in a pattern of social relationships.
2 A role consists of the form(s) of behaviour associated with that status.

Each status is a position in a particular pattern of interaction. The individual person can have several statuses, depending on which patterns of interaction (s)he participates in, and the part played in each. Statuses that are assigned to individuals automatically, by virtue of their possessing certain socially defined characteristics, are said to be *ascribed.* Statuses which can only be taken on as a result of demonstrating certain skills or accumulating sufficient wealth, are said to be *achieved.*

The notion that everyone is accountable to everyone else (or, as Radcliffe-Brown's school would have put it, to the collectivity that constitutes society) is implicit in this simple typology. The implication appears naive wherever certain members of the society have exclusive control of productive resources such as land, livestock, equipment or human labour. In any such context, those in power have the means to impose their wishes upon others. This vital Marxist insight was lost sight of by the Functionalists. The smallest-scale societies, particularly hunter-gatherers living in unpredictable environments (see chapter 6), conform best to the Functionalist model of social control.

Functionalists conceived of the social structure as a network of statuses connected by the associated roles. Four types of intermediate structure are recognised, illustrated in Figure 2.1. *Dyadic* relationships

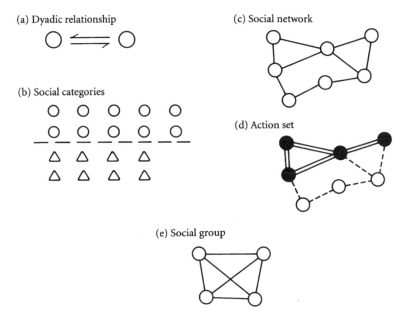

Figure 2.1 Intermediate structures in Functional analysis

exist between two complementary statuses, such as friend ↔ friend, patron ↔ client, or wife ↔ husband. *A social category* consists of a number of people who have some status in common, but do not inter-act in an organised fashion on the basis of that common status. In many small-scale societies people inherit membership of social cate-gories called moieties (halves of society), which govern whom they can marry. If the moieties are *exogamous* (i.e. if you cannot marry someone in your own moiety) a member of moiety A must marry a member of moiety B, and vice versa.

A *social network* is composed of many dyadic links. Each person in the network is related to at least two others, but no one is related to all other members. The members of a social network do not share common property or organise their action for a common purpose. A network tends, therefore, not to be clearly bounded. Each link may be built on a different role. If some members of a network activate their relationships with one another to perform a particular task, they can be said to constitute an *action set* (Fichter 1957). The beer parties of the Fur (see chapter 4) are action sets.

A *social group* has several characteristics which distinguish it from social categories, networks or action sets. It has defined limits which establish who is a member and who is not. It has an internal structure, such that all members stand in a definite relationship towards all others, even when there are several roles within the group. Each group has a common purpose, which may be to administer common property, to defend members against outside attack, or to worship a deity. Groups are relatively permanent. Many of the groups found in small-scale societies recruit their members at birth and each child joins the group to which their mother or father belongs. A group which has presumed perpetuity, that is, which is expected to last indefinitely, is called a *corporate group*. A group which has a limited life-span, such as a household which will dissolve when the married couple who established it die, can be called a *quasi-group*.

Functionalists working in the Durkheimian tradition, particularly Radcliffe-Brown and his students, attached greatest importance to status and role (the elementary particles of the social system), and to the corporate groups which outlived individuals and gave permanence to the social structure. Networks, action sets and quasi-groups assumed greater importance with the development of interactionist theories, which returned to Malinowski's approach, and interpreted social systems as the product of negotiation, rather than predetermined structures within which each new individual was assigned a place (see chapter 4). These concepts became particularly useful when anthropologists began to study social relationships in urban communities, especially those consisting of working-class families who held no property in common (Barnes 1954; Mayer 1966).

Some examples
The usefulness of these concepts can be illustrated by considering how they clarify four different social systems: those of Greek shepherds; East African cattle herders; a pre-colonial West African kingdom; and a

Latin American shanty town. The African cattle herders are a classic instance of a society dominated by autonomous, corporate descent groups, but such groups are absent from the social organisation of the Greek shepherds and shanty-town dwellers. Although corporate descent groups are present in the African kingdom, they are incorporated into the hierarchical structure of the state, and are not politically autonomous. While the Sarakatsani own their flocks of sheep and goats the shanty-town dwellers, lacking legal rights to their houses and working for others, have little material basis on which to build social relations.

The Sarakatsani

When Campbell studied them in the 1950s, the Sarakatsani of northern Greece were transhumant shepherds. In summer, the 4,000 Sarakatsani of Zagori grazed their flocks of sheep and goats on mountain sides between 3,000 and 6,000 feet above sea-level. During the winter, when the high mountains were snow-covered, and the lower slopes less parched by the sun, the Sarakatsani moved their flocks down. The Sarakatsani did not own the pasture on which they grazed their livestock, but were obliged to rent it from villages or monasteries. While Campbell was in the field, between 100 and 300 shepherds attached themselves to each high village in summer, accompanied by up to twenty-five times their own number in livestock. Each household, containing a nuclear family (parents and children) managed its animals independently. In winter, associations were formed between sets of households who rented pasture jointly and managed their flocks collectively. The associations were called *stani* (companies), and they can be characterised as quasi-groups, since they dissolved each spring. The 4,000 Sarakatsani living in the district of Zagori did not constitute a corporate group. They never united to take common action against outsiders, and they shared no common property. Campbell found them none the less to be united as a community which shared common values, held together by networks of interpersonal relations. They passed judgement on each other's actions according to an ethical code, and competed to achieve honour in the eyes of their fellow Sarakatsani. In the following account, the present tense will be used to describe the organisation studied by Campbell in the 1950s (many Sarakatsani have now taken up residence in towns).

The Sarakatsani kinship terminology is *bilateral*, that is, no distinction is made between relatives on the mother's and father's side. This, as will be seen below, is related to the absence of corporate descent groups. Every individual recognises matrilateral and patrilateral kin (i.e. kin on his mother's and father's side) to the level of second cousins (Figure 2.2). These relatives constitute the individual's *kindred*. For any individual, the total Sarakatsani community is divided into two categories: those who are kin, and those who are strangers. Relatives by marriage (*affines*) form a third, intermediate category. Confidence, trust and a genuine concern for the other's welfare can only exist between kin. There are no other institutions which enable people to co-operate.

Campbell calculated that a kindred would contain about 250 people, about half of whom would be second cousins, and therefore on the margins. As Figure 2.2 shows, only full brothers and sisters will have the same kindred and even they will have different affines once they marry. The overall pattern of social relationships among the Sarakatsani can therefore be characterised as a network, in which each person has dyadic relationships with a number of others who, in turn, have relationships with others. A person's kin are often scattered through the region and, when a family travels in search of pasture, their kin can provide the hospitality and local information which pride prevents a man from seeking from strangers. When a man is involved in a fight, or a difficult court case, his kinsmen will help and advise him. Because he is their relative, they will lose standing if he acts dishonourably and, because he needs their support, he will listen to their advice (exemplifying the Functionalist theory of social control). A man must not steal animals from the flocks of his kinsmen, seduce their sisters or gossip about their private lives outside their own circle of kin. No one may marry a kinsperson. Affinal ties are necessarily established between non-kin, obliging both men and women to turn outward from their kin and create new social relationships. Goody (1983) has argued that the prohibition on marriage between kin was a creation of the early Christian church.

Two forms of social unit are central to Sarakatsani social organisation. Both are small and neither is corporate. The minimal unit is the nuclear family, to which the individual 'owes almost exclusively his or her time, energy and loyalties' (Campbell 1964: 8). The Sarakatsani household is not a corporate group because it lacks perpetuity. Not only must the members of a corporate group recognise common rights

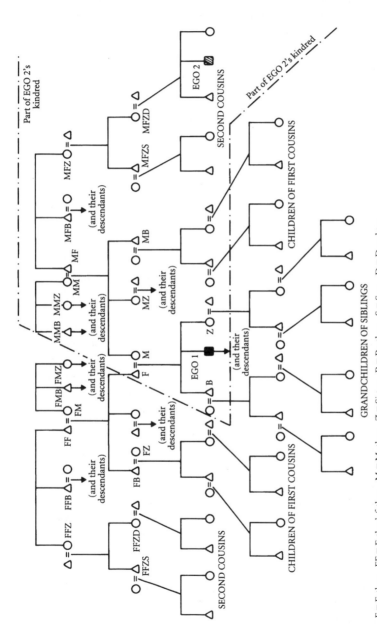

F = Father   FF = Father's father   M = Mother   Z = Sister   B = Brother   S = Son   D = Daughter

Note: The diagram shows the extent of *ego 1's* kindred and part of *ego 2's* kindred

Figure 2.2 Sarakatsani kinship and the extent of personal kindreds

and obligations to one another, as do the members of the Sarakatsani household, they must also have a means of recruiting new members to replace those who die or leave. The Sarakatsani household only lasts for the lifetime of the married couple who establish it, and is therefore best regarded as a quasi-group. As their children grow up and marry, they leave. Gradually, the household dissolves, and is replaced by those of its children. A corporate group must also possess shared property, ownership of which is transmitted, undivided, to each successive generation of members. The Sarakatsani household undoubtedly possesses common property. It has a herd of sheep and goats, it lives in a single hut, it has a collection of religious icons (paintings) and the equipment it needs to subsist. When sons marry, however, each son receives a portion of the flock, which becomes the sole property of his household. Each daughter receives a number of the icons and household utensils. Instead of successive generations within a line of descent having collective rights to these goods (as is the case in the two following examples), each child receives an exclusive right to a discrete portion, and sheds the mutual obligation to avenge the rape or murder of his siblings in favour of undisputed loyalty to his own household (Figure 2.3).

The process by which a household dissolves, to be replaced by others, is a gradual one. Before any brother has married, their unity against outsiders is complete. Once by one, however, their interests diverge. A married man owes it to his wife not to risk his life avenging wrongs against his own siblings, and the obligation is reinforced by the birth of children, for whose sake he must strengthen relationships with his wife's kin. None the less, married brothers often continue to live and work together, and jointly manage their respective herds of sheep and goats. The vehicle through which they do so is the second social unit, the company. To rent good winter pasture an agreement must be negotiated with a government official or person of influence within the village. To produce cheese that will sell for a good price requires careful management of the flock and of the company's purse. Each company chooses one man to act as its leader, or *tselingas*. Most companies consist of households led by married brothers who, although their own portion of the herd is clearly marked, continue to co-operate for their mutual benefit. A company led by an influential *tselingas* will attract other households, headed by uncles, nephews, brothers-in-law and cousins of its leader.

The power which can be gained from membership of a company is

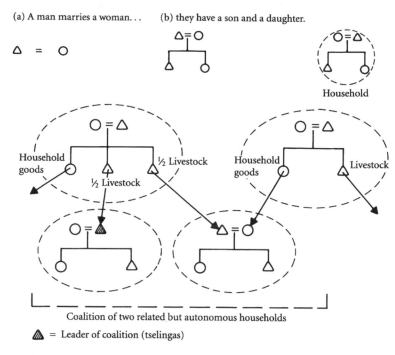

(a) A man marries a woman. . .   (b) they have a son and a daughter.

Household

Household
goods   ½ Livestock   Household   Livestock
½ Livestock   goods

Coalition of two related but autonomous households

⧫ = Leader of coalition (tselingas)

Figure 2.3 Sarakatsani inheritance

exemplified by an incident which occurred in 1954. Ten years earlier, a company consisting of eighty people owning 2,000 sheep and goats found that the Muslim villagers from whom they habitually rented winter pasture had been obliged to flee as refugees to Albania. The company's right to continue grazing the pasture was challenged by the Christian villagers who had usurped the Muslims' land and who eventually persuaded the local governor to support them. In 1954 the Sarakatsani were told they could not return. They responded by hiring two influential lawyers and instructing them to enter a plea 'that they were simple men, but easily tempted to violence in a crisis' (Campbell 1964: 90). Nothing more happened until word reached the village that the company had reassembled and was on its way down the mountain. At this point, the decision was overturned on the grounds that such a large body of persons and animals had to be accommodated somewhere to avoid violence and political embarrassment.

Sarakatsani social organisation functions to enable the mobility transhumant shepherds require, but at the cost of the fragmenting effect of feuds sparked off by murder, rape and revenge. It is also clear that, if the Sarakatsani were able to coalesce as corporate groups, they would gain even more power than that conferred by membership of a company.

The Samburu

The Samburu of Kenya are also pastoralists but, unlike the Sarakatsani, they have corporate groups. They belong to a cluster of pastoral societies extending from the Nuer and Dinka of the Sudan in the north, to the Maasai of Kenya and Tanzania in the south. Probably historically related to the 'Ethiopians' described by Herodotus, these societies are ultimately descended from communities who emigrated south centuries ago in response to desertification of the Sahara. The region in which these peoples now live was colonised by the British in the early twentieth century, not because its economy offered the opportunity for making a profit, but to pre-empt an Amharic Ethiopian advance. Unlike the traditional kingdoms to the south, the pastoral nomads had a political system unfamiliar to their colonisers; they remained difficult to subdue, as did the Scythian nomads described by Herodotus. Evans-Pritchard set out to solve the puzzle posed by the resilience of these uncentralised peoples in his fieldwork among the Nuer.

One key to their social organisation is the age-grading which frees young men from family responsibilities while they fulfil the role of warrior (*moran*); the other is the collective management of livestock by corporate groups, membership of which is inherited from father to son (patrilineal descent). Spencer, who studied the Samburu during the 1960s and 1970s (Spencer 1965, 1973), concluded that the role of warrior was not so much dead as dormant among the Samburu (Spencer 1973: 95); elsewhere it is an active role, albeit one sadly transformed in potency by the acquisition of high-powered guns left over from the various wars that have been fought in the region over the past two to three decades.

To understand the way in which status is allocated on the basis of age, the distinction between *age-grade* and *age-set* must be appreciated. An age-grade is a *social category* through which everyone must pass. Each grade is associated with a status, which defines the *role* a person must adopt towards other members of the grade, and towards members of other grades. Samburu boys who are circumcised over a period of about a decade are admitted to a particular age-set. This age-set is a quasi-group which survives for the remaining life-span of its members. An age-set can be compared to a class of children at school, and age-grades to the years (grades) through which they will pass in the course of their school career. The principal grades for males are *boyhood* (birth to adolescence), *warriorhood* (adolescence to early manhood) and *elderhood* (mature manhood) (see Figure 2.4). Women do not belong to age-sets, but two female age-grades are recognised. Girls are initiated at about the same age as boys but, whereas boys have to remain unmarried during their time as warriors, girls are expected to marry soon after initiation.

	AGE GRADES (Statuses)	LOCATION OF AGE SETS
	[DECEASED]	[SET A]
		SET B
		SET C
		SET D
ELDERS	[FATHERS OF THE MORAN]	SET E
ELDERS	[FIRESTICK ELDERS]	SET F
MORAN	[ADJACENT SET]	SET G
MORAN	[EGO]	SET H
BOYS		

Figure 2.4 Samburu age grades

Within an age-set relationships are friendly and egalitarian. Authority is primarily exercised between alternate age-sets. The 'Firestick elders' organise the initiation of boys who are entering the set two sets below them. They can delay the initiation of unruly boys. Once that set is closed and admitted to warriorhood, the Firestick elders educate and discipline them. The future children of disobedient *moran* can be cursed, rendering the warriors effectively unmarriageable and therefore unable to graduate to elderhood. The Samburu consider the disciplinarian role of Firestick elder to warrior incompatible with the relationship of father to son, and the fathers of the *moran* belong to the age-set above the Firestick elders. The large difference in age between father and son is possible because of the delayed age at which men marry. *Moran* are obliged to live in a separate camp to that of married men and women, and are forbidden from eating meat cooked by a married woman (a convenient way of reducing the opportunities for women to visit desirable young men of their own age in the bush). Free from family responsibilities, the warriors are strategically placed to defend their own hamlet from cattle-raiders, and to venture out on raiding parties themselves. Moran may have unmarried girls as lovers, and enter into illicit affairs with older men's wives, but they are not deemed to be legally responsible for any child born. The moran may be a *genitor* (biological father) of a child, but not its *pater* (social father). It is already possible to see how a functional analysis of social structure reveals the greater complexity of Samburu society, when compared to the Sarakatsani.

Patrilineal descent among the Samburu confers membership of the father's corporate descent group. Functionalist theory assumes that descent group membership is *ascribed* at birth although there is, in practice, some flexibility allowed by adoption (see Verdon's re-analysis of Nuer descent, discussed in chapter 4).

Unilineal descent, that is descent which is traced exclusively through the social father (termed patrilineal descent) or the mother (matrilineal descent) ensures that everyone in society will automatically belong to a group, and to one group only: the group to which the father, or mother, belongs. Figure 2.5 shows who would belong to particular descent groups among the Sarakatsani, were such groups to exist. Whenever lineages are exogamous (i.e. people cannot marry other members of their own lineage), everyone will also have a personal kindred which includes people outside his or her lineage. Links in this network have been created by the marriages of relatives. Functionalist theory interprets such networks as the means for mediation during disputes between lineages and, therefore, one of the ways in which the units of Durkheim's segmentary society are held together.

The simplest model of a lineage assumes each couple have one son and one daughter (Figure 2.6 (a)) but, in practice, some couples have many children and others have few, or none. Thus lineages tend to be *segmented*. Each segment at a higher level (A and B in Figure 2.6 (b)) contains segments at a lower level (1, 2, 3 and 4 in Figure 2.6 (b)). In the

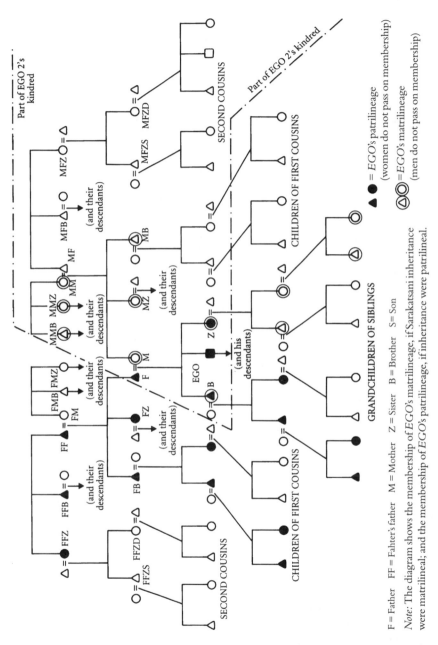

F = Father   FF = Fahter's father   M = Mother   Z = Sister   B = Brother   S = Son
FF = Father   FF = Fahter's father   M = Mother   Z = Sister   B = Brother   S = Son

Note: The diagram shows the membership of *EGO*'s matrilineage, if Sarakatsani inheritance were matrilineal; and the membership of *EGO*'s patrilineage, if inheritance were patrilineal.

Figure 2.5 Sarakatsani kinship, with the composition of putative descent groups indicated

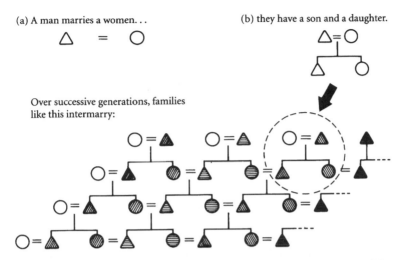

(a) A man marries a women. . .

(b) they have a son and a daughter.

Over successive generations, families like this intermarry:

and within this pattern four lines of patrilineal descent can be recognized, designated thus: i: ▲◍ ii: ▲⬤ iii: ▲◍ iv: ▲ ... Everybody belongs to *one* descent group only; the group of their father. Only sons transmit this membership to their children.

(b) In reality, some families have many sons, others many daughters, and so descent groups fluctuate in size. The fortunes of one group might proceed as follows:

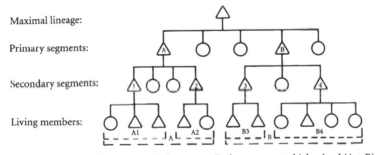

Branches within the lineage are called *segments*. Each segment at a higher level (A + B) contains lower level segments (1, 2, 3, 4).

Figure 2.6 Single lines of descent and segmentary lineage

case of patrilineal descent, where a man has two or more sons, each son is potentially the founder of a discrete segment of the lineage. The converse is true of matrilineal descent, where it is a woman's daughters who become the founders of lineage segments. A lineage traces its descent from a known ancestor, but lineages are often clustered into wider descent groups whose members believe they share common descent, even though they cannot specify genealogical links to a common ancestor. Such groups are known as *clans*.

The Samburu patri-clan is the most significant corporate group among the Samburu. Spencer found that within each clan there was a spirit of co-operation based on the principle that the clansmen shared rights over each other's cattle. Each man acknowledges that fellow clansmen are entitled to gifts from his herd, especially to feed their households or contribute to marriage payments. Although such gifts must be repaid, 'it is this element of reciprocity which creates the assumption of a larger herd belonging to the whole clan' (Spencer 1973: 77). Clansmen also advise each other on how to manage their herds, encouraging husbands to respect their wives' rights and younger brothers not to compete with older, unmarried brothers. Warriors who belong to the same clan perform their ceremonies together, to the exclusion of all outsiders. Social interaction is more cohesive, and larger groups can act together than is the case among the Sarakatsani.

Samburu daily life is regulated by the intersecting roles ascribed by descent and age, which function to organise camp life. The pastoral economy and semi-desert ecology make nomadism essential. Household heads prefer to camp with other men of the same clan and age-set, because they can rely on their trust and co-operation. The huts and cattle of the married men and women are protected by a thorn fence around the camp. Within the enclosure, the elders meet to plan camp life. The warriors of the households must camp outside, to defend the camp. They are excluded from decision-making and, in principle, from the elders' wives.

Corporate descent groups are conspicuously absent from Sarakatsani society and the greater social cohesion achieved by the Samburu is demonstrated by the absence of feuding. Gaining recompense for murder is not the sole responsibility of the dead person's household, as it is among the Sarakatsani, but extends to the whole clan, or segment of it, which stands opposed to the victim's group. A murderer is driven out of his own camp for the first five days, and must wear women's clothes for several months, making him a general object of ridicule. Any person who gains revenge by killing the murderer is held to be responsible for *both* murders. Some time after the murder, the victim's patrilineal kin go and seize the murderer's cattle or, if he is a poor man, the herd of one of his close relatives. The owner should not resist, since the cattle are *restitution* for the murder. If a killing is deliberate, public opinion will favour a quick seizure of cattle to avert the possibility of revenge. If the killing were accidental, seizure might be delayed or never carried out.

Why does the clan not keep its livestock together in a single herd? Spencer concludes that the scattered and unpredictable distribution of water and pasture oblige each household to manage its portion of livestock independently. In the dry season, a father may even have to send some of his sons with cattle to one water-hole, and others to another. Even when conditions are good only about four households can camp together, otherwise surrounding pasture is quickly exhausted (Spencer 1973: 21–22).

Since the Samburu clan is exogamous, bridewealth moves cattle between clans. Although Spencer found inter-clan relationships to be marred by disputes over cattle, whether designated as bridewealth or as compensation for murder, the links established by inter-clan exchange are the basis for alliances between clans. There are no positions of authority which extend beyond the clan and even the affairs of the clan are managed collectively by the elders. A coherent society exists, in which collective action can be taken without overall leadership. Evans-Pritchard's account of the Nuer was the first to elucidate this type of social structure.

The Asante

The Asante kingdom, now incorporated into the nation state of Ghana, had a political system which the British found easier to comprehend. The Asante belong to a larger category of people speaking Akan languages and their state developed in conflict with an older Akan kingdom called Denkira. There had been centralised states in West Africa for many centuries, the oldest known, Ghana, having been founded before AD 800. At first the Asante consisted of a confederation of independent states but later, at around 1760, were transformed into a single, centralised state, which was at its most powerful in the early nineteenth century.

The leader of the first British expedition to record its visit to the capital, Kumasi, was dazzled by its wealth and artistry. He described his impression of their arrival in 1817 as follows:

> An area nearly a mile in circumference was crowded with magnificence and novelty ... The sun was reflected, with a glare scarcely more supportable than the heat, from the massy gold ornaments,

which glistened in every direction. More than a hundred bands burst
at once on our arrival, with the peculiar airs of their several chiefs . . .
At least a hundred large umbrellas, or canopies, which could shelter
thirty persons, were sprung up and down by the bearers with brilliant effect. The chiefs, as did their superior captains and attendants,
wore Ashantee cloths of extravagant price . . . They were of incredible
size and weight, and thrown over the shoulder exactly like a Roman
toga. Gold and silver pipes and canes dazzled the eye in every direction. Wolves' and rams' heads as large as life, cast in gold, were suspended from the gold-handled swords.

> (McLeod 1981: 7, quoting Bowdich 1819)

Trade had always been essential to the power and wealth of West
African kingdoms. Early states such as Ghana traded north across the
Sahara to Muslim empires. Participation in trade was, however, only
possible because of local production. In the Middle Ages, gold and kola
nuts (kola nuts were chewed to suppress thirst on the desert journeys)
were traded north, in exchange for cloth and slaves. Literate scribes
travelled south to assist in the administration of the kingdoms. By the
fifteenth century, European traders on the coast were receiving Akan
gold and slaves in exchange for cloth and guns. New World crops such
as maize, cassava and ground-nuts increased the productivity of farming just as did those, such as the potato, which were introduced to
Europe at the same time. Slaves were probably also put to work within
the West African states to pan for gold and cultivate crops to sustain the
growing towns (see chapter 5). By the eighteenth century, the population of Kumasi was about 20,000, fed by the produce of surrounding
farms. Craftsmen such as the blacksmiths, goldsmiths and umbrella-
makers each occupied a designated district of the capital.

It took six wars for the British to defeat the Asante. Even after defeat,
the Asante state retained much of its structure, which allows a reconstruction of how the state was organised. The Asante are divided between
eight matriclans, which are exogamous and dispersed throughout
Asante territory. Each clan consists of numerous matrilineages. Every
free-born Asante belongs to his mother's matrilineage and is a citizen
of the chiefdom to which that lineage belongs, from which he derives
the right to cultivate forest land within the chiefdom. The living members of a matrilineage normally occupy a 'ward', containing up to
twenty households, in one village. Each village contains representatives of between four and eight of the clans. The lineage which is said to

have founded the village and first cleared the surrounding land, has the right to provide the village headman, but he is advised by the heads of other lineages living in the same community.

The Asante matrilineage is a corporate group, owning the land farmed by its members, performing their funerals and caring for its ancestors' shrines. It is exogamous. When a girl marries, her husband presents bridewealth to the lineage head. No member can divorce without the head's consent. The head settles disputes between members of the lineage and represents it at the village council. A senior woman is chosen to resolve disputes between female members and to initiate girls into adulthood. She is often the authority on the lineage's genealogy. Most marriages occur between lineages in the same village. Although a father is expected to feed and clothe his children he does not have legal authority over them, because (as among the Trobriand Islanders) they belong to their mother's lineage and fall under her brother's authority. Many men live with their sisters rather than their wives and Fortes found that less than 50 per cent of children under fifteen years lived with their fathers (Fortes 1950: 262).

Whereas Samburu lineages are politically autonomous, Asante lineages have been incorporated into the hierarchical administrative structure of the state. Within the original confederation, the chief was drawn from a royal lineage and the chief's community was the capital of the chiefdom. The elders of lineages within his community were not simply responsible for the internal affairs of their own lineage, but also for liaison with a designated cluster of other villages in the chiefdom (Figure 2.7). The elder acted as a 'friend at court', relaying messages to or from the villages and collecting tribute. When the confederation underwent centralisation into a single state, each of the original chiefdoms became an *oman* or 'division' and its chief became an *omanhene*.

As Kumasi emerged from a position of equality with the other chiefdoms, and became the seat of central government, so its chief became the *Asantehene* or king. His council of elders, drawn from the lineages resident in the capital, assumed responsibility for running the state. Some governed conquered areas, others supervised gold production. The structure of the Asante state can be described as 'segmentary', since smaller administrative units are grouped into larger units with the same structure, but it is not segmentary in the sense seen in Samburu society, where each corporate descent group is politically independent. Central authority has been assumed by certain lineages, whose members

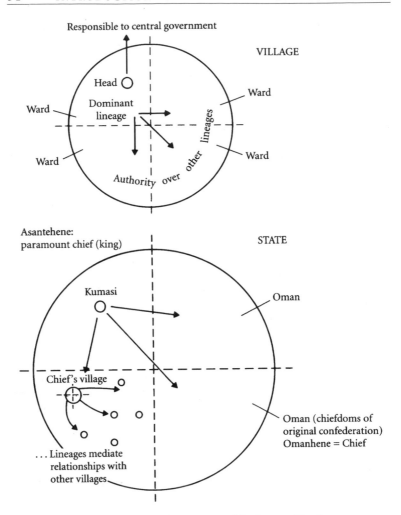

Figure 2.7 Diagrammatic structure of the Ansante kingdom

have extended their control over the members of other lineages. The power of central government rests, to an important degree, on the exclusive control over long-distance trade and the weapons obtained through such trade.

Los Peloteros, a shanty town in Puerto Rico

Los Peloteros, a shanty town in Puerto Rico studied by Helen Safa, has several structural features in common with the Sarakatsani. The fundamental feature of shanty-town members' social life was their exclusion from the corporate groups functioning in the wider society. Although the main thrust of Safa's analysis is Marxist, demonstrating its inhabitants' powerlessness against the urban elite, Safa uses Functionalist constructs in her analysis of shanty-town social structure. Like the Sarakatsani, shanty-town society lacks corporate groups. The shanty-town community was largely excluded from meaningful participation in dominant institutions such as political parties, trade unions and the church. The inhabitants of Los Peloteros mistrusted unions, regarding them as corrupt.

Over 70 per cent of Los Peloteros' inhabitants had begun adult life as landless wage labourers on farms or plantations (Safa 1974: 20). Much rural land belonged to US corporations. Low pay, seasonal unemployment and lack of residence rights drove shanty-town dwellers out of rural Puerto Rico. They settled in squalid shanty towns on the edge of the capital, becoming the core of an urban, industrial workforce. Their dwellings were built on public land on the city's margins. In 1935 the first arrivals settled on what were then mangrove swamps. Still beset by job insecurity, many could only find part-time or intermittent employment. No sewerage system or refuse collection services were ever provided, nor were there opportunities for employment within the shanty town. Although houses were bought and sold, inhabitants had no title to the land on which they were built. By 1962, most of Los Peloteros had been cleared and its inhabitants rehoused.

In the absence of corporate groups, kinship networks were crucial to social action. During the thirty years of its existence, new arrivals to the shanty town often settled close to kin. Although many people stayed less than five years, a core of 'old-timers' consisting of some of the original inhabitants, gave stability to the neighbourhood. Twenty per cent of households in Los Peloteros are headed by women, usually older women. Safa argues that, in the absence of property, there is little to keep a man and woman together. This is probably the most salient difference between the social structure of the Sarakatsani and shanty-town dwellers. A kin network linking households provides vital support, and husband and wife remain closely linked with their own kin. Although sets of kin group no longer co-operate to earn money as a team, as they may have done on a rural farm, the kindred still operates as a closely knit social unit providing support and companionship to its members (Safa 1974: 41).

Like the Sarakatsani community of Zagori, the shanty town was bound together by a network of reciprocal relationships. 'We always have something for someone in need' a resident told Safa (Safa 1974: 61). None the less, the inhabitants of Los Peloteros resembled the Sarakatsani in their assumption that, beyond the circle of relatives, neighbours and close friends, 'everyone is out for himself' (Safa 1874: 65). Co-operation was generally *ad hoc*, with *action sets* coalescing to help at childbirth, house fires and other emergencies. There was no central authority in the community, and social control was exercised by overlapping sets of neighbours. Sometimes, action sets emerged in response to particular problems. In 1959, a group of neighbours went to the aqueduct authority to complain about the shortage of water in one part of the shanty town. They were told no funds would be made available, because Los Peloteros was about to be demolished. They rallied support among their neighbours, who refused to pay their water bills. Signatures were collected for a petition to the mayor. Eventually a new pipeline was installed. Committees were also formed to protest against the unpaved and unlit streets. The only significant formal association was the housing co-operative.

For the Functionalists, the crucial difference between Samburu and Asante social structure is that Samburu corporate lineages are politically independent. The balance of power in Samburu social structure is created by the equal strength of lineages, and their shared desire to maintain peaceful relations mediated through the network of relationships between members of different lineages. In the Asante case, the balance of power exists between the palace organisation and the collectivity of commoner lineages. In Functionalist theory, the Asante correspond quite closely to Hobbes' model of the social contract between a sovereign and people, whereas the Samburu exemplify the solution to the problem of creating a stable society without a literal sovereign. Gluckman compared the social structure of East African pastoralists to international relations between nation states (Gluckman 1970). As part-societies, who depend on others for access to essential resources, communities like the Sarakatsani of Zagori and Los Peloteros lack corporate, property-owning groups. None the less, the networks which grow up through mutual aid can, on occasions, provide the means for collective action through action sets recruited to tackle particular problems.

The classification of social systems

Radcliffe-Brown's main contribution to anthropology was to devise ways of classifying the numerous non-Western societies which were studied during the first half of the twentieth century into types and subtypes. This is exemplified by his classification of Australian Aboriginal societies. Although he carried out fieldwork in Western Australia, it was in an area where Aboriginal life had been severely disrupted by colonial settlement. Many of his data were collected at an isolation hospital for victims of venereal disease on an island, where he was able to obtain genealogies and statements of marriage rules but, unlike Malinowski, he did not observe how these procedures were translated into daily interaction during traditional life in the bush (Kuper 1983: 44–5).

Radcliffe-Brown demonstrated that all of the 130 Australian 'tribes' whose social organisation had been documented by 1930 had certain common dimensions in their social structure:

(a) a local organisation made up of families grouped into bands;
(b) the division of the tribe into social categories such as moieties (defined above, p. 38);
(c) the use of a particular type of classificatory kinship terminology, each associated with a particular marriage rule (these marriage rules are described in chapter 3);
(d) a totemic religion.

These common strands in social organisation were shown to vary in regular ways (Radcliffe-Brown 1930–1). The kinship terminology corresponded to both the rule of marriage and the categories created by the moiety and section systems. The local group corresponded to the men of a totemic clan with their wives and children. Radcliffe-Brown showed that a limited range of types of Aboriginal society could be identified, and named each after a representative 'tribe': the Kariera system, the Aranda system, the Murngin system, and so forth (see Figure 2.8). Each of the 130 cases documented was assigned to one or another of these types.

When Radcliffe-Brown attempted to relate the different 'species' of Aboriginal society to one another, he did so by implicitly relying on the nineteenth-century notion of social evolution as an increase in complexity. He tended towards a Spencerian view that lower levels of social

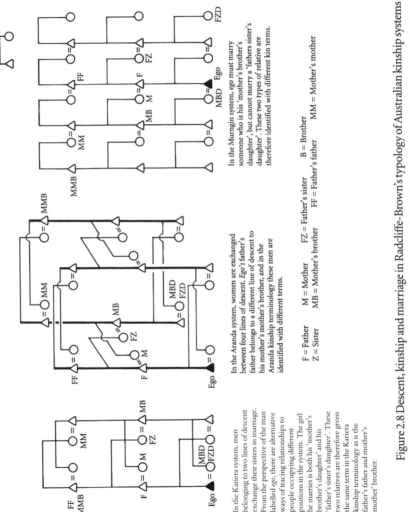

(a) A man marries a woman. . .   (b) they have a son and a daughter.

In the Kariera system, men belonging to two lines of descent exchange their sisters in marriage. From the perspective of the man labelled ego, there are alternative ways of tracing relationships to people occupying different positions in the system. The girl he marries is both his 'mother's brother's daughter' and his 'father's sister's daughter'. These two relatives are therefore given the same term in the Kariera kinship terminology as is the father's father and mother's mother brother.

In the Aranda system, women are exchanged between four lines of descent. Ego's father's father belongs to a different line of descent to his mother's mother's brother, and in the Aranda kinship terminology these men are identifed with different terms.

In the Murngin system, ego must marry someone who is his 'mother's brother's daughter', but cannot marry a 'fathers sister's daughter'. These two types of relative are therefore identified with different kin terms.

F = Father   M = Mother   FZ = Father's sister   B = Brother
Z = Sister   MB = Mother's brother   FF = Father's father   MM = Mother's mother

Figure 2.8 Descent, kinship and marriage in Radcliffe-Brown's typology of Australian kinship systems

integration gave way to higher levels, through time. Since Radcliffe-Brown saw accurate prediction as the hallmark of a successful scientific hypothesis, he attempted to show that he could predict the structure of Aboriginal societies from this hypothesis of evolving complexity. Spencer and Gillen had already documented the Aranda social system of central Australia (Spencer and Gillen 1899). Radcliffe-Brown considered that the Aranda kinship terminology and subsections derived from a simpler form of organisation which, he predicted, would be found in north-west Australia. It did indeed exist there, among the Kariera and other communities (Figure 2.8 shows how the Aranda system can be visualised as a more complex version of the Kariera system). Unfortunately, the Kariera system had already been documented in north-west Australia by Daisy Bates, an amateur anthropologist who had retired to the bush after it was discovered that she had been bigamously married to two men, one of whom was executed for shooting prisoners during the Boer War. Bates claimed Radcliffe-Brown had plagiarised her field notes: a claim later supported by Needham (1974). Isobel White argues that the matter is more complex. Radcliffe-Brown would have known of elements of the Kariera system from Bates' work, but may have fitted them together into a general appreciation of the structure of the system himself (White 1981).

Late in his life, Radcliffe-Brown wrote that classification was an essential prerequisite for scientific study, and that he had devoted his career to devising means for classifying human societies (Radcliffe-Brown 1951). He could be described as the Linnaeus of social anthropology. Linnaeus was a creationist, who believed that much of the variation between biological species was due to the original divine creation, and that little had occurred since. Like Linnaeus, Radcliffe-Brown was less interested in the history of societies than in devising a typology of what were seen to be essentially stable types. Radcliffe-Brown's method was to deduce the norms of conduct and, while the resulting typologies did clarify the range of human social systems, they diverted attention away from the individual strategies studied by Malinowski. Typologies tend to be inimical to the study of variability within types.

Radcliffe-Brown and his followers were later ridiculed by Leach for indulging in 'anthropological butterfly collecting' when they classified societies into types and subtypes, as if each new ethnography brought into the study was pinned to a board in its appropriate place according to some arbitrary principle such as the colour of the butterflies' wings or the length of their legs (Leach 1961a). How helpful is it to class the social structures of Greek shepherds and Puerto Rican shanty-dwellers together? Is the presence of centralised government among the Asante, and its absence among the Samburu, the most salient difference in their political systems? There is no doubt that, as ethnographies began to accumulate, some means for describing societies according to certain agreed criteria such as the rule of descent was needed to facilitate comparison and generalisation. One of the classic compilations of Structural Functionalist ethnographies in the Radcliffe-Brownian style is *African Systems of Kinship and Marriage* (1950), edited by Radcliffe-Brown and Daryll Forde. The other is *African Political Systems* (1940) edited by Fortes and Evans-Pritchard. In his introduction to *African Systems of Kinship and Marriage*, Radcliffe-Brown wrote that: 'to understand any kinship system it is necessary to carry out an analysis in terms of social structure and social function. The components of social structures are human beings, and a structure is an arrangement of persons in relationships institutionally defined and regulated' (Radcliffe-Brown 1950: 82). In his introduction he classifies kinship systems into several basic types. Kinship is based on descent, and therefore the type of descent is the diagnostic feature. Descent may be cognatic (i.e. bilateral, as seen among the Sarakatsani and Peloterenos), patrilineal (as among the Samburu), matrilineal (as among the Asante) or double unilineal. Cognatic descent (i.e. bilateral kinship) gives rise to personal kindreds, unilineal descent to lineages. Marriage rearranges the social structure by creating new relationships between groups of kin. Radcliffe-Brown demonstrates that such a typology not only allows the classification of African kinship systems, but allows them to be compared with Indian, North American, Teutonic and Tudor English kinship.

The typology of African political systems devised by Fortes and Evans-Pritchard in *African Political Systems* was essentially a reworking of pre-Functionalist models of social evolution: from hunter-gatherers lacking land-ownership, through uncentralised subsistence farmers and pastoralists with land or livestock vested in descent groups, to traditional, tribute-paying states. In the preface to *African Political Systems*, Radcliffe-Brown defines political organisation as: 'the maintenance or establishment of social order, within a territorial framework, by the organised exercise of coercive authority through the use, or the possibility of use, of physical force' (Radcliffe-Brown 1940b: xiv). Two principal types of African political system were identified: states (such as the Asante), which have a centralised authority, and stateless societies (such as the Samburu), where order is maintained because the segments of society have equal power, and balance each other in disputes.

One of the main weaknesses of this approach to anthropology is that it is largely descriptive. There are no hypotheses to explain why the variety of human societies should take particular forms. The pseudo-historical theory that matrilineal descent is a survival from an earlier phase in social evolution was rejected, but no alternative causal theory of human social behaviour is put in its place. Radcliffe-Brown wrote that 'All the kinship systems of the world are the product of social evolution. An essential feature of evolution is diversification... and therefore there is great diversity in the forms of kinship systems' (Radcliffe-Brown 1950: 82). Unfortunately Radcliffe-Brown's concept of diversity is misleading. He failed to relate it to any concept of adaptation and, like Herbert Spencer, visualised the social system evolving in its own right, not as a consequence of the changing behaviour of individuals. One reason why any such theory would have been difficult to arrive at, is that social institutions have been reified. Instead of keeping Malinowski's insight that patterns of social behaviour are the consequence of people furthering their interests through interaction, institutions take on a life of their own. Evans-Pritchard's argument that it is because the lineage structure of the Nuer is so 'deeply rooted', that Nuer can actually move around and attach themselves to any community they like by whatever cognatic or affinal tie they find it convenient to emphasise is a classic example (see chapter 4)! Function has become defined by a tautology: the function of a custom is the contribution it makes to social solidarity. Why do customs take the form they do? Because that is the form they must take to perpetuate that type of social system.

An equally serious criticism of Structural Functionalism has been advanced by Asad (1973). While it is true that Malinowski was concerned by the impact of colonialism, little or nothing of this appears in the monographs written by Radcliffe-Brown's disciples. Asad argues that the Functionalists deliberately played down social change because they depended on colonial governments for access to the field. Consciously or otherwise they sought to reconstruct how their communities would have been if colonialism had never taken place, and in doing so minimised not only the dynamics of indigenous African history, but the consequences of the slave trade, and the introduction of taxation, wage labour and freehold title to land by colonial governors. Asad argued that 'it is because the powerful who support research expect the kind of understanding which will ultimately confirm them in their world view that anthropology has not very easily turned to the production of radically subversive forms of understanding' (1973: 17). This explains why Safa relied on a Marxist analysis to explain the powerlessness of the shanty town's inhabitants. The response to this criticism by other anthropologists will be considered in chapters 5 and 7.

CHAPTER THREE

Structuralism

The Structuralism advocated by the French anthropologist Claude
Lévi-Strauss during the 1950s and 1960s is closely related to the
Structural Functionalism practised by Radcliffe-Brown and his
students. Both were heavily influenced by the theories of Durkheim.
The principal difference is that Radcliffe-Brown studied the regularities in social action, which he saw as an expression of social structures made up of networks and groups, whereas Lévi Strauss located
structures in human thought, and saw social interaction as the outward
manifestation of such cognitive structures. Structuralism is opposed to
the Marxist theory that people's beliefs and ideas are determined by the
material conditions of their existence. In the United States, cognitive
anthropology developed a parallel approach to the analysis of cultural
structures during the 1960s and 1970s exploring, like Lévi-Strauss,
kinship, symbolic communication and indigenous classifications of the
natural world. D'Andrade suggests it was the development of artificial
logic in computer languages during the 1950s which stimulated interest in discovering the natural logic of the human brain during the
following decades (D'Andrade 1995: 10).

Durkheim and the origin of Structuralism

The earliest Structural analysis appeared in 1903, when Durkheim and
his nephew Mauss published a study of *Primitive Classification*
(Durkheim and Mauss 1963) in which they tried to reconstruct the
origin of logical thought in the collective consciousness of the earliest

societies. Returning to the problem posed by Rousseau concerning the origin of language, Durkheim and Mauss took the opposite approach to that of later structuralists, arguing that taxonomies of the natural world are too complex for the individual human mind to construct, if it has only its innate capacities to rely upon. They therefore asserted that such classifications are collective in origin. Durkheim and Mauss further argued that the structure of natural taxonomies cannot be derived from simple observation of nature. The hierarchy of families and genera is not empirical. Therefore, they concluded, society also provides the structure upon which classifications of nature are built. After all, the term *genus* originally referred to a Roman kin group.

Taking the indigenous societies of Australia to be the simplest human societies to have survived, they reconstructed the development of clan totemism into the form recorded in central Australia by Strehlow, and Spencer and Gillen (Strehlow 1907–20; Spencer and Gillen 1899): the same authors who later influenced Radcliffe-Brown. Supposing that the simplest, and therefore earliest, form of a compound society would be one with two segments, they envisaged moieties as the earliest social divisions. Moieties often have totemic emblems which form opposed pairs, such as eaglehawk (a hunting bird) and crow (a scavenging bird). Subsequent development of a section system (known to Durkheim and Mauss as 'marriage classes') would impose a generational division on each moiety, creating a four-fold division of society as in Table 3.1. Since clans are more numerous than this, they imagined that the division of society into many clans would be a third stage of development. At both moiety and clan level, it was argued, the classification of nature derives from the classification of people in society.

Durkheim and Mauss contended that once a totemic system had been established it could 'react against its cause' and bring about increasing social differentiation. If Australian Aboriginal societies became increasingly divided into larger numbers of clans, this could be the consequence of philosophical reflection upon the form of society, which had been made possible by the development of the system of thought. They argued that the Aranda of central Australia had developed the more complex system of eight subsections, rather than the four-section system already recorded in eastern Australia, as a consequence of this supposed process. Here, too, can be seen the theoretical tradition on which Radcliffe-Brown was to draw in his argument that the Aranda kinship system had developed from an earlier system of the

Table 3.1 *Durkeim and Mauss' hypothetical reconstruction of the development of Australian Aboriginal social systems*

Moiety I (Eagle)	{ marriage class A { marriage class B	{ emu clan { snake clan { caterpillar clan ...
Moiety II (Crow)	{ marriage class A' { marriage class B'	{ kangaroo clan { possum clan { lizard clan ...

Kariera type. Outside Australia, the consequences of this developmental sequence could be found in the allegedly more complex systems of native North Americans such as the Zuñi. Chinese Taoist philosophy was claimed to carry the process forward towards the abstract and 'relatively rational' order seen in the earliest philosophies.

Durkheim and Mauss' extraordinarily speculative theory makes many unjustifiable assumptions. Social causality of cognition is never demonstrated. Unilinear evolution is assumed, and taken to justify ranking historically unrelated cultures on a single ladder of complexity. While it will never be possible to reconstruct the circumstances in which the first totemic classifications appeared, Needham (1963) has pointed out that a simple comparison of Australian societies with others of comparable complexity, such as the Basarwa or San of the Kalahari, would have shown that clans and totemism are not invariably associated with such hunter-gatherer cultures (Barnard 1989; but see Lee 1979: 340–1, where he suggests some form of totemism may have existed among the Ju/'hoansi (!Kung San) in the nineteenth century).

Durkheim took the analysis of totemism further in his subsequent book *The Elementary Forms of the Religious Life* (1915 [1912]). Here he argued that religion originated in the deification of the collective consciousness. To reconstruct the origin of religion it would therefore be necessary to discover the circumstances in which people had first become aware of the collective consciousness. Durkheim still supposed that indigenous Australian societies were the simplest known. The central Australian ethnography of Spencer and Gillen (1899) described how some central Australian rituals culminate in a moment when the participants rush together to the centre of the dance ground. Durkheim interpreted this episode as a re-enactment of the moment when the members of the clan first met each other. He seems to have visualised a primal condition not unlike that imagined by Rousseau, in which people normally wandered as solitary individuals through the vast outback but, in Durkheim's image, periodically emerged from the bush to meet together. The meeting, like the start of a nuclear chain reaction, initiated a social current which swept through the minds of the participants and was perceived by them as a spiritual force acting upon each from the outside.

Durkheim argued that, although the Aborigines were aware of the social current generated when the clan assembled, they could only express their awareness through 'symbols'. These symbols were supplied by clan totems. Durkheim had learned from the central Australian ethnographies that people attached particular importance to the material objects used in ritual to represent clan totems. 'If left to themselves,' he concluded, 'individual consciences are closed to each other; they can communicate only by means of signs which express their internal states' (Durkheim 1915 [1912]: 230). Sacred objects were the concrete realisation of the sense of a collective force felt by members of a clan when they interacted. Celebration of the clan's totemic ancestor in ritual was a reaffirmation of the group's identity within the wider compound society. Indeed, he argued, the survival of the society as a system depended on such periodic reaffirmation of each segment's place in the whole. The association of each clan with a particular animal emblem was arbitrary. It did not matter whether a particular clan had snake, possum or kangaroo as its emblem. Once the association was established within the collective consciousness, however, it seemed natural and immutable.

It is extraordinary that such a speculative theory could have been so fruitful, but this is probably because Durkheim failed fully to appreciate that an explanation for the function of a custom in contemporary society does not need to be based on a speculative reconstruction of its origins. Durkheim's theory of the function of symbolic action stimulated three lines of development in the social sciences: structural linguistics, the structural theory of myth and ritual, and the Functionalist theory of religion.

Structural linguistics

The Swiss linguist Saussure was presenting his structural theory of linguistics through general lectures in Geneva at the time Durkheim was developing his theory of totemism (1906–11). Although Saussure died

Table 3.2 *Durkheim's model of clan totemism*

GROUP	clan A	clan B	clan C...etc.	(social group)
motif	Emu	Python	Kangaroo	(animal emblem)

Table 3.3 *Saussure's model of the linguistic sign*

IDEA	RIVER	STREAM	RIVULET...etc.	(SIGNIFIED)
sound	'river'	'stream'	'rivulet'	(signifier)

before he had committed his lectures to writing, several of his former students relied on their lecture notes to reconstruct his theory. Saussure had given his course three times, changing his ideas to some extent each year. Even those who had listened to the same lecture found their notes did not always agree. The published book expressed what they considered Saussure had intended (Saussure 1959: xiv–xv). Several writers have subsequently argued that Saussure interpreted Durkheim's model of clan totemism as a special case of a more general phenomenon, and developed it into a general theory of communication through signs (e.g. Barthes 1967: 23; Ardener 1971: xxxiv). Saussure took issue with the idea that language originated by imitating the sounds of things, so that the message DOG might be communicated by barking, or the message BEE by buzzing. Like Rousseau, he realised that in all extant languages, the vast majority of words derive their meaning from the arbitrary or conventional association of sound and meaning. Even if onomatopoeia could explain the way hypothetical, early languages conveyed meaning, it could not explain how language has functioned throughout history. Language has all the qualities Durkheim attributed to the collective consciousness; it exists prior to the birth of those who use it, and seems to impose itself upon people, as if they had no choice but to accept its conventions. Saussure concluded that, as in Durkheim's model of clan totemism (Table 3.2) each clan is arbitrarily associated with a particular totemic emblem carved on its sacred objects, so each idea in language is arbitrarily associated with a sound (Table 3.3). The sound is the *signifier*, and the idea the *signified*. Together, they constitute a linguistic sign. The significance of each clan's totemic emblem derives from its place in the structure of a segmentary society. The meaning of each linguistic sign is determined by its position in the total language. A 'stream' is smaller than a 'river', but larger than a 'rivulet'.

Saussure's theory was more complex than Durkheim's, and one of the crucial additions that he made was to introduce the distinction between *language* and *speech*. Speech draws upon the vocabulary and grammar of the language to construct a limitless series of statements. Saussure showed that signs can be related in two ways, firstly as a *syntagmatic* chain such as a subject and object linked by a verb ('the woman threw the ball') and secondly as a *paradigmatic* series, consisting of alternatives that could be substituted for any of the signs in a syntagmatic chain ('the *child* threw the ball'; 'the woman *found* the ball', and so forth). Saussure also pointed out that a language gradually changes. A sign can be studied *synchronically*, that is, in terms of its position in the structure of the language at any time, and *diachronically*, as its meaning is transformed by changes in the structure of the language.

The Structuralist theory of ritual

The British Functionalists such as Malinowski and Radcliffe-Brown took from Durkheim's theory the inference that a people's religion will both 'reflect' the structure of their social system and function to maintain that system in its present state. Variations between myths told by neighbouring peoples would be expected to reflect differences between their social systems. Centralised political systems will be associated with beliefs in a high God, who has lesser beings to mediate between himself and ordinary people. Uncentralised political systems will be associated with religions in which there are a number of deities of equal status. In particular, lineage-based societies such as the Nuer and Tallensi will be associated with ancestor cults.

In continental Europe, anthropologists more closely linked with Durkheim took up the proposition that a culture's belief system had an internal logic which gave meaning to ritual actions. Like the British school, they were reacting against earlier writers who had interpreted customs as survivals from what were supposed to be earlier stages in human social evolution. The British argued that the presence of each custom should be explained in terms of its contemporary *effect* on the social system. Writers such as Hertz (1960 [1909]) and van Gennep (1960 [1905]) argued that the *meaning* of each custom had to be deduced from its place in a cognitive structure. In his essay 'The Preeminence of the Right Hand' (originally published in 1909, and reprinted in Hertz 1960) Hertz documented a general tendency among many cultures to associate the right hand with strength and order, the left with chaos and weakness. He concluded that the structural opposition between right and left stood for a more general opposition between right and wrong. He regarded this as one case of a general tendency for 'primitive man' to think in terms of dual oppositions. What is, in biological terms, a statistical tendency for more people to be right- rather than left-handed is transformed by culture into an absolute opposition filled with meaning. 'The vague disposition to right-handedness, which is spread throughout the human species,' he wrote, 'would not be enough to bring about the absolute preponderance of the right hand were this not reinforced and fixed by influences extraneous to the organism' (Hertz 1960: 91).

In *The Rites of Passage* (originally published in 1905), van Gennep argued for the widespread occurrence of three-part, rather than binary cultural structures. He contended that there is a general tendency among human societies to conceive of a change in status on the model of a journey from one town or country to another or, as he put it, a 'territorial passage' (van Gennep 1960: 18). Territorial passage had three aspects: separation from the place of origin, transition and incorporation into the destination. Just as the opposition between right and left hands could stand for more general, moral oppositions, so territorial passage could stand for any change of status in society. 'Marriage by capture', where the groom and his brothers ride to the bride's house, snatch her and carry her back to the wedding is not a survival from some fancied early epoch in human evolution when cave men clubbed women and dragged them home, but a symbolic enactment of the separation of the bride from her status as an unmarried girl in her parents' house, and her incorporation into the groom's household. Rituals of birth, entry into adulthood and death may all have the same structure. As van Gennep emphasised, 'The primary purpose of this book is precisely to react against the procedure which consists of extracting various rites from a set of ceremonies and considering them in isolation, thus removing them from a context which gives them meaning and reveals their position in a dynamic whole' (van Gennep 1960: 89). Although van Gennep's case of territorial passage is not the only image around which passage rites are constructed, many others have the same tripartite structure, as set out in Table 3.4.

Table 3.4 *Tripartite structures in the symbolism of rites of passage*

	Separation	Transition	Incorporation
(a)	leave home	travel through wasteland	arrive at destination
(b)	eaten by monster	lie in belly	reborn
(c)	immoral order	destroyed by flood	replaced by new order

Lévi-Strauss

Lévi-Strauss developed the theories of Structuralism in two directions, first in his analysis of the structure of kinship systems and later, in his study of the structure of myth. His study of kinship centred on the discovery that strikingly similar marriage rules existed among historically unrelated peoples in Australia, Asia and the Americas. All such societies were characterised by rules which specified that an individual should marry his or her *cross-cousin*. Cross-cousins are children of siblings of the opposite sex (i.e. children of a brother and a sister). Such kinship systems differ from those with which British anthropologists who had worked in Africa were familiar. In the so-called *descent* systems of Africa, corporate descent groups frequently consist of 200 or more people and are sometimes much larger. The descent group is internally divided into segments and marriage occurs more or less at random outside the lineage, giving each member a distinctive network of kin relations traced through the in-marrying parent. Children are generally forbidden from finding a spouse in the in-marrying parent's lineage, further diversifying the ramification of kin relationships between lineages. In the *alliance* systems studied by Lévi-Strauss lineages, while still exogamous, are smaller, having perhaps 50–100 members. Such lineages enter into regular alliances with other lineages by regularly exchanging marriage partners. Successive generations of one lineage are expected to marry into one other lineage. In consequence one's cross-cousins become preferred marriage partners.

What is cross-cousin marriage?

The character of such a social system can be illustrated with reference to the Yanomamö of southern Venezuela and adjacent parts of Brazil. Although now sadly disrupted by the logging and gold-mining perpetrated by colonial settlers, the Yanomamö may number around

10,000 people. Prior to colonisation, they lived in villages of between 40 and 250 inhabitants. The average village housed about 80 people. The Yanomamö environment was densely forested, but each village was surrounded by gardens in which plantains (a banana-like fruit) were cultivated. Politically uncentralised, the Yanomamö belonged to small, autonomous patrilineages, which depended upon the exchange of women in marriage to maintain alliances with other lineages, either resident in the same village or in neighbouring communities.

Yanomamö frequently move the location of their settlements. They do so partly because garden soil becomes exhausted and must be allowed to return to fallow but, more frequently, they move to escape the raids perpetrated by other Yanomamö. Chagnon, the anthropologist who described the Yanomamö marriage system, reports that ruthlessness in warfare was the foremost male virtue (Chagnon 1968). All men must constantly demonstrate their bravery and lack of mercy in daily behaviour. There is constant fighting between neighbouring villages. Sometimes whole villages move to escape from neighbours' raiding. On other occasions a village which has exceeded the critical size of around 150 members splits, because irreconcilable feuds have broken out within the community, and the members of one lineage move away.

It is hard work felling trees to open a new garden. Plantain seeds and cuttings must be carried to the new site, together with sufficient stored food to sustain people until the new gardens bear fruit. During the first year yields from new gardens are irregular. Successful marriage alliances are crucial, because they forestall the need to move by providing the lineage with allies. Chagnon estimates that a village must have around 50 inhabitants if it is to defend itself successfully, but only persistent enemy attacks will compel a village of above 150 to remain intact. He cites the case of a village known to him which contained 200 people, who split into three factions, each of which established a new village. After suffering persistent raids, the factions reunited and even then endured twenty-five raids in fifteen months. The smallest villages are most dependent on alliances with other villages; the largest are most dependent on alliances within the village.

The sequence by which a Yanomami alliance is established and maintained can be exemplified by taking two model lineages, each of which contain one man and one woman in each generation. In the first generation, the two unrelated men exchange their sisters in marriage

A new alliance...

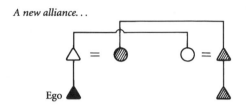

Ego

Whom should ego marry to maintain the alliance?

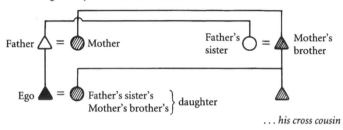

... *his cross cousin*

Where are ego's parallel cousins?

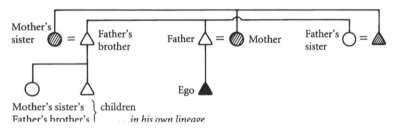

...*in his own lineage*

Figure 3.1 Development of a Yanomamö marriage alliance

(Figure 3.1). When their sons repeat the exchange, each is now marrying a woman to whom he is already related. The Yanomamö marriage rule requires marriage with a cross-cousin. The relationship can be traced both through the father and the mother. The woman whom the man marries is both his father's sister's daughter and his mother's brother's daughter. The woman is marrying a man who is both her mother's brother's son and her father's sister's son. Radcliffe-Brown, who studied such marriage rules in Australia, termed this *bilateral cross-cousin marriage.*

In practice there are, of course, several men and several women in each generation of the lineage. All the men, however, address each other as 'brother' (or 'fellow-male-member-of-my lineage'), and all the women address each other as 'sister'. Men address women of the lineage to which they are allied as 'wife', or 'marriageable woman', while women address the men as 'husband' or 'marriageable man'. Members of the same sex in the other lineage will be addressed as 'brother-' or 'sister-in-law'. The marriage rule is, therefore, that a man must marry a woman he calls 'wife', and a woman a man she calls 'husband'. *Parallel cousins* (children of one's father's brothers and mother's sisters) are addressed as brother and sister, and cannot normally be married. They are, in fact, members of one's own lineage, because the father's brother has married the mother's sister (see Figure 3.1). The rule is only broken when senior men of an over-large lineage precipitate a split by starting to address women in distantly related segments as 'wife', not 'sister'.

The pattern of relationships created by the Yanomamö marriage rule is exactly the same, at least in the model, as that in the Kariera system of north-west Australia (see Figure 2.1 (a)). It was the remarkable convergence of such kinship systems on opposite sides of the world which prompted Lévi-Strauss to develop his theory of cross-cousin marriage.

Lévi-Strauss' theory of cross-cousin marriage

Lévi-Strauss' theory of kinship is built in some important respects upon Radcliffe-Brown's analysis of Australian kinship systems, although this is not as explicitly stated in Lévi-Strauss' writing as it might be. The British Structural Functionalist's influence is apparent from the fact that Lévi-Strauss adopts Radcliffe Brown's three forms of cross-cousin marriage (bilateral, matrilateral and patrilateral) as his basic typology; he re-analyses Australian kinship systems in the first of the ethnographic sections of his book *The Elementary Structures of Kinship* (first published in France in 1949, second edition 1967, English translation 1969), and his theoretical position is frequently framed by placing it in opposition to Radcliffe-Brown's. Like Radcliffe-Brown, Lévi-Strauss is interested in the life of social systems, not individuals, and the needs of the individual are subordinated to the alleged needs of the system. One of the shortcomings of Radcliffe-Brown's typological approach noted by Leach was that there is no apparent limit to the number of types and subtypes of society that can be devised (see chapter 2). Lévi-Strauss set out to demonstrate that there were logical limits to the number of types among what he termed 'elementary social systems'.

Mauss' theory that exchange perpetuates social relationships was equally influential upon Lévi-Strauss' work (see chapter 4), but Lévi-Strauss argued that the structure created by exchange was itself determined by the structure of human thought, developing the ideas of Hertz and van Gennep. Lévi-Strauss' work follows closely earlier Dutch studies of kinship in Southeast Asia, especially Van Wouden's analysis of the practical consequences of different types of cross-cousin marriage and their representation in myth (Van Wouden 1968 [1935]). Structuralist theory explains the structure of society as the product of ideas rather than the material conditions of existence.

Lévi-Strauss pointed out that cross-cousin marriage is a phenomenon which occurs in many parts of the world: not just Australia (as among the Aranda, 'Murngin' and Kariera), but lowland South America (the Yanomamö and others), Southeast Asia and India. Lévi-Strauss accepted that this could not have occurred through diffusion of the custom from a common point of origin, and saw it as an expression of universal patterns of human thought. Durkheim and Mauss had attributed the origin of logical thought to the experience of structure in the segments of a compound society. Lévi-Strauss reversed this hypothesis, and argued that it was the structure of human cognition which generated structure in social relationships. He argued that the exchange of gifts and marriage partners were forms of communication and should be treated like language, the best-studied medium of human communication. While regarding the most basic structures of cognition as universal, Lévi-Strauss accepted Durkheim's caution that supposedly universal psychological mechanisms could not explain human cultural diversity, and he interpreted the *content* of structural thought as the property of specific cultural traditions, paralleling the enormous diversity of languages.

Radcliffe-Brown's theory of kinship was that relationships were built outward from the nuclear family, increasing in scale as social systems achieved higher levels of complexity. Lévi-Strauss followed Saussure in arguing that kinship terms only gained meaning from their place in a structural system, that is, in opposition to other kinship terms, and not by extension from close relatives to more distant ones. One of the simplest might be the four-fold division created by the combination of patrilineal and generational moieties, and expressed through the Australian four-section system (see Table 3.5). In this structure, there are only four basic positions, since grandparents and

Table 3.5 *A four-section system created by combining generational and patrilineal moieties*

		Patrilineal moiety A	Patrilineal moiety B	
	Generation			
A1	Other }	Father and father's sister	Mother and mother's brother	B1
A2	Own }	Ego and siblings	Spouse and sibling-in-law	B2

Note: The table shows how ego's closest relatives are distributed between the four sections, A1, A2, B1 and B2.

grandchildren belong to ego's generation. In the Kariera kinship terminology, which is based on this four-fold division, the father's father and the mother's mother's brother are therefore called by the same term because they occupy the same position (see chapter 2, Figure 2.1 (a)). Parallel cousins occupy the same position as ego's siblings (his brothers and sisters), and are therefore also called 'brother' and 'sister'. Even the closest kinship relationships are thus determined by the structure of the system, and not extension (such as, from father's father to mother's mother's brother, or from sibling to parallel cousin). Just as people are unconscious of the structure of their language, so they are unconscious of the structure of their kinship system and accept it implicitly (Lévi-Strauss 1969: 177).

Lévi-Strauss classified the world's kinship systems into three types: elementary, intermediate and complex. In elementary systems, everyone known to a person stands in a definite kinship relationship to them, even if they have no known genealogical link. There are precise rules of marriage, which specify what type of relative a person must marry. This is the type of kinship system found in Aboriginal Australia. At the other extreme are the complex systems found in Europe. Here only a fraction of the people known to anyone are regarded as their kin. Marriage is regulated by a principle that close kin should *not* marry, and people normally marry non-kin (the Sarakatsani, outlined in chapter 2, exemplify this type of kinship system). Intermediate kinship systems are of the sort found among native North American and many African peoples. Crow-Omaha systems are of this type (Figure 3.2). Here, Lévi-Strauss argued, the social universe is divided into a determinate number of lineages but these are not linked by a regular pattern of marriage alliances. Ego can therefore only specify kinship relationships with members of other lineages into which (s)he or their close relatives happen to have married.

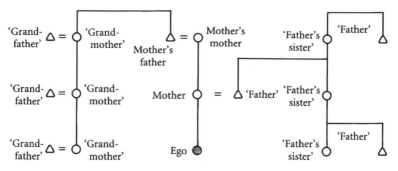

In this example, descent is traced through women. Men marry women of other lineages. The diagram shows the links which *Ego*, in the third generation, has with the lineages of their father and mother's father. In the father's lineage, all women regardless of generation are addressed by the same term as the father's sister and all men born into the group are addressed by the same term as the father. All women of the lineage into which the mother's father was born are addressed as 'grandmother' and their husbands as 'grandfather'.

Figure 3.2 Example of a Crow-Omaha type kinship terminology

Lévi-Strauss' study of *The Elementary Structures of Kinship* is only concerned with kinship systems of the first type. He argued that all systems of this form can be classified according to three subtypes, depending on which rule of cross-cousin marriage they follow. Exchange, he argued, is the universal basis of kinship systems, and is made possible by three properties of the human mind: to accept that rules must be followed, to regard reciprocity as the simplest way of creating social relationships, and to consider that a gift, once given, binds giver and receiver in a continuing social relationship. The structures created by exchange depend on the type of marriage rule followed. In making these claims, Lévi-Strauss was clearly influenced by the work of Malinowski and Mauss (exchange theory will be discussed further in the following chapter). He follows Radcliffe-Brown, however, in arguing that the ultimate beneficiary of relationships created by exchange is the social system, not the individual participants in it.

The Yanomamö case study showed how, wherever a society contains exogamous, unilineal descent groups, cross-cousins will always belong to a different group to ego. Once such lineages are linked by regular marriage exchanges, parallel cousins will always belong to ego's group. Any social system which depends on such regular alliances can therefore specify cross-cousins as the ideal marriage partners and forbid marriage with parallel cousins. Cross-cousins function as 'markers' who, even if they do not themselves become ego's marriage partners, signal the identity of the group into which he or she should marry. Logically, as Radcliffe-Brown had already appreciated, there are only three types of cross-cousin: patrilateral (the father's sister's child), matrilateral (the mother's brother's child) and bilateral (where the father's sister's child and mother's brother's child are one and the same or, at least, occupy the same position in the structure of the kinship system).

Lévi-Strauss' most fascinating discovery was to realise that each type of cross-cousin marriage produces its own structure of exchange. Van Wouden had earlier made the same discovery and it is hard to believe Lévi-Strauss was unaware of his work (see Van Wouden 1968: v, vii, xii). The insight can be illustrated with models which again assume each line of descent has only one man and one woman in each generation. If the men of the two lines of descent exchange their sisters, the mother's brother marries the father's sister. Ego's marriage partner will be at once his mother's brother's child and his father's sister's child. Repeated over several generations, a closed alliance develops between two lines of descent, of the type exemplified by the Yanomamö (Figure 3.3 (a)). One alternative is to open up the pattern of alliance by following a rule that, while the men of one group give their sisters to the men of a second one, they themselves receive their wives from a third. This is the pattern generated by following a rule that men must marry their mother's brother's daughters, but not their father's sister's daughters (Figure 3.3 (b)), which Van Wouden called *asymmetric connubium* (Van Wouden 1968: 86–7). This system can be extended indefinitely, creating a chain of allied groups which only terminates when the chain closes in upon itself to become a circle. For this reason, Lévi-Strauss referred to bilateral cross-cousin marriage as *restricted* exchange, and matrilateral exchange as *generalised*. Both the Kariera and the Aranda have restricted exchange but the so-called Murngin (Yolngu) of northern Australia, whom Radcliffe-Brown chose to exemplify another of his types of Aboriginal society, practise matrilateral cross-cousin marriage.

The third possibility is for a series of lineages each to transfer the members of one sex in marriage one way in one generation, as in matrilateral exchange, but to reverse the direction of exchange in the following generation, as if to repay the debts incurred by the receipt of marriage partners in the previous generation. This is what happens if a

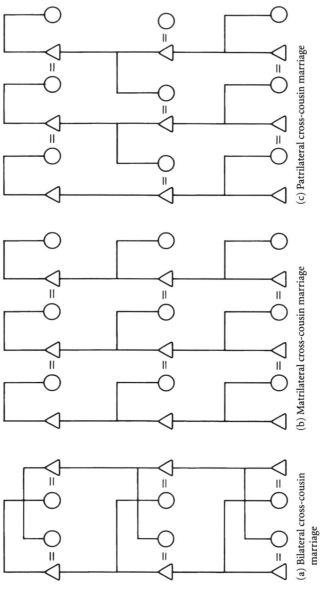

(a) Bilateral cross-cousin marriage

(b) Matrilateral cross-cousin marriage

(c) Patrilateral cross-cousin marriage

Figure 3.3 The structures created by the three types of cross-cousin marriage

rule of patrilateral cross-cousin marriage is followed (Figure 3.3 (c)). Van Wouden anticipated this would have a disruptive effect on social relations, while Lévi-Strauss regarded it as tantamount to a sudden loss of confidence in the stability of the system. Both matrilateral and patrilateral exchange create patterns of debt and credit linking a chain of lineages, but in the case of matrilateral exchange, each lineage has to accept the cost of being permanently indebted to the group who give them their wives, even though it remains permanently in credit with the group to whom it is giving its sisters. Even in bilateral exchange, the two lines remain in a balanced state of debt and credit over successive generations. In the case of patrilateral exchange, the system constantly 'returns to a point of inertia' (Lévi-Strauss 1969: 444) from which social relationships must once more be re-initiated. It is a system with inherent internal contradictions, which will either succumb to these contradictions and collapse, or transform itself into a more stable condition (Lévi-Strauss 1963: 311). Lévi-Strauss' theory appears to be supported by the fact that patrilateral cross-cousin marriage is in fact the rarest of the three types.

To what extent do the participants in such a system need to be aware of its structural consequences? Like Malinowski, Lévi-Strauss considered that there was no more need for them to be aware of the total structure than there was for native speakers of a language to be capable of consciously articulating its grammatical rules. They *do* need to recognise the obligations incumbent on them by virtue of their position in that system. Lévi-Strauss admits that matrilateral cross-cousin marriage seems a 'risky venture' from 'an individual and psychological viewpoint', because each man gives his sister to one group, but relies on the goodwill of another to receive a wife (Lévi-Strauss 1969: 451). He quotes two proverbs from a Sumatran people who practise matrilateral cross-cousin marriage. One, explaining the prohibition on marrying a patrilateral cross-cousin, asks 'how is it possible that water can flow up to its source?' The other, justifying confidence that anyone who has given away his sister in marriage will receive a wife, states 'the leach rolls toward the open wound' (Lévi-Strauss 1969: 449).

Criticisms of Lévi-Strauss' theory of cross-cousin marriage

Two principal lines of criticism have been directed by British and American anthropologists at Lévi-Strauss' theory. The first is generally known as the 'preference or prescription' debate. Critics ask what proportion of marriages have to follow the rule of cross-cousin marriage for Lévi-Strauss' predictions about the structural consequences of cross-cousin marriage to be realised. The Asante told Fortes that they considered the ideal marriage to be with a bilateral cross-cousin, but Fortes found that only 8 per cent of marriages actually accorded with this ideal and alliances between different lineages were rarely perpetuated (Fortes 1950: 279). Chagnon, on the other hand, found that 70 per cent of Yanomamö marriages took place between members of already-allied lineages, and many of them were with first cousins (Chagnon 1968: 73). It is clear that, while the Yanomamö exemplify Lévi-Strauss' predictions concerning the type of structure generated by bilateral cross-cousin marriage, the Asante do not. Another version of the criticism asks how tightly the pool of marriageable women has to be defined to generate Lévi-Straussian structures. Even the Yanomamö allow marriage with second cousins, or more distant relatives, providing they are members of the same lineage as ego's cross-cousins. Suppose the whole of a small-scale society were simply divided into three categories, such that (from the individual's perspective) one-third were members of his own category, one-third were potential wife givers and one-third potential wife receivers? The Purum of Burma, a small community of four villages containing a total of ninety households, appear to have organised matrilateral cross-cousin marriage somewhat in this way (Wilder 1971). Unfortunately for the Purum, their villages came under attack by the Japanese during the Second World War and their marriage system was not available for reinvestigation at the time of the debate stimulated by Lévi-Strauss' theory.

The second critique concerns what Leach termed the 'structural consequences' of cross-cousin marriage. Will the structures generated by a particular marriage rule be the same, even where it is embedded in otherwise very different social systems (Leach 1961b)? Leach pointed out that the Katchin of Burma, whom he had studied, were hill-dwelling, dry-rice cultivators who used matrilateral cross-cousin marriage as a means of creating closed alliances between aristocrats and similar alliances among small groups of commoners. Each alliance might embrace no more than three lineages. Certain women were given in marriage between aristocrats and commoners to create links of dependence. Leach argued that the alliances were unstable. Commoners sought to maintain equality, while aristocrats attempted to extract tribute, in the way that neighbouring princes did in the wet-rice cultivating valleys, but without their access to agricultural surpluses (Leach 1954). The 'Murngin' of Australia, on the other hand, were egalitarian hunter-gatherers, whose use of the same marriage rule created chains of relationships among numerous clans. Leach's study suggests the material conditions of existence may have a radical effect on the way that cognitive structures are expressed.

Just how the Murngin system really worked became the subject of intense debate. Lloyd Warner, an American student of Radcliffe-Brown, had carried out extensive fieldwork among the Murngin. In his book *A Black Civilisation* (Warner 1958 [1937]), Warner had published the Murngin kinship terminology (Figure 3.4) which clearly identified seven lines of descent. Many anthropologists assumed each line on Warner's chart corresponded to a distinct clan, or descent group, on the ground. Since Warner had also written that the Murngin had patrilineal moieties, some assumed that Warner must have missed an eighth line of descent, otherwise the two outer lines whom, it was inferred, closed the circle of the alliance, would be guilty of intra-moiety marriage. Lawrence and Murdock published an interpretation along these lines (1949) which was ridiculed by Radcliffe-Brown as demanding a greater complexity of kinship relationships than even native Australians, masters of kinship though they are, could handle (Radcliffe-Brown 1951)! It is clear from Warner's own work that the Murngin do not create such tidy marriage alliances (Figure 3.5). Yolngu marriages in fact create a network of alliances which sometimes turn back on themselves, so that two local groups appear to be engaging in bilateral exchange. Leach realised this was because some clans consisted of more than one exogamous lineage (Leach 1961b: 70; compare Warner 1958: 26 and Morphy 1978: 217).

When the second edition of *The Elementary Structures of Kinship* was published in 1967, Lévi-Strauss responded to earlier criticisms by contending that, even though in practice matrilateral cross-cousin marriage might involve no more local groups than were needed in the Aranda system, the potential of the two types was always different: the Aranda system would always tend to close in upon itself, whereas the Murngin system would always tend to open out into longer chains of alliance. His argument has received support from Keen's comparison of marriage practices among the Yolngu (Murngin) and their neighbours the Gidjingali, who have an Aranda-type system (Keen 1982).

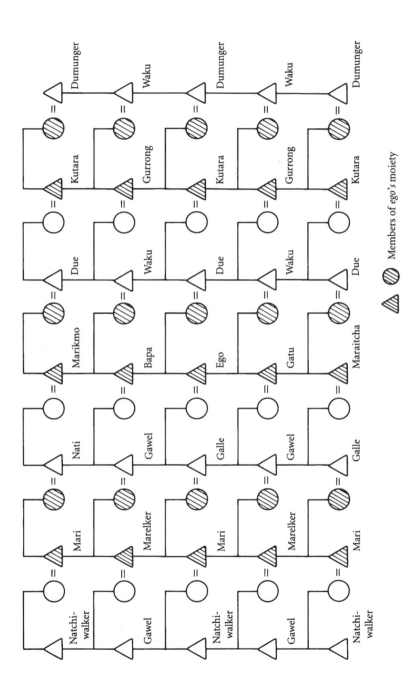

Figure 3.4 'Murngin' (Yolngu) kinship terminology

Members of *ego's* moiety

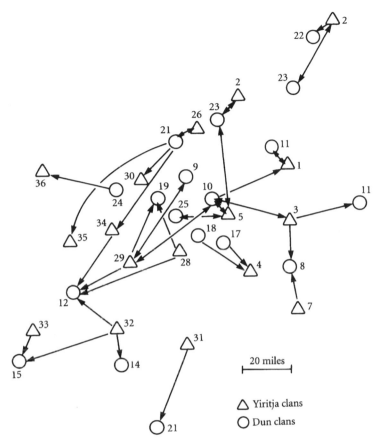

Figure 3.5 Actual marriage exchanges between 'Murngin' (Yolngu) clans

Lévi-Strauss on myth and totemism

Lévi-Strauss' earliest monograph on the structure of myth and ritual was *La Pensée Sauvage* (1962), translated as *The Savage Mind* (1966). Lévi-Strauss here develops Durkheim and Mauss' insights in *Primitive Classification* and in Durkheim's *The Elementary Forms of the Religious Life*. He starts from two observations. Small-scale cultures appear to draw on the natural world in an apparently random or arbitrary way for symbols which represent ideas, values or fears characteristic of that community. There appears, none the less, to be an apparently universal desire to impose order on the world through schemes of classification.

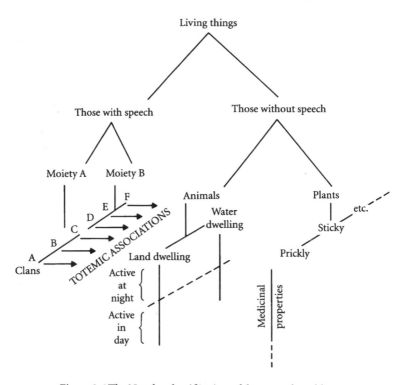

Figure 3.6 The Navaho classification of the natural world

The characteristic form of such classificatory schemes is illustrated in Figure 3.6. Lévi-Strauss outlines numerous examples of what have become known as ethno-taxonomies from traditional societies in Africa, South America and elsewhere. He notes these classifications are often botanically or zoologically accurate or, one might prefer to state, accord with Western taxonomies. The Navaho classification appears quite unlike Western taxonomies, however, in the existence of another order (or axis) of classification, by means of which the Navaho draw equations or correspondences between living beings such as animals and plants, and natural entities such as sky, sun, mountains and water. The sky is associated with the crane, the sun with a songbird, the mountains with the eagle and water with the heron. It is on the basis of such correspondences that plants and animals are used in ritual. Different cultures construct different sets of correspondences, and each particular set appears arbitrary. The Iban of South Borneo, for instance, contend that the cry of the crested jay sounds like the crackling of burning wood and so, if it is heard, is taken to signal success in clearing forest for swidden cultivation. The alarm cry of the trogon, another bird, is said to sound like a dying animal, and therefore to signal good hunting. As Lévi-Strauss observes, many other systems of the same type would have been equally coherent, and no single system of divination from bird calls could be chosen by all cultures. Only the history of the culture can explain why certain associations have been chosen over time; to understand why the Osage of North America associate the eagle with the land rather than the air, we have to know that eagles are associated with lightning, a form of fire, and fire is associated with coal, which comes from the ground. 'It is not the elements themselves but only the relations between them (i.e. the structures) which are constant' (Lévi-Strauss 1966: 53). There are no archetypal, universal symbols. If the same symbols appear among different cultures, it is either through diffusion, or because the intrinsic properties of the symbolic objects have suggested the same associations to members of different historical traditions. Lévi-Strauss concludes, following Durkheim, that the place in which objects are put within any system of significance is more important than their intrinsic properties. The same object may be used in very different ways.

Somewhat contentiously, Lévi-Strauss concludes that 'primitive' people are driven by an insatiable desire to impose order on the world, an argument developed by Douglas in her book *Purity and Danger* (1966) and, to a lesser extent, by Sahlins in *Culture and Practical Reason* (1976a). Any disruption to their system of classification will cause the system to be readjusted, in order to avert the primeval cognitive chaos which threatens to overwhelm them. Lévi-Strauss poses a hypothetical example. Suppose there were a totemic society with two clans called the Bears and the Turtles. If the Bear clan died out, and the Turtle clan increased in size then, in order to restore the two-part structure, the Turtle clan would split into two, known by two different species of turtle (perhaps as freshwater and saltwater turtles). Totemic classifications are, as Durkheim realised, codes for conveying messages in which social groups can be represented in terms of their animal emblems (Lévi-Strauss 1966: 76).

Ethnography shows that such symbolic associations can be expressed in a number of ways; in native North America, clanspeople may be said to be like their totem in behaviour (the Fox clan is cunning, the Moose clan timid) whereas, in Australia, clanspeople may be forbidden from eating their totem since that would be tantamount to eating their own kin. Lévi-Strauss termed such rules 'totemic operators' which function to maintain the significance of the symbolic equations. It is the 'operators' which turn the cognitive structures into structured interaction.

Perhaps the most interesting chapter of *The Savage Mind* is that in which Lévi-Strauss shows that totemism and the Indian caste system, despite their association with very different social systems, have logical structures which are similar in their organisation. They differ in that one is the mirror image, or converse of the other. Both the exchange of women and the exchange of food between groups can be seen as logical 'operators' which maintain the distinctiveness yet interdependence of the groups. In a society based on totemic clans, each clan is exogamous (that is, it exchanges marriage partners with other clans), and avoids eating its totemic emblem. The totemic species is the animal guardian, or transformation, of the clan's founding ancestor. In the Indian caste system, each caste is endogamous (marriages take place within the caste), and associated with a particular occupation: farming, making pottery, weaving and so forth. In the same way that the totem is emblematic of the clan, the occupation is emblematic of the caste. Yet, instead of exchanging women in marriage, the members of the castes exchange the products of their labour.

Through ritual, rather than practical work, the totemic clan exploits its special relationship with its totem to perform 'increase rites' which its members (mistakenly, from a Western perspective) suppose will increase numbers of the totemic species to benefit other clans. In a contrary fashion, by supposing that higher castes will be polluted by contact with the occupations of lower ones, the Indian culture artificially creates a system of occupational interdependence between the castes present in a local community.

Both cognitive systems postulate that the division of society into groups is paralleled by a division of the non-human world into species or the products of work. Yet in one case the species are natural, and wrongly thought to be subject to increase through ritual, whereas in the other the artefacts are genuinely human-made. In one case, women provide the means of linking groups in alliance, in the other they are kept within the group. In one, all clans are equal in status, in the other castes are ranked.

The comparison of caste and totemism shows that the same type of logical thought or *modus operandi* can be found behind social structures traditionally regarded as totally dissimilar. The European folk tales portraying animals as *individuals* with the characters of humans (the wise owl, the timid rabbit) can, Lévi-Strauss proposes, be seen as yet another variation or transformation of this type of thought. Other cultures use the parts of the human body to represent aspects of the environment, such as the points of the compass, or kinship relationships.

Lévi-Strauss' analysis of South American mythology
In his later work on South American mythology, Lévi-Strauss looked in considerable detail at the myths of neighbouring peoples across the Amazon Basin. The parallels that he found between such myths convinced him that the symbolic systems they revealed were not, as he had earlier thought, completely arbitrary but 'motivated' by their natural properties or the way they were commonly used by the peoples of the Amazon. Animals eat raw food, but people cook it. The invention of cooking thus becomes a metonym (i.e. a part exemplifying the whole) for the origin of culture. Animals mate at random (Lévi-Strauss believes) but people construct marriage alliances; thus the first men to exchange their sisters also originate culture. Marriage exchange also becomes a metonym for culture. Lévi-Strauss did not suppose that such myths had any historical validity. It was, indeed, irrelevant to a myth's cognitive value whether it related a genuine historical event or an imaginary one. In this, Lévi-Strauss agreed with the Functionalist rejection of history.

Lévi-Strauss identified a number of mythical themes which recurred throughout lowland South America, each culture having a distinct variant. Some South American bees make deliciously sweet honey, 'so much so that the eater of honey wonders if he is savouring a delicacy or burning with the fire of love. These erotic overtones do not go unnoticed in myth' (Lévi-Strauss 1973: 52). Honey has another property: it is eaten raw. To cook honey would be to mistreat it. Cooking honey is therefore sometimes equated in myth with incest. Equally, refusing to give honey to someone else is associated with incestuous behaviour. The exchange of food parallels the exchange of marriage partners (Lévi-Strauss 1973: 27, 43). Tobacco is another unusual substance. It has to be burnt to be consumed. In one sense, then, honey and tobacco are conceptually opposed: one is untreated by culture, the other is over processed. A three-part cognitive structure

Table 3.6 *Lévi-Strauss' model for the symbolism of food*

Nature	Culture	Spirits
Honey	Cooked food	Tobacco
Promiscuity	Cross-cousin marriage	Incest

can thus be imagined, in which honey, cooked food and tobacco each stand for more general ideas (see Table 3.6).

One myth recounted by Lévi-Strauss depicts the jaguar as the giver of a wife to the first men. He behaves courteously, protects his brother-in-law and allows men to steal his fire; whereas the men keep all the meat they have hunted for their own use and indulge in unrestrained intercourse with the wives they have been given. The animal behaves like a cultured human; the humans behave savagely. By inverting normal behaviour, cultural categories are thrown into relief. Another myth describes how honey was acquired while people were still animals. This is what one might anticipate, as honey does not have to be cooked. The myth extols hunting and gathering. While cooking meat epitomises the origin of culture, people who exceed the bounds of culturally accepted behaviour are burnt alive. One myth describes how the villains are burnt alive in a prison into which tobacco smoke is injected while, in another, tobacco originates from the ashes of a hero burnt on a funeral pyre. Inhaling tobacco instead of exhaling it for the spirits causes people to be turned into animals.

There is no doubt Lévi-Strauss was able to show striking parallels between the symbolic oppositions found in different cultures. In fact, he appears to have a Midas touch, so that whatever he reads falls into a universal scheme of oppositions and equivalences. Leach pointed out that the history of the kings and queens of England can be retold in the form of Lévi-Straussian structural oppositions. Henry VIII was a strong man, who had many wives, while Elizabeth I was a strong woman, but celibate. Elizabeth was succeeded by James, a weak man with one wife. One of the most memorable moments in my Australian fieldwork was, none the less, when Sam Woolagudja, a Worora man of the Western Kimberleys, told me the myth accounting for moiety exogamy:

> There were two men called Wodoy and Djunggun. They agreed to give each other their sisters in marriage. Wodoy started ceremonial

exchange by giving Djunggun a sacred object he had made, and telling Djunggun he must fetch him honey in return. But Djunggun was lazy, and immediately reciprocated with another sacred object to discharge the debt. Then Djunggun started cooking wild honey to eat himself. Wodoy said, 'that's not the way... you're spoiling good tucker'. Wodoy took a stick and killed Djunggun, and they were both transformed into birds (Owlet and Spotted Nightjar).

Although Lévi-Strauss' structural oppositions sometimes appear artificial or strained, he has undeniably drawn attention to widespread patterns in culture.

Cognitive anthropology

During the 1920s the Prague school of linguists, including Jakobson and Trubetzkoy, developed Saussure's theory of the structure of language. Jakobson, who emigrated to the United States, influenced both Lévi-Strauss and the American school of cognitive anthropology (Lévi-Strauss was himself in the United States during the Second World War). Jakobson argued that the sounds of speech are organised into opposed pairs. We intuitively distinguish *fitter* from *sitter*, or *fitter* from *fibber* by identifying which of the alternatives *f/s* or *t/h* the speaker has articulated (Jakobson and Halle 1956: 3). Jakobson thus revived Durkheim and Mauss' hypothesis that the earliest and simplest cognitive structures were based on binary oppositions, a view which harmonised with the development of computer languages based on a binary code. Jakobson further proposed that speech could explore two types of structural relationship. Metaphoric relationships are based on similarity between ideas drawn from different realms. The relationship between a clan and its totem is a metaphoric one. Metonymic relationships are based on what Jakobson called 'contiguity', in which a part stands for the whole: 'the crowned heads of Europe' stand for kings and queens (cf. Jakobson and Halle 1956: 76–80). Leach pointed out that Jakobson's distinction is similar, but not identical, to Saussure's concept of syntagmatic and paradigmatic relationships (Leach 1976: 15).

The American cognitive anthropologists applied Jakobson's Structuralist concepts to the analysis of kinship terminologies and indigenous taxonomies, thus paralleling the work of Lévi-Strauss without apparently being influenced by him. D'Andrade's history of cognitive anthropology, for example, makes very little reference to Lévi-Strauss

(D'Andrade 1995: 248). The work of the cognitive anthropologists is illustrated by Lounsbury's work on Crow-Omaha kinship terminologies and Frake's study of the classification of illness among the Subanam of the Philippines.

Crow-Omaha kinship terminologies exemplify what Lévi-Strauss referred to as 'intermediate' kinship systems. The society is made up of a determinate number of kin groups, but ego can only apply kin terms to those groups into which s/he or their close relatives have married. Within such related groups, however, ego often calls relatives of different generations by the same term (see Figure 3.2). Thus, if descent is traced through men, ego's mother will come from a different group. All members of the mother's group, regardless of generation, may be called 'mother' and 'mother's brother'. Radcliffe-Brown had interpreted this as an expression of the solidarity of the lineage, that is to say, if ego has the same rights and obligations towards all members of his or her mother's group, all members will be called by the same terms. Lounsbury pointed out that Radcliffe-Brown's functional explanation accounted for the presence of Crow-Omaha terminologies in societies with corporate lineages, but not for their occurrence in other types of society, nor for the fact that many societies with corporate lineages do not have Crow-Omaha kinship terminologies. Lounsbury argued that such terminologies must be understood as expressions of a logical system of thought which could be applied in various functional contexts, and showed that the system could be reduced to a set of three rules for classifying different relatives under common terms (Lounsbury 1964: 353, 384).

Frake describes how disease is a frequent topic of conversation among the Subanam. When people were ill they often sought others' advice to try and diagnose their illness. Frake, who eventually recorded 132 Subanam names for diseases, realised that he would never be able to participate in daily conversations until he had mastered the Subanam classification. The same word could have different meanings when used in different contexts. Frake found that the Subanam classified complaints in a structural hierarchy, part of which is reproduced in Figure 3.7.

Many terms such as 'sore' had a more or less specific meaning, depending on the term to which they were opposed. Frake found that people rarely disagreed on what made one disease different from another. In other words, they agreed on the cognitive structure of the

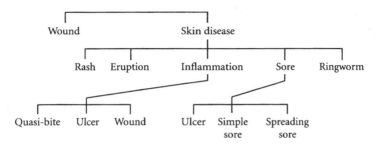

Figure 3.7 Some skin diseases in Subanam

system. If disagreement occurred, it concerned the diagnosis of a particular case: whether an ulcer was 'deep' or 'shallow', for example, or ringworm 'exposed' or 'hidden' (Frake 1961: 130).

Structuralism in Britain

The first, and most influential Structuralist analysis by a British anthropologist was Douglas' *Purity and Danger* (1966). Douglas proposed that Biblical ideas about impurity could be illuminated by studying the place of purity and impurity in the religions of small-scale societies. Douglas argued that beliefs about what is impure and how it should be handled must not be understood as an evolving knowledge of hygiene, but as a series of symbols embedded in a structural system. This was true even of our own notions of dirt: 'upstairs things downstairs; under-clothing appearing where over-clothing should be ... our pollution behaviour is the reaction which condemns any object or idea likely to confuse or contradict cherished classifications' (Douglas 1966: 36)

When the Old Testament book of Leviticus defines certain creatures as unclean, the creatures condemned must be seen as elements in a cognitive scheme. Creatures that live in water but lack fins and creatures which have hands but walk on four limbs are associated with human actions which are morally crooked, or breach social categories, such as theft or incest. The fact that we respond with similar horror to shoes left on the dining table, or food in the bedroom, shows such patterns of cognition to be universal rather than specific to 'primitive' thought.

Leach developed Douglas' application of Structuralism to biblical imagery in his 1976 book *Culture and Communication*. Like the American cognitive anthropologists, Leach also drew upon the work of

Jakobson (Leach 1976: 15, 31; cf. Jakobson and Halle 1956: 81). He explicitly compares the binary opposition of human cognition to the binary code of a computer (Leach 1976: 57). The purpose of cultural logic, Leach argued, is to impose measurable boundaries on a world where, in reality, things merge into each other or change instantaneously. Because the mind depends on creating clear-cut categories and oppositions to make sense of the world, experiencing boundaries and ambiguities induces anxiety. The rites of passage studied by van Gennep impose a transitional phase between leaving the old status and entering the new one to eliminate such anxiety. The meaning of the simplest gestures and the most complex myths can only be understood by discovering the structure of opposed meanings they draw upon. Since, however, the logical operations of the human mind are universal, it should be possible to 'decode' exotic cultures and translate them into the analogous cognitive oppositions of our own culture (Leach 1976: 39).

Criticisms of Lévi-Strauss' theory of myth

How significant is variation in the telling of myth?
Lévi-Strauss' data suffer from the same weakness as Radcliffe-Brown's (see chapter 2). Just as Radcliffe-Brown failed to observe the minutiae of daily life in the field, so the South American myths Lévi-Strauss analyses are derived almost entirely from secondary sources, often from missionaries who may not have been good anthropologists. Lévi-Strauss tends to assume each culture consists of a Durkheimian 'collective consciousness' such that any member can be asked for the 'myth of X' and will give the same account or, where variants occur, they are irrelevant because the same structure is represented (see, for example, Lévi-Strauss 1970: 6–7; 1973: 56–7).

Detailed ethnographic studies have invariably shown the situation to be more complex. Biebuyck's account of the ritual expert among the Lega of the Congo (Central Africa), gives outstanding examples. The expert dazzles his audience by showing how many different interpretations he can derive from one object handled during ritual: the beak of the hornbill may be used to evoke the proverb 'the chick, the tender care of both mother and father', which tells people that even bad children should not be neglected; or the proverb 'Hornbill, the miserable one, has tried to imitate the call of animals', ridiculing a man aspiring to join the Bwami ritual association who has failed to accumulate sufficient wealth. Likewise, the spotted hide of the genet may be used to evoke 'bad kinship, here light coloured, here dark coloured', or to remind people that as the genet's coat is stained by spots, so living people are affected by the deeds of their ancestors (Biebuyck 1973).

Giddens is among those who have argued that structure and performance interact (Giddens 1979). Speech, and the performance of rituals, are real; language, or the structure of the ritual system, are inferred. If participants have learned to construe each others' intentions correctly, then the abstractions which the social scientist describes as *language* or *culture* approximate to reality. But it is through novel performances that culture is changed: each new reading of the hornbill beak or the genet's coat will change the way in which Lega participants at an initiation will understand future occasions when such objects are produced. Giddens calls this process 'structuration'.

Each time a legend is told it similarly takes a particular form which depends on the speaker's interests, and the level at which (s)he wants the anthropologist to understand its references to initiation, ceremonial exchange, clans' title to land and so forth. Members of the community share ideas about what is an acceptable performance of the legend, but there is no standard 'text' against which other performances are judged. Even in the 1950s, Kaberry and Leach showed how different parties to a political dispute in Cameroon or Burma may tell a myth of origin in different ways, so as to justify their claim, and dispute that of their rivals (Kaberry 1957; Leach 1954).

Structuralism as 'code breaking'

A more serious criticism of Structuralism is that it attempts to decode exotic cultures, to show that familiar messages can be found behind unfamiliar signifiers. Lévi-Strauss believed that, by sitting in his study in Paris and reading books about South America, he could penetrate the symbolism of exotic myths. This was because he believed the myths embodied structures that were a direct product of universal cognitive structures, by which the human mind made sense of the world: a belief taken from Durkheim and Mauss' work on primitive classification. The myths made thought possible, by clothing these universal structures in particular imagery. 'Myths operate in men's minds without their being aware of the fact' (Lévi-Strauss 1970: 12), and can do their work equally effectively in the tropical forest or the urban study. The same themes appearing in the myths of different people can be analysed as variants of a single myth (see, for example, Lévi-Strauss 1973: 35ff.).

Suppose, however, that Amazonian people make sense of the world in a wholly unfamiliar way: what they read into the myth will be very different. In a rather trivial sense this is illustrated by the following anecdote: during the mid-1970s, the Australian government decided that the Australian national anthem would no longer be 'God Save the Queen'. Many Australians argued that the new anthem, whatever it was, should be sung to the tune of 'Waltzing Matilda', since that was recognised throughout the world as a musical emblem of Australia. Reporting the debate, a left-wing paper (*The Melbourne Age*) summarised 'Waltzing Matilda' as 'a song about the eternal struggle of the common man against the forces of property and power', whereas a right-wing paper (*The Australian*), on the same day, characterised it as 'a song describing how a sheep thief is brought to justice by the forces of law and order'. This kind of variation, which is meat and drink to contemporary literary theory, has now been shown to be just as characteristic of Aboriginal Australian culture (Morphy 1984; Keen 1994), and its implications for anthropology will be assessed in chapter 7.

The Structuralist critique of Marxism

Structuralists have convincingly shown that human social action is meaningful because it is expressive of cognitive structures. The German sociologist Weber took issue with Marx on this point (Weber 1930) in his foundational study in interpretative sociology, asking whether people's consciousness was, as Marx had claimed, wholly determined by their place in society, or whether beliefs existed independently of the experience of social interaction. Weber asked why a devout commitment to Protestant Christianity had become associated with the growth of capitalism in Western Europe. He argued that Protestant beliefs, and the practices they advocated such as condemnation of indulgence in the arts and self-denial for future gain, already existed in the teaching of Calvin (1509–64), and were taken up by the emerging middle class during the Industrial Revolution because they could be used to validate the ethic of hard work and investment in the future which such people wished to promote. What was, in Weber's assessment, a chance coincidence of an existing set of beliefs and new economic practices led to the paradox that a class of people engaged in intense material economic activity also became deeply religious.

Despite having published a Marxist analysis of social processes in *Stone Age Economics* (1974), Sahlins turned to a Structuralist analysis of social process two years later, in *Culture and Practical Reason* (1976a). Marvin Harris traces Marshall Sahlins' interest in Structuralism to the time he spent with Lévi-Strauss in Paris between 1967 and 1969, while writing *Stone Age Economics* (Harris 1979: 233). Sahlins contends that 'individuals and social groups, in struggling against one another, transforming nature, or organising their life in common, bring into play a system of concepts which is never the only possible one and which [none the less] defines the very form of their action' (Sahlins 1976a: 20). The environment or subsistence economy can never wholly determine the form of a people's beliefs and values, and yet the way in which they interact will be determined by their values and beliefs. Sahlins considers that non-Western societies pose this problem for analysis in particularly acute terms since, in contrast to Western society, 'Archaic' societies appear relatively unchanging, or impervious to history. How can this be? Sahlins takes the example of the culture of island communities in eastern Fiji, where he had himself conducted fieldwork.

Sahlins found the structure of eastern Fijian culture to be characterised by pairs of opposed concepts. Among the most important were the opposition of chief and commoner, in which the commoners own the land, but the chief protects it and is therefore given tribute, and the opposition between sea and land, in which chiefs are associated with the sea and commoners with the land. A third structural opposition exists between patrilineal descent and matrilateral kinship. Secular authority is transmitted in the male line, but ritual authority is held by the children of women born into the group.

When a Fijian house is built, its form reproduces the structure of the culture in microcosm. It has, for instance, a 'chiefly side' facing the sea, and a 'commoner side' facing the land. Representatives of the chiefly category build the 'noble' side; representatives of the commoner category build the landward side. If only the members of one settlement are involved in building the house, who will all belong to the same moiety, a subdivision of the moiety comes into effect: the higher-ranking semi-moiety takes the part of the chiefs, the other that of the commoners. If more than one community is involved, all members of the chiefly moiety work on one side. 'The house functions as the medium by which a system of culture is realised as an order of action' (Sahlins 1976a: 36).

The same is true, in Sahlins' assessment, of economic exchange. Goods are classed into spheres of exchange according to whether they are considered chiefly or common, sea or land, male or female. The economic basis of society is therefore not determinative of the social order but on the contrary becomes the realisation of a given meaningful order. Economic transactions express and perpetuate culturally ordered social relationships. 'Any cultural ordering produced by the material forces presupposes a cultural ordering of these forces' (Sahlins 1976a: 39). When a new village was created in the late nineteenth century it was founded exclusively by master fishers attached to a chief who were all 'sea/chiefly' people, but the villagers achieved the reproduction of the dual structures of the culture by deeming the first arrivals more landward, and therefore tantamount to commoner, than those who came later.

The approach of Structural Marxism attempts to reconcile Marxism and Structuralism (see chapter 5). Sahlins claims that, in his earlier writing, Marx would not have wholly disagreed with the Structuralist argument. A mode of production includes concepts of exchange and property rights. Marx considered that becoming a slave, or using machinery as capital equipment is only possible within certain social formations (Sahlins 1976a: 133). In Sahlins' assessment, Marx's material determinism grew as he became increasingly committed to bringing about a transformation of society. Although Marx may appear to be referring to mental constructs when he writes of becoming a slave, or an entrepreneur, Sahlins' reading of Marx is an unlikely one. Marx's early writing was explicitly directed against Hegel's theory that social change is driven by transformations in human ideology. Marx's argument was that one can only experience the condition of being a slave or a factory owner where the material conditions of society allow (see Marx 1973 [1857–8]: 156; Marx and Engels 1970 [1845–6]: 42).

Although Sahlins contended in 1976 that the structure of the culture defuses or emasculates the impact of historical change, his later analysis of the colonisation of Hawaii takes a position closer to that of Giddens, conceding that Hawaiian cultural structures entered into a dialectic with the economic and political exigencies of colonial conquest. 'Culture is a gamble played with nature' (Sahlins 1985: ix). Sahlins argues that Captain Cook's first two visits to Hawaii coincided with the feast of the god Lono, which celebrated the regeneration of nature. The Hawaiians' reaction to Cook and his crew, which appeared bizarre from a Western perspective, was entirely comprehensible when interpreted in the light of Hawaiian belief. The outcome of their behaviour, in particular the spread of venereal disease and the influx of anxious Protestant missionaries who sought to eradicate what they regarded as twenty forms of illicit intercourse, was entirely beyond the Hawaiians' control and ultimately compelled a radical restructuring of Hawaiian culture.

The Structuralists are, however, undoubtedly right in claiming there is an essentially arbitrary dimension to human culture. In the course of human social evolution, patterns of social interaction have been extended well beyond the limits of biological kinship, and languages have developed as elaborate but arbitrary codes for transmitting information by means of sounds made with our mouths. Mary Douglas has applied Structuralist theory to an understanding of economic behaviour in the West. She argues that all advances in social anthropological theory have come about through cutting interpretation free from the material and biological level of existence (Douglas and Isherwood 1979: 59): 'Forget that commodities are good for eating, clothing, and shelter; forget their usefulness and try instead the idea that commodities are good for thinking; treat them as a non-verbal medium for the human creative faculty' (Douglas and Isherwood 1979: 62).

Cultures have come into being because different communities within the same (human) species have, by consent or negotiation, accumulated distinctive sets of conventional strategies in the organisation of behaviour and the attribution of meaning to actions. This, in Douglas' view, is the proper level for social anthropological analysis. 'Instead of supposing that goods are primarily needed for subsistence. . . let us assume that they are needed for making visible and stable the categories of culture' (Douglas and Isherwood 1979: 59). Sahlins argued that North Americans avoid eating horse and dog because they are classed as almost human, named and loved by their owners, and not because it is uneconomic to eat them. It is, however, questionable whether the freedom to use goods to think with is absolute, and the limits which may be imposed upon it will be considered in the following three chapters.

CHAPTER FOUR

Interactionist theories

Introduction

Three years after the publication of Malinowski's *Argonauts of the Western Pacific* the French anthropologist Marcel Mauss published his essay on *The Gift* (1954 [1925]). Mauss placed Malinowski's account of the *kula* exchange network within the context of other ethnographic studies of exchange such as the potlatch of the north-west coast of North America (outlined later in this chapter), together with written references to gift exchange in Roman and Hindu literature. Mauss argued that gift exchange, not (as Adam Smith supposed) barter, was the process which created and maintained social relationships in small-scale societies. Gift exchange, he pointed out, is not just an eco-nomic transaction, carried out for material gain, but also a moral transaction. His theory was exemplified through Elsdon Best's account of Maori exchange. Best understood that if one person gave another a gift, that gift contains a 'spirit', the *hau*, which travels from one gift to the next, and must eventually be returned to the original giver (Mauss 1954: 8–9). Hence, Mauss concluded, to give something is to give a part of one's self. Because acceptance of a gift is believed to impose an oblig-ation to reciprocate, social relationships persist beyond the moment when the actual transaction takes place. Mauss challenged the Western assumption, legitimated in the work of Adam Smith, that market exchange was 'natural', and showed that gift exchange was no more dis-interested than buying and selling, even though it was conducted to a different end. Although Malinowski had rejected a simple distinction between gift and market exchange, arguing that Trobriand exchanges consisted of numerous types, many of which were intermediate in character (Malinowski 1922: 176), Mauss showed that it was useful to distinguish between the two ideal types of exchange. Two key ideas emerge from Mauss' essay:

1   Social relationships are generated through exchange, rather than being 'given' as part of an existing social structure. 'I have not described [social systems] as if they were fixed, in a static and skeletal condition . . . We see them in motion' (Mauss 1954: 77–8).

2   The significance of exchange depends on the meaning it has in the culture of the participants (an argument taken up by Sahlins and others in their critique of Marxism).

Modes and spheres of exchange

Mauss' approach was elaborated and developed, during the Second World War, by the historian Polanyi (Polanyi 1944; English edition 1945). Polanyi attributed the suffering of the Great Depression of the 1930s and the subsequent World War to the uncontrolled operation of a market economy. Like Mauss, he challenged the assumption that market exchange was the original and natural form taken by human transactions. Polanyi used the ethnography of Malinowski and Firth (Firth 1929; 1939) to question the claims of Adam Smith and Herbert Spencer that barter was the foundation of human social organisation. He argued that people have always been more interested in protecting their social standing than in the possession of material goods. 'In the long run, all social obligations are reciprocal, and their fulfilment serves also the individual's give-and-take interests best' (Polanyi 1945: 53). Rather than posit that structure or exchange have primacy, Polanyi contended they were interdependent. The division of society into moieties makes the recognition of reciprocal obligations easier, but the division is itself the product of previous acts of reciprocity (Polanyi 1945: 56). Unlike Marx, whom he rarely cites, Polanyi does not consider ways in which transactions may transform the structure of relationships. In his view the market could only become all-pervasive after Western governments had taken action to break down both the barriers that previously separated local from long-distance trade, and the social regulations that prevented labour, land and money itself being bought and sold. Polanyi considered such deregulation responsible for the decay of society.

Out of Polanyi's work developed the idea of distinguishing between modes and spheres of exchange. A *mode of exchange* is a type of transaction, governed by particular principles such as those of the market. A *sphere of exchange* delimits a set of items which can be exchanged for one another, but not for items outside that sphere. In Western, industrial society, methods of production are complex, using many technical processes. Distribution is, however, largely achieved by a single method, that of market exchange. In small-scale societies the opposite is the case: methods of production are simple, but distribution is more elaborate. Anthropologists frequently use Polanyi's (1945, 1957) distinction between three modes – *the market, redistribution* and *reciprocity* – to appreciate the relationships between transactions and social organisation. Polanyi also recognised *householding* as a fourth type of production. He defined it as 'production for a person's or group's own sake' (Polanyi 1945: 60), but did not recognise that it is associated with another mode of exchange, namely, *inheritance*. He did appreciate that two or more of these modes of exchange have often existed side by side within a society, and this has given rise to the concept of spheres of exchange, in which different types of goods circulate.

In a market economy, items can be exchanged between people who are not already linked by a direct social relationship, and the exchange does not create such a relationship. If you are on holiday in France, you can call into a supermarket and buy bread and wine for lunch, pay at the check-out counter and leave without having incurred any further obligation. Market economies operate most efficiently where there is a form of money. Money is a standard of value: all goods being bought and sold can be valued in terms of the sums of money they are worth. Money is also a medium of exchange. While one could exchange goods of equal monetary value for one another (two pence worth of bananas for two pence worth of sweet potato), it is usually more efficient to sell one for money and then buy the other. Money can also be a store of value, and can be used to pay for non-material items such as hours of work rendered to an employer. Markets can operate without money but, to do so, they must rely on barter. In this case, goods are swapped directly for one another and the equivalence of value between the goods must be negotiated by the parties to the exchange, which is a time-consuming process. In any market economy, the price or value of goods is usually considered to be determined solely by supply and demand (but see Smith and Marx's alternative labour theory of value outlined in chapter 1). Polanyi argued that where the market predominates, it inverts the relationship between exchange and social relationships associated with other modes. Instead of the economy being embedded in social relations, social relations become embedded in the economic system (Polanyi 1945: 63).

Redistribution is the systematic movement of goods to an administrative centre, and their reallocation by the central authority. In Western society, taxation is a form of redistribution, which is used partly to provide public services, partly to support the central government and partly to assist those with an inadequate, or no income. Polanyi recognised that those who control a system of redistribution will often use it to increase their own status (Polanyi 1945: 58), and that redistribution, like reciprocity, is as much a political process as it is an economic one. In small-scale societies, redistribution may operate at a village level, as in the potlatch of the north-west coast of North America. Redistribution also played an important role in sustaining the pre-colonial Asante state, outlined in chapter 2.

Reciprocal exchanges differ from redistributive ones because they normally take place between equals, although permanent indebtedness created by the inability to reciprocate fully will create inequality. Reciprocal exchanges differ from market exchanges because they are used to create or maintain ongoing social relationships between the participants. A classic example of reciprocity is the exchange of sisters that takes place in some small-scale societies (see chapter 3). Women are exchanged to create or maintain political alliances. Having obtained their wives from another lineage, men remain permanently indebted to that lineage, unlike the case of purchasing food in a supermarket mentioned above. Supply and demand does not govern such reciprocal exchanges. Each group of men could be said to have its own supply of women, but 'chooses' to exchange them for the women of another group in order to create social relationships.

A fourth mode of exchange, not considered by Polanyi, is the transmission of property by inheritance. Although the current created by the transfer of property flows more slowly than in any other mode it is, none the less, the means by which such essential resources as land and livestock are often acquired in small-scale societies (see the Samburu and Asante case studies in chapter 2).

Spheres of exchange

One of the characteristics of a monetary economy is that, because all items are valued in the medium of a single currency, virtually anything can be compared on a single scale of value and therefore exchanged for anything else. Even in Western society, however, we keep certain things out of the market economy. Husbands, wives and children are not bought and sold, nor should political offices be available for money.

In economies which lack a currency that can provide a universal medium of exchange separate spheres of exchange can be maintained much more easily. Items belonging to the same sphere can be exchanged for one another but not items belonging to different spheres, because they are incommensurate. Often, although not invariably, different spheres are governed by different modes of exchange. Over the last few years a special sphere of exchange has grown up in parts of the English Midlands and north-east, known as the LET (local exchange token) or 'button' economy. Neighbours in communities with high unemployment pay each other for house decorating, car repairs, baking and other services in a special currency which only circulates in that sphere, and reinforces neighbourhood networks (see Robertson 1985: 179).

Spheres of exchange among the Tiv

The classic account of an economy with several spheres of exchange is Paul Bohannan's analysis of the Tiv of northern Ghana, in West Africa. Bohannan identified three spheres of exchange in the Tiv economy, as it operated before 1927, and showed how the existence of these spheres constrained the transformation of wealth into power.

Subsistence goods were known as *yiagh*. All locally produced foodstuffs (vegetables, and animals such as chickens, sheep and goats), household utensils and agricultural tools belonged to the subsistence sphere of exchange. There was no money, and transactions were carried out by barter, at local markets. Bohannan describes the morality governing such transactions as that of the 'free and uncontrolled market' (Bohannan 1963: 248–53). Everyone aimed to trade something for which he had relatively little need, for something else of equivalent or greater value, to his personal profit.

Shagba (prestige goods) consisted of slaves, cattle, positions in local religious cults, white cloth, magic and medicines, and brass rods. Almost none of these goods was ever brought to market and they changed hands at ceremonies. Within this sphere, however, brass rods performed all the functions of money, acting as a medium of exchange, a standard and store of value, and a means of paying for services. The only 'leak' in the otherwise impermeable barrier between the subsistence and prestige spheres was that brass rods might, in moments of dire need, be used to purchase subsistence goods.

The third sphere regulated the exchange of women in marriage between men in different lineage segments. Such exchange was abolished by the British colonists in 1927, who made the 'payment' of bridewealth mandatory. In the simplest expression of marriage exchange prior to 1927, two men actually exchanged their sisters. In practice, however, one man might have several sisters, while others had none. Each lineage segment therefore 'pooled' its female members, and every girl became the ward of a man, whose marriage he would arrange in exchange for a wife. Not surprisingly, women sometimes eloped rather than submit to an arranged marriage. Their custodians could still marry, but had to balance the transaction temporarily by handing over cattle and brass rods to the new brother-in-law as a signal of the intention to supply a ward at a later date. Brass rods and cattle could never fully repay the debt incurred by receiving a wife because, until the introduction of bridewealth, women were incommensurate in value with anything else. This sphere was clearly governed by reciprocity rather than market values.

The Tiv believe that everyone is born equal, being endowed with equal amounts of *tsav*, a quality which Bohannan translates as luck or good fortune. In practice, some become wealthier, and hence more influential than others. How does this happen? Demographic processes ought to ensure that there are equal numbers of men and women and hence each man could only expect to have one marriage ward. Growing many vegetables and rearing many chickens cannot enable someone to accumulate slaves or other prestige goods. Inequality comes about because the spheres are not impermeable, and transactions, which Bohannan terms 'conversions', can be made between them. To convert upwards brings prestige (more *tsav*); to convert downwards leads to loss of prestige.

A man giving a large feast may need more food than his household can produce. In such circumstances he will reluctantly go to market with brass rods and use them as currency to buy food. He risks losing prestige, although the lucky person who sells the food gains it. Brass rods are not divisible (there is no change for a brass rod), and one rod will normally buy a huge quantity of vegetable food; in the case of peppers, an absurdly large quantity.

There existed an inferior form of marriage, one which was never balanced by sister exchange, which was achieved by 'paying' bride-wealth in brass rods. A woman obtained in this way was known as a *kem* wife. The husband acquired rights over the woman's labour and, if he gave a sufficient quantity of prestige goods, he also gained exclusive rights to her children. A *kem* wife's daughters were not put into the lineage segment's 'pool' of marriageable women, but could be used by the husband to obtain wives for his own sons. A successful man could thus increase the size and productive capacity of his household. Men who successfully converted goods from lower to higher spheres were said to have a 'strong heart' (synonymous, presumably, with having much *tsav*).

Bohannan thus demonstrates that social structure seems to be 'con-structed' within the idiom of Tiv culture, as individuals pursue their own, sometimes competing, interests. Exchange theory develops Malinowski's transactional form of Functionalism and turns away from the Structural Functionalism of Durkheim and Radcliffe-Brown.

Exchange among the Nuer

The Nuer are famous in social anthropology because Evans-Pritchard's analysis of them was the first in British anthropology to use the concept of the segmentary lineage as an analytical tool. The story of how Evans-Pritchard repudiated Malinowski's analytical techniques for Radcliffe-Brown's, was related in chapter 2. Evans-Pritchard substituted the concept of structure, manifested in corporate lineages, for that of exchange expressed in such institutions as the *kula* (Figure 4.1).

A careful reading of Evans-Pritchard's writings on the Nuer has led a number of later anthropologists to question whether the Nuer do actu-ally have lineages, in the sense of corporate groups which outlive indi-vidual members, and whether it may not be exchange which creates the groups studied by Evans-Pritchard (Glickman 1971; Verdon 1982). The Nuer have a clear territorial organisation. The tribe is the most inclusive political unit. Within a tribe, mechanisms exist to resolve feuds. Cattle can be paid in compensation for murder and mediators known as 'leopard-skin chiefs' can intervene in disputes to negotiate compensation. Each tribe 'has its particular territory and owns and defends its own building sites, grazing, water-supplies and fishing

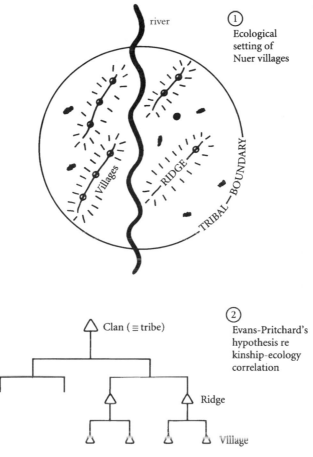

Figure 4.1 Diagrammatic representation of the relationship between the segmentary lineage and the ownership of territory among the Nuer, as proposed by Evans-Pritchard

pools' (Evans-Pritchard 1940a: 119). Tribes are separated by stretches of no-man's land, and tend to move in different directions during drought. The tribe's land is shaped by ecology. Within each tribe is a series of spatially defined segments and sub-segments, nesting within one another. Evans-Pritchard postulated that each level of geographical segmentation was associated with the genealogical segment of the tribe's dominant clan. He noted, however, that individual households, and even groups of brothers, frequently moved about within the tribe's territory to avoid disputes or to find grazing, so people would often not be living in that part of the tribe's land which should be associated with their lineage segment. Nor does every member of the tribe belong to the dominant clan. There are smaller lineages, some of which originated through the incorporation of neighbouring Dinka as the Nuer conquered Dinka territory (Evans-Pritchard 1940b: 286). Both the dominant clan and the smaller autonomous lineages are exogamous and therefore linked by the exchange of women in marriage for bridewealth. In Evans-Pritchard's words, 'the kinship system bridges the gaps in the political structure by a chain of links which unite members of opposed segments' (1940a: 226).

During the wet season, Nuer retreat to ridges of high ground, where they live in villages and cultivate millet (and a little maize), arduous work which has to be undertaken to compensate for the seasonal decline in milk yields from their cattle. The people who assemble in the hamlet form close-knit relationships. 'Scarcity of food at times and the narrow margin that for most of the year divides sufficiency from famine cause a high degree of interdependence among members of the smaller local groups, which may be said to have a common stock of food' (Evans-Pritchard 1940a: 84). Although each settlement is associated with a segment of the dominant clan, and named after that segment, many of its inhabitants at any time are not members of the 'owning' segment but people who trace links to the segment through the marriages of their sisters, mothers or more distant relatives. 'The result tends to be that a local group is a cognatic cluster round an agnatic core' (Evans-Pritchard 1940a: 286).

The Nuer distinguish between relationships of patrilineal descent, which they call *Buth*, and bilateral kinship, which they call *Mar*. Evans-Pritchard's analysis thus suggests that there will be two distinct fields of social interaction, each associated with different rights and obligations: mutual aid within the village, associated with bilateral kinship links; and the ownership and inheritance of cattle within lineages. Is this in fact the case? The primary function of the lineage system seems to be to regulate feuding. Lineage segments are supposed to oppose one another in feuds, yet unite against a common enemy. The dead man's 'people' seek cattle in compensation for a murder, from the killer's 'people' (Evans-Pritchard 1940a: 153). Are these 'people' lineage segments? Evans-Pritchard writes that a homicide involves not just the murderer but his close agnates (patrilineal kin), and that 'for years after cattle have been paid close agnates of the slayer avoid close agnates of the dead man' for fear of being killed in revenge. Yet Evans-Pritchard does not categorically state that it is the murderer's patrilineal kin who provide the cattle paid in compensation for a killing merely that the leopard-skin chief 'finds out what cattle the slayer's people (*jithunga*) possess and that they are willing to pay compensation' (Evans-Pritchard 1940a: 153, 158).

In practice the distinction between patrilineal and other kin is sometimes blurred. 'Small local groups pasture their cattle in common and jointly defend their homes and herds' (Evans-Pritchard 1940a: 17). 'Within the complex of village kinship ties and the circuit of daily contacts all relationships are given equal weight, for what is significant is less the category or degree of kinship than the fact of living together in a small and highly corporate community' (Evans-Pritchard 1950a: 370). Except when they find themselves on opposite sides, as defined by the segmentary lineage structure, all members of a village will fight together when drawn into a feud. Feuds normally develop between different villages in the same district, because the disruptive effect of a feud within the village is so great that people are most willing to submit to the mediation of a leopard-skin chief. The behaviour of the village community as if it were a corporate lineage is put even more strongly in the following passage: 'In its external relations the village is a single lineage, and, because marriages have taken place between its component hamlets whose members have originated from different localities, it "can be presented as descended from a common ancestor"' (Glickman 1971: 312, quoting Evans-Pritchard 1951: 17). Such descent would, of course, in fact be traced through a mixture of maternal and paternal links. The Nuer can, however, create fictive patrilineal descent by transforming past links through women into links alleged to be through men, and by deeming distant patrilineal links to be close ones (Glickman 1971: 309).

Verdon (1982) argues that patrilineal and matrilateral relationships are both generated by the transfer of cattle. *Buth* (patrilineal descent) is created by the inheritance of cattle, and *Mar* (cognatic kinship) by the transfer of cattle in bridewealth, thus legitimating the relationships of children with the kin of both parents. The opposition between patrilineal and cognatic kin resembles the cultural oppositions Sahlins identified in eastern Fiji between chief and commoner, sea and land (Sahlins 1976a; see chapter 3). As Sahlins argued with reference to Fiji, actual exchanges in the *idiom* of culture generate relationships which realise the *structure* of the society. Yet expediency, which among the Nuer requires movement in search of grazing or plots on which to grow millet, or to avoid disputes, constantly threatens to undermine the existing structure. Patrilineal kin who live a long way away are no help in pursuing a feud, and cannot be called on to provide cattle in compensation for murder. On the other hand, people with whom one co-operates on a daily basis can do both these things, and thus the interpretation of who acts like, or observes the rules of patrilineal descent is constantly being renegotiated during inter-household politics. Ironically, then, had Evans-Pritchard drawn a parallel between the transactions in cattle among the Nuer, and the exchange of *kula* valuables in the Trobriands, he might have succeeded in following Malinowski's analytical methods.

Social change

Although many actual markets depend on relationships of credit extended by shopkeepers to regular customers, pure market transactions do not create or perpetuate durable social relationships between the individuals who buy and sell from each other. This does not result in pure market transactions operating outside a social system. On the contrary, market transactions tend to generate a particular type of social system, one in which there are differences of wealth, but achieved status predominates over ascribed status. As Adam Smith wrote, money confers the power to buy others' labour. Reciprocity, on the other hand, tends to promote negotiated, egalitarian relationships. While redistribution appears to promote equality it never does so completely, because the central authority which undertakes the redistribution invariably keeps some of the wealth which it receives. This was one of the fundamental weaknesses of the Communist regimes of Eastern Europe: redistribution tends to perpetuate existing structures of authority. The consequences of inheritance depend on whether everyone has access to inherited resources, or not. In the classic type of lineage-based societies studied by the Functionalists, inheritance binds everyone to the corporate groups in which rights to land or livestock are vested. In a feudal system, where certain rights are restricted to members of a particular social class, a stable but inegalitarian social system will result.

Polanyi argued that the extension of market principles to new areas of social interaction tends to have a destabilising effect. Numerous instances of this can be found in Africa during the colonial period. There is said to have been a legend which arose at that time in East Africa, that the Devil invented money but was so frightened by it that he threw it away. Man, on his way to market, picked it up, not knowing what it was (Mary Douglas, personal communication).

Spheres of exchange in Darfur

Fredrik Barth used the concept of spheres of exchange to provide an effective analysis of social change among the Fur of south-west Sudan (Barth 1967b; but see the critical reassessment in de Waal 1989). The Fur live on a mountain massif called Jebel Marra, surrounded by savannah grassland. Unlike the surrounding grassland, Jebel Marra is watered by permanent streams. Nomadic pastoralists occupy the savannah, but the Fur cultivate millet and other crops. Their principal subsistence crops are millet, grown in summer, and onions, grown in the winter. Subsistence crops are supplemented with cash crops, including tomatoes, garlic and wheat. Land belongs to lineages, and a lineage custodian allocates use-rights to individual members. Husbands and wives cultivate separate fields, belonging to their respective lineages, and dispose of their crops independently.

Transactions in labour and farm produce take place in two spheres: one concerned with subsistence crops, the other with cash crops. Subsistence exchange is regulated by reciprocity while cash crops are, by definition, exchanged through the market. Working for wages is considered shameful, since it causes permanent dependence upon an employer. Help with planting and weeding subsistence crops is obtained through reciprocal beer parties. One of the wife's few obligations to her husband is to brew beer from his millet (in return, the husband provides his wife and children with clothes he makes himself). The person who recruits labour with a beer party will later have to help those who worked for him by attending their beer parties, thus balancing the exchange. There is, however, some non-reciprocal labour rendered during infrequent but major projects such, for example, as house-building. On such occasions, the obligations of the house-owner are discharged immediately through the gifts of beer he provides. Although such events are customarily interpreted as parties, they are the means by which a relatively prosperous majority have become differentiated from a minority who, through bad management, old age or disease, tend to join non-reciprocal work parties to obtain food (in the form of beer), thus 'selling' their labour to others rather than devoting it to the cultivation of their own fields.

Barth calculates that a day's labour can be obtained from another adult in exchange for five litres of beer; 1.7 pounds of millet are needed to brew five litres of beer. Yet, in Barth's assessment, an average day's labour spread over the growing season will yield five pounds of millet. It is therefore better to work in your own field than work for someone else's beer, and even better to recruit others' labour through non-reciprocal beer parties. The existence of the two spheres of exchange none the less limits the opportunities to exploit such potential inequality.

The scope for market transactions is limited. Cash crops can be sold on local markets, but there is little one can do with the cash. It can be used to buy calves, which can be raised and sold again, or it can be saved towards bridewealth. Several considerations tend to keep the two spheres separate. There are several points at which 'conversions' can be made, but their scope is limited by economic conditions or local custom. Some millet is sold in local markets, for example, but almost everyone grows their own millet, and therefore demand is low. Millet is heavy and bulky in relation to the price it commands and therefore scarcely worth transporting to market. Beer parties can be recruited to plant cash crops, but only if the recipient of the labour has enough millet left over after satisfying his subsistence needs.

The economic system of the Fur therefore appears substantially closed, and in equilibrium. Barth shows, however, that some individuals had found innovatory ways of breaking out of the closed circuits of exchange. Cultivating fruit trees is an alternative to growing traditional winter cash crops. The labour needed to plant them can be recruited through a beer party. The trees take four years to mature and during those four years traditional cash crops can be grown between the saplings. Fruit crops are very profitable, yielding twenty to thirty pounds per year at the time of Barth's fieldwork (Barth estimated the cash needs of a man to be around eight pounds a year, and those of a woman, between one and three pounds). Once fruit trees are mature, however, nothing else can be grown under them and they are therefore unavailable for reallocation among the lineage's members. When the implications of growing fruit trees became evident, the custodians of some lineages pressed for a general rule that fruit trees should not be planted on lineage land. Others evicted fellow-members of their lineage, and usurped their land to grow fruit trees themselves, while yet others sold lineage land into private ownership. Since land had hitherto been transmitted by inheritance rather than sale, there was no guide to the value of land in the market sphere and its price was greatly underestimated in early sales. In one of the most dramatic 'conversions', a field was sold for seventeen pounds. While the fruit trees were maturing, the new owner grew onions between them which earned him twenty-seven pounds in the first year alone, twenty-two pounds in the second and twenty-five in the third. He had made a handsome profit even before his trees bore fruit.

A second innovation was effected by an Arab merchant who usually visited Jebel Marra each year to trade. In 1961 he asked permission to stay with the Fur through the winter, and grow a tomato crop on borrowed land. He and his wife brewed a large quantity of beer from millet they had bought, at a cost of five pounds, from a distant market beyond reach of the Fur. The tomatoes cultivated by labour recruited through beer parties were sold for a hundred pounds at a local market. A local man, who followed the Arab's example, bought three pounds' worth of millet on a local market and was still able to recruit sufficient labour to cultivate thirty-eight pounds' worth of tomatoes.

Barth anticipated that the Fur would respond to such innovations by reordering their spheres of exchange. Either the value of labour, expressed in beer or cash, would rise, or people would refuse to attend non-reciprocal work parties, or visiting entrepreneurs would no longer be able to borrow suitable land. In fact, such changes are often very difficult to resist. The entry of previously inherited land on to the market has been particularly damaging to subsistence economies. An example of the consequences during the present century (Maiurno) is given in chapter 5, exemplifying the causes of growing poverty in contemporary Africa. The classic nineteenth-century case is that of the potlatch, an exchange system destabilised by the advent of European fur traders. The availability of new goods for exchange, and the devastating impact of European diseases on the population exacerbated the inherent tendency of the potlatch to promote social change.

The potlatch

The potlatch was a form of exchange which developed among the hunter-gatherer societies of the north-west coast of North America, in what is now Alaska and British Columbia (studies of the potlatch include Boas 1966; Drucker and Heizer 1967; Garfield and Wingert

1966; and Rosman and Ruebel 1971). Living in a seasonally rich environment, these people were sedentary rather than nomadic. Small lineages, tracing descent either matrilineally or ambilineally, owned hunting and berry-picking patches, and fishing grounds at sea which they defended against members of other lineages. Each lineage appointed a leader to co-ordinate its activities. Land could be captured in warfare, and the members of a defeated lineage enslaved by the victors. Several lineages lived side by side in each winter village, providing between 100 and 500 people to defend themselves against raids. The constituent lineages then dispersed to their respective territories in spring, and began accumulating the food they would need to survive the lean months of winter, from November to February. The native people of the north-west coast had developed sophisticated techniques for preserving food. Salmon and the meat of mountain goat were smoked, berries were stored in lard and oil extracted from fish. Woodcarvers, sometimes slaves but often freemen, were commissioned to make totem poles and carve masks representing the spirit guardians of the lineages. Other artefacts, including elaborately decorated blankets, were made to exchange in the potlatch. Potlatching took place in the winter villages. The occasion for a potlatch varied from one community to another; sometimes it was the initiation of young members into secret cults, sometimes marriage or the installation of a new lineage head. When a lineage held a potlatch it provided a feast to which other lineages were invited. Gifts were given to all visitors according to their rank.

Unlike the stable equilibrium created by exchange among the Trobrianders, the north-west coast potlatch was, during the time it was studied by anthropologists, a competitive institution. The wealth each lineage could accumulate depended on how many active members of the lineage there were, how many slaves they had working for them, and how effectively their activities were co-ordinated by the lineage head. He set goals for the lineage to achieve. The quantity of food provided at a potlatch and, more importantly, the scale of the gifts given away, expressed the lineage's economic position. The potlatch cemented alliances and advertised the lineage's power. The gifts distributed also expressed the rank of the recipients, since those with higher rank received bigger gifts. It is uncertain how competitive the system was before the arrival of European traders, but it is clear that the fur trade exacerbated its competitiveness. Russian and English traders (the latter working through the Hudson Bay Company) bought pelts from the Native Americans in exchange for woollen blankets, guns, traps and other goods. The enormous influx of wealth unbalanced the ranking of chiefs and lineages and, even more destructively, introduced diseases killed many people. Among the Tsimshian, who held potlatches to inaugurate lineage heads and village chiefs, the pace of potlatching rose as new leaders had to be installed ever more frequently. People from many communities left their traditional winter villages to congregate around trading posts, meeting new lineages and having to potlatch with them in order to determine their relative rank. Among the Kwakiutl, elaborately decorated blankets formed the principal item of exchange. Totemic crests were associated with each level of social rank, and wealthy Kwakiutl men engaged in potlatch 'duels' of feasting and counter-feasting, through which each attempted to better the other and achieve the right to display a certain crest. Realising the value of blankets, the Hudson Bay Company imported hundreds of thousands from the factories of the English Midlands, resulting in runaway inflation in the value of blankets exchanged at potlatches. It was like printing too many bank notes. Some Kwakiutl then destroyed all their property in an attempt to achieve the ultimate competitive challenge. Late in the nineteenth century the governments of the United States and Canada made the potlatch illegal. When it was reintroduced in the 1950s, it became a non-competitive exchange designed to cement unity among indigenous communities who now formed an ethnic minority within the nation state.

A language of social relations

During the 1950s and 1960s, many anthropologists abandoned the analysis of static social structures for a study of the social processes created by exchange. Fortes was perhaps the first to question the usefulness of a static model of social relationships in his *Time and the Social Structure* (Fortes 1949a). He showed how several household structures could be identified among the Asante of Ghana, and argued that, rather than create a static typology of household types, these structures could best be represented partly as stages through which a household invariably passed during the life-cycle of its members, and partly as the outcome of choices individuals made at certain points in the cycle. A household which at first only contains a married couple will later contain a nuclear family and may, if a child marries, eventually contain members of three generations. Since descent among the Asante is matrilineal, men had to decide whether to live with their sisters (whose children would be the man's heirs), or with their own wife and children. Fortes compared social structure to the vocabulary and grammar of a language, and social relations to the spoken word (Fortes 1949a: 304).

A more striking recantation from Radcliffe-Brown's methodology was made by Evans-Pritchard in a public lecture delivered in 1950 (Evans-Pritchard 1950b). Evans-Pritchard declared his dissatisfaction with the theoretical basis of Functionalism, and its attempt to ground social anthropology in the natural sciences. Is anthropology a natural science, he asked, or is it a humanity?

The distinction between science and history was already current in German philosophy, and had influenced both Boas and Weber. Boas drew on his training in the German philosophical tradition to distinguish between the scientific search for general laws and the historian's quest to understand particular traditions. Although trained as a scientist, Boas became attracted by the idea of interpretive understanding and argued that the validity of ideas and conceptions is relative to the civilisation in which they originate (Stocking 1982: 9–13). Boas refers to the 'old controversy' between historical and physical (scientific) methods: the search for general laws and the attempt to understand individual events (Boas 1940b [1887]: 641–2). He termed the historical method the 'cosmographic' one, which 'lovingly tries to penetrate into [the] secrets' of actions and events 'until every feature is plain and clear' (Boas 1940b [1887]: 645).

Evans-Pritchard traced the idea of anthropology as a natural science to the eighteenth-century philosophers who first studied society as a system. In their view societies were to be construed as natural organisms, studied empirically and explained in terms of general laws or principles that must hold good for all societies. One version of the doctrine was employed by the nineteenth-century Social Evolutionists such as Herbert Spencer, who classified societies according to their supposed stage of development and attempted to discover the laws of social evolution. Social Evolutionism had been attacked by the Diffusionists, who argued that societies do not change independently of one another. The diffusion of customs from one society to another was held to have 'contaminated' the evidence upon which the Evolutionists depended to so great an extent that their theories were invalidated. Although rejecting extreme forms of Diffusionism, Evans-Pritchard suggested that their arguments had more force than was generally appreciated in mid-twentieth-century British anthropology.

Functionalism had arisen as a second critique of Social Evolutionism. Its proponents rejected the study of history as irrelevant to the present functioning of a social system, thereby discounting both speculation about social evolution and the plucking of customs out of their social context which the Diffusionists had practised. But Functionalists still considered it axiomatic that social life should be 'reduced to laws or general statements about the nature of society *which allow prediction*' (Evans-Pritchard 1950b: 120, my emphasis). The Functionalist method had produced good ethnographies, Evans-Pritchard conceded, but its theoretical basis was unsound. Directing his remarks particularly against Radcliffe-Brown's method, he asked five questions. Are societies really organisms? Does every custom really have a social value? Must every institution necessarily take the form it does? Has social anthropology ever discovered a law of social behaviour comparable to the laws formulated by natural scientists? Can societies really have come to take on their present form by a series of unique and irrelevant events?

Like the nineteenth-century Social Evolutionists, Functionalists still aimed 'at proving man is an automaton and at discovering the sociological laws in terms of which his actions, ideas and beliefs can be explained and in the light of which they can be planned and controlled' (Evans-Pritchard 1950b: 123). Against this view, Evans-Pritchard argued that behaviour must be *understood* as the outcome of people's beliefs and understandings; an approach which originated, perhaps, with Herodotus' analysis of the Persian wars. Social life, Evans-Pritchard maintained, has a pattern because humans are reasonable creatures and must live in a world in which social relations are ordered and intelligible. Fieldworkers should therefore aim to understand the people they studied in their own terms; to think in their concepts and feel in their values. These experiences must then be translated into the conceptual categories and values of the anthropologist's own culture. As a trained observer, the anthropologist can make the implicit categories of the 'native' culture explicit, in the same way that a trained linguist can reveal the rules of grammar a native speaker uses implicitly. Social anthropology should model its methods on those of the humanities, especially history. Societies should be studied as moral rather than natural systems; patterns rather than scientific laws should be sought; and social life should be interpreted rather than explained. Paradoxically, he concluded, it is only when this transformation has been achieved that social anthropology will become truly scientific.

Two years after Evans-Pritchard's public lecture, Lévi-Strauss published a paper on 'Social Structure' (Lévi-Strauss 1952) in which he made more thorough use of the analogy between language and social life. He argued that communication operates at three levels of social life: the exchange of women in marriage, the exchange of goods and services, and the exchange of verbal messages through language. Radcliffe-Brown had 'lowered' social anthropology to the level of biology through his use of the organic analogy. Lévi-Strauss proposed to 'raise' it to the level of communication theory. Radcliffe-Brown had failed to distinguish between social *structure*, a static model of social organisation, and social *relations*, the organisation of the processes of interaction. Lévi-Strauss cited Fortes' model of a language of social relations with approval.

The American anthropologist Goodenough developed the linguistic analogy further in a reanalysis of the concepts of status and role, which had been introduced by Linton. He wrote, 'I have found it useful to look upon the content of social relationships as containing (among other things), "vocabularies" of different kinds of forms and a "syntax" or set of rules for their composition into (and interpretation as) meaningful sequences of social events' (Goodenough 1965: 1, his parentheses). Goodenough took issue with Linton's formulation of status as a position in a social structure and role as the rights and duties incumbent on the occupant of the status (see chapter 2). Goodenough argued that status was a social *identity*, and that the occupant always had some latitude in how (s)he might interpret that identity. Such latitude could, however, only be interpreted within the idiom of the culture, which provided the 'syntactic principles' governing the composition of social relationships. Drawing on his own fieldwork on the island of Truk, Goodenough showed how, if a man wishes to flatter a superior, he can act as if offering more duties than are required and, if wishing to insult him, he can offer fewer duties.

Social life as a game

Having cited the model of social life as a language in his 1952 paper on social structure, Lévi-Strauss went on to propose a second model, that of social life as a *game*. The advantage of this model was that it would focus attention on how individuals use strategies in choosing between the alternative courses of action open to them (Lévi-Strauss 1963: 298). The 'rules' merely set the limits on possible strategies. Explaining the rules of football, for example, will not convey a sense of what a football match is like, nor will it enable one to predict which team will win the match.

Of all the anthropologists participating in the shift of paradigm away from Radcliffe-Brown's concept of social structure, Raymond Firth had remained closest to Malinowski's vision of anthropology. Firth presented his own formulation of social process in two papers (Firth 1954; 1955). While acknowledging the influence of Lévi-Strauss, Firth chose not to use a linguistic analogy. Instead he distinguished between *social structure*, which he defined as the major patterns of existing social relationships which constrained the possibilities of future interaction (Firth 1954: 4), and *social organisation:* the constant process of responding to fresh situations by adopting appropriate strategies. A study of social organisation would reveal how people made decisions or accepted the responsibility expected of them by virtue of their position in the social system. Although every society has a procedure for replacing office-holders when they die, to characterise the procedure in structural terms, as matrilineal or patrilineal succession, is inadequate. Such rules do no more than provide a general frame of reference and a witless, irresponsible or lunatic person will not usually be chosen for office, even if he is genealogically qualified.

The analogy of life as a game was most thoroughly developed by the Norwegian anthropologist Fredrik Barth, who treated individuals as rational actors seeking their personal advantage, like the liberal economist's Economic Man. In a paper called 'On the Study of Social Change' (Barth 1967a) he argued that anthropologists working in the intellectual tradition of Radcliffe-Brown found it difficult to explain social change. Their method of description is to aggregate individual observations of behaviour into patterns which they call 'customs' which, they claim, people are required to follow. Radcliffe-Brown had, in fact, rejected Malinowski's technique of including accounts of individuals' actions in an ethnography, arguing that examples should be confined to the fieldworker's notebook (see chapter 2). Barth dismissed Radcliffe-Brown's approach as depending on a 'morphological' concept of custom, as if custom were the observable organs of the social body. Customs cannot be directly observed, they are only revealed by observing a series of what are taken to be more or less representative examples of the behaviour required by the custom. Barth argued that customary patterns of behaviour should rather be seen as the outcome of strategic decisions which people make about how to allocate their time and resources in certain circumstances. The social structure is not something that people, let alone 'society', seek(s) to maintain. It is an *epiphenomenon,* an unintended by-product of people's strategies. Technical and ecological conditions favour certain strategies and doom others to failure. The presence of other actors imposes constraints and opportunities on each person, qualifying what they can, or wish to do. The guest at a non-reciprocal Fur beer party does not think, 'how will my attendance contribute to social stratification in the community?' None the less, his decision not to cultivate his own fields contributes to the emergence of two social classes: those who work their own share of lineage land, and those who work for others.

Barth regarded the explanation of social change as particularly problematic for the Functionalists. Although Radcliffe-Brown recognised that social structures do change, as one institution replaces another, it is difficult to characterise this within the terms of the organic analogy, which would represent the transition from a compound to a complex society as if it were the transformation of, for instance, a starfish into a mammal (see chapter 2); hardly a likely event! Barth argued that the problem could be overcome if change is seen as the consequence of individuals modifying their allocation of time and labour. Among Fur farmers there is little co-operation between husband and wife, since each cultivates land belonging to their own lineage. If a Fur household decides to abandon farming and take up nomadic pastoralism in the surrounding savannah, however, the husband and wife adopt complementary, and mutually dependent strategies. The husband specialises in herding and husbanding his livestock. The wife continues to grow some millet, but also churns butter from cream produced by the livestock, sells the milk and cooks food for the whole household. As it happens, this is how local Arab pastoralists organise their households. Have the Fur who take up nomadism become Arabs? No, replies Barth; this is simply the most effective allocation of time and labour for pastoralists. He concludes that it is the rates and kinds of pay-off from alternative strategies in any social system that determine which strategies will become institution-alised, and which rejected (Barth 1967a: 668).

The game of Swat

Barth's most ambitious attempt to analyse social interaction from the perspective of individual strategies was his study of politics in the Swat valley of northern Pakistan (Barth 1959a; 1959b). During the sixteenth century the valley had been conquered by Pathans belonging to the Yusufzai lineage, who established themselves as feudal overlords dom-inating the existing peasant farmers. According to Yusufzai legend, an institution known as *wesh* was introduced shortly after conquest, according to which each feudal lord would move to a different part of the valley every few years. This ensured that all members of the lineage benefited equally, despite the uneven quality of land in different parts of the valley.

Although Barth paid attention to the valley's history and social insti-tutions, he interpreted society in the valley as existing in an unstable equilibrium brought about by actors competing, in a Hobbesian fash-ion, for their personal advantage. Barth found that the segments of the Yusufzai lineage did not exhibit the phenomenon of 'segmentary opposition' typified by the Nuer and Tallensi, in which smaller seg-ments of the lineage fuse, to present a united front, when members of one such segment are confronted by outsiders. Rather than groups at a particular level of segmentation allying with each other against com-mon opponents, the fiercest opposition in the Yusufzai lineage was expressed between closely related segments, each segment seeking allies among more distant members of the lineage (Figure 4.2).

Barth concluded that disputes arose over competition for land at the times when *wesh* required landlords of each segment to move to another part of the valley. The quantity of land available was fixed, and only some landlords could get the best, yet their rivals were their closest kin. In order to free it as far as possible from its specific cultural con-text, Barth sought to characterise this behaviour in terms of von Neumann and Morgenstern's theory of games, a theory which has since been applied to the evolution of social behaviour by Socio-ecologists (von Neumann and Morgenstern 1953). Barth argued that the Yusufzai were playing a zero sum majority game. In von Neumann and Morgenstern's terms a *zero sum game* is one in which the winnings are fixed. Successful coalitions between players will always give way to

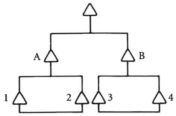

'Nuer' model:
1 + 2 unite to confront 3 + 4: proximity creates a common interest

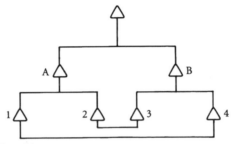

'Pathan' model:
1 + 4 unite to confront 2 + 3: proximity creates competition for resources

Figure 4.2 The 'Nuer' and 'Pathan' models of segmentary opposition

Opening teams:

			Coalition 1		□		Coalition 2		
1	2	3	4	5	□	6	7	8	9

One player defects from the weaker team:

Coalition 1	□	Coalition 2

Splits into 1a   1b

| 1 | 2 | 3 □ 4 | 5 | 6 | □ 7 | 8 | 9 |

Now coalition 2 can place itself in a stronger position by soliciting defections from coalition 1a or 1b:

Coalition 1	□	Coalition 2

1a   1b

| 1 | 2 | 3 □ | 4 | 5 | □ 6 | 7 | 8 | 9 |

Figure 4.3 Segmentary opposition in the Swat Valley

conflict over how the winnings are to be shared. A *positive sum game* is one in which the total winnings can be increased by co-operation, in which case coalitions of players will tend to persist. The Yusufzai were playing a *majority* game, because the opposing teams were never of the same size.

In the simplest model of the Yusufzai game, there are five players. If any two players combine to form a coalition, to help each other obtain the best feudal tenures in their respective parts of the valley, the others must combine against them. If the fifth player remains on his own, he will fall prey to both coalitions. Whichever coalition he chooses to join will become the stronger and yet, because it is larger, the land it gains will have to be divided between a larger number of players, tempting team members to divide into smaller coalitions in competition for the spoils. No coalition will ever be eliminated from the 'game' because the winning coalition will always tend to break up over arguments. Members will attempt to evict each other from the team in order to increase their own gains. The example in Figure 4.3 is based on a game with nine players. If Barth is correct in his assessment, the Nuer are presumably playing a non-zero sum game in defence of pasture, livestock and crops. Evidence suggesting this may be so will be considered in chapter 6.

Order out of chaos?

The theory that social systems were generated through interaction, rather than having a life of their own which outlived particular actors, encouraged a return to the eighteenth-century idea of reconstructing the origin of society. Parallel developments in sociological theory aimed to explain how social institutions could emerge from sponta neous patterns of interaction. Blau's *Exchange and Power in Social Life* (1964) exemplifies the approach. Blau took dyadic interaction (inter-action between two individuals – see chapter 2) as the starting point for the generation of social forms, and constructed a model of the possible outcomes of transactions in goods, services or information. A relation-ship is started when one individual renders a service for another. There are three possible outcomes. If the recipient reciprocates, the first indi-vidual is encouraged to offer further services, and a balanced (equal) social relationship is established. If the recipient of the initial transac-tion does not reciprocate, he suffers a loss of 'credit' and risks exclusion from further transactions. A recipient who is unable to return services upon which he depends becomes a subordinate. One who has the necessary resources to reciprocate, but refuses to do so, will take on a superior position if the other goes on rendering him services. The two general 'functions' of social exchange are thus to establish relationships of equality or inequality between the participants. Blau accepts that such exchanges cannot create an entire social system. The values attached to exchange vary from one culture to another, and such values influence the outcome of transactions. Structured organisations based on the laws of contract cannot be generated through interpersonal interaction, since they depend on existing legal frameworks. Blau is principally interested in the relationships which develop in what Marx termed the 'interstices' of the formalised social order.

A more ambitious theory was proposed by Berger and Luckmann in their study of *The Social Construction of Reality* (Berger and Luckmann 1966). People perceive the world as meaningful and yet, Berger and Luckmann argue, this meaningfulness originates not in a pre-existent collective consciousness, but in the thoughts and actions of individuals. Out of random interaction, agreed understandings will be negotiated. Meanings then become embedded in routine and choices are narrowed as certain strategies become formalised (Berger and Luckmann 1966: 72). While people in fact live in a cultural milieu where meanings and practices have already been negotiated, Berger and Luckmann believe that, in principle, such 'institutionalisation' will occur even when two strangers meet upon a desert island, having only salvaged from their respective shipwrecks their perception of themselves as 'selves'. The strangers' interaction passes through several stages. First, they attribute meaning to each other's actions and, by a process of trial and error, test such predictions against the outcome of their actions. Then, they detect regularities in each other's behaviour and hence attribute roles to each other. Life becomes predictable and labour can be divided. By the time the two erstwhile strangers get around to having children, the objectivity of their intersubjective world has thickened and hardened. The real reasons for the origins of their institutions have been forgotten, and the children have to invent rationalisations.* Only parts of experience are remembered, or 'sedimented'. Only where a 'sign system' allows, can experiences selectively be shared, reinterpreted and simplified.

---

* Berger and Luckmann's reading in anthropology is confined to Lévy-Bruhl and Lévi-Strauss. The book is littered with armchair speculation about the practices and beliefs of people in small-scale societies.

From one perspective, Berger and Luckmann's argument is an important contribution to intellectual debate leading from phenomenological (interpretive) sociology to Postmodernism. It is now generally accepted that cultural meanings *are* intersubjectively negotiated, that they change through time and that individuals may well differ in the significance they attribute to others' actions and messages. But there is, from another perspective, a fundamental difficulty with their model. They concede that the desert island is an unlikely situation for the origin of culture, but not that it is entirely atypical. Durkheim was surely correct when he pointed out, against the social contract theorists, that all known human societies have developed out of earlier societies, and there has never been a time when people were able to come together of their own free will, and construct a society uninfluenced by existing customs. Berger and Luckmann concede that the juxtaposition of individual uniqueness and collective social identity is a false one (Berger and Luckmann 1966: 194).

Durkheim himself coped with the problem of the origin of institutions through his notion of the emotional currents that sweep through crowds. Crowds are more or less random aggregates of individuals and he considered that no prior institutional framework was needed to explain the waves of passion that flow through them. None the less the sentiments are, from the start, collective ones (see chapter 1). Lévi-Strauss also succumbed to the temptation to identify certain contemporary situations as replicating the conditions under which the first society emerged. In *The Elementary Structures of Kinship* (1969), he depicts the relationship created by two strangers meeting in a French café and exchanging a glass of wine as 'an example, rare in our society. . . of the formation of a group for which. . . no ready-made formula exists' (Lévi-Strauss 1969: 59). Finding themselves sitting at the same table, each offers the other a glass of wine from his own carafe, even though the wine has come from the same barrel. From a purely material point of view, each might as well have drunk his own wine. Rather than recognising this as an established French custom, Lévi-Strauss interprets it as an instance of the 'non-crystallised' forms of social life which are also exemplified in communities arising spontaneously out of accidental or enforced circumstances such as earthquakes or concentration camps. He argues these reveal traces of primitive psycho-social experiences, considerably less developed than what he terms 'savage institutions', and compares the meeting in the café to 'an infinitely distant projection... of a fundamental situation, that of individuals of primitive bands coming into contact for the first time' (Lévi-Strauss 1969: 60).

A re-analysis of the 'game of Swat'

The problems with this type of Interactionist theory are exemplified by a re-analysis of social interaction in the Swat valley of north-west Pakistan. Asad and Ahmed have both criticised Barth for attempting to detach the 'game of Swat' from its social context. Asad's analysis is based on a re-analysis of Barth's own material, while Ahmed writes with first-hand knowledge of the region.

Asad argued that Swat social order is not the outcome of independent actors making free choices, but of cumulative historical processes which led to a particular form of class structure: the domination of the valley's population by the minority who are Pakhtuns, that is, recognised members of the Yusufzai land-owning lineage. This social system has not emerged spontaneously from playing games, but was deliberately regulated by the landowners. Only they can play the 'game of Swat'. Although they compete with one another to increase the quality of their fiefs, they act in concert to exploit their tenant farmers, from whom they have in the past taken up to four-fifths of all crops in tithes.

There are, moreover, two types of Pakhtun: large landlords and smallholders. Barth stated that any Pakhtun who loses his land is expelled from the Yusufzai lineage to become a landless tenant like any member of the indigenous population (compare Marx's analysis of the ancient mode of production), but Barth did not take this into account in his description of how the 'game' operated. If this rule *is* taken into account, then the number of players should become progressively smaller, until ultimately one winner held all land in the valley. The legendary rationale for *wesh* was to ensure that every Yusufzai had a feudal tenure of equal value. Since the observed outcome is one of unequal holdings, the process of eliminating players may be under way. Whereas Barth portrayed a state of equilibrium, Asad sees a process of unilinear, irreversible change.

Asad's interpretation is confirmed by Ahmed's research. Barth viewed the emergence of a centralised state in the Swat valley, prior to its incorporation into British India early in the twentieth century, as a consequence of British domination. Ahmed argues that, although supported by the British, centralisation was the logical outcome of the 'game'. As land holdings became concentrated in the hands of success-ful feudal lords, so increasing numbers of descendants of the original Yusufzai invaders were threatened by total loss of their land and there-fore surrender of their Pakhtun status. The vertical relationships between tenant and landlord, based on the payment of tribute, were undermined by an emerging class consciousness among the peasantry. In the mid-nineteenth century a charismatic, unorthodox Sufi leader, the Akhund of Swat, led a rebellion against the Yusufzai and nomi-nated a non-Yusufzai as king of the valley. Ahmed points out that the Akhund was the product of a specific historical and cultural tradition whose significance Barth had underestimated. When the Akhund died, his descendants battled among themselves for supremacy, giving rich Yusufzai maximum opportunity to play the 'game'. They did so by supporting first one candidate for the kingship, then another, con-stantly shifting their allegiances in an attempt to prevent any one con-tender from achieving an outright victory. Eventually one of the Akhund's grandsons, the Wali of Swat, succeeded in turning the fac-tional processes of Yusufzai politics to his own advantage. Before invading any part of the valley he always formed an alliance with the weaker bloc in that district. Having defeated the dominant faction in each district he destroyed his opponents' forts and disarmed the popu-lation. Generally, he allied himself ideologically with the peasant majority against their Yusufzai landlords. The Wali abolished the rem-nants of *wesh* and converted the supposedly mystical right of the Yusufzai to receive tribute into a simple cash tenancy, diverting some of the income into state funds and thereby maintaining a standing army of 10,000 men. He called on British engineers to construct a telephone system who installed 1,500 miles of telephone lines to keep the Wali in touch with regional centres.

This re-analysis demonstrates that not only the cultural form, but also the cumulative effects of exchange must be taken into account. Life is more than a game or an exchange of intangible messages. It involves power. As differences of power accumulate over time they can trans-form the structure of social relations.

The analysis of interaction led to several developments. While social anthropology rediscovered Marx's theory of exchange and power, games theory was developed by Socioecologists to model the evolution of social behaviour. The concept of social interaction as a form of 'speech', in which participants interpret each other's actions as meaningful, contributed to the rise of Postmodernism. The different approaches that arose within Interactionism laid the grounds for the divergence in anthropological theory currently represented by Socioecology and Postmodernism.

CHAPTER FIVE

Marxist anthropology

Thanks to the attacks of Boas and his students in the United States, and Radcliffe-Brown and Malinowski in Britain, the nineteenth-century unilinear theories of evolution had been discredited by the 1930s. During the 1940s, however, Leslie White wrote a series of papers arguing, against Boas' historical particularism, that there were general laws of social evolution. White revived Morgan's evolutionary typology and, although White did not refer to Marx by name, it is generally agreed that the tenor of his theory was Marxist. White's efforts to 'revive the work of Morgan must rate as one of the most courageous intellectual stands ever taken by an anthropologist ... especially in light of the regnant McCarthyism' (Murphy 1977: 28; cf. Sanderson 1990: 90).

White replaced Marx's emphasis on the control of human labour and access to productive resources with the idea that the decisive force driving social evolution was the control of energy (White 1943; 1949). He retained Marx's causal paradigm, recognising three subsystems of culture: technology, social relations and ideology. Technology drives change in the social system, and social life shapes ideology: 'there is a type of philosophy proper to every type of technology ... but experience of the external world... is filtered through the prism of social systems also' (White 1949: 366). White argued that because the earliest cultural systems exploited the energy of the human body alone, they were condemned to remain simple in form. Around 10,000 years ago, the Agricultural Revolution harnessed the energy of domesticated crops and animals, gaining control over sufficient power to enable the growth of cities and empires, but also allowing the exploitation of primary producers by a ruling class who appropriated surplus production (White 1949: 382). The 'Fuel' (Industrial) Revolution transformed the form of exploitation exercised by the dominant class and inaugurated colonial expansion in search of new markets. 'No industrial nation had or could have purchasing power sufficient to keep and absorb its own output; the very basis of the industrial profit system was an excess in value of the product over the cost of production in terms of wages paid to the industrial workers' (White 1949: 387).

White's approach also owes something to Durkheim in his insistence that social processes are to be explained in terms of the intrinsic characteristics of social systems, rather than appeals to biology or psychology (White 1949: 364, 392). White's theory is entirely within the mould of the nineteenth-century progressive Evolutionists. It allows no role for adaptation, and puts to one side the influence of the environment: 'The functioning of any particular culture will of course be conditioned by local environmental conditions. But in a consideration of culture as a whole, we may average all environments together to form a constant factor which may be excluded from our formula of cultural development' (1949: 368n). Having chosen to use a single criterion, the amount of energy captured and the efficiency with which it is used, White could only measure cultural variation on a unilinear scale. His scheme is at times closer to that of Herbert Spencer than it is to Marx's multilinear model of social change.

No British anthropologist advocated a Marxist approach during the 1940s but in 1956 Peter Worseley published what was, at the time, regarded as a revolutionary, Marxist reinterpretation of Fortes' analysis of Tallensi society. The Tallensi are subsistence farmers who traditionally lacked centralised leadership. They live in what is now northern Ghana.

Fortes carried out two years' fieldwork with the Tallensi between 1934 and 1937. He analysed their society from a Functionalist perspective (see chapter 2). He found that the Tallensi had localised patrilineal descent groups, grouped into patrilineal clans that contained about 400 people. Clanspeople sometimes occupied a single village, sometimes several villages. Each lineage had a leader. The lineage was a landowning, corporate group. Together with Evans-Pritchard's analysis of the Nuer, Fortes' analysis of Tallensi lineages became the leading Structural-Functionalist ethnography.

The Tallensi were composed of two historically distinct sets of people, the 'original inhabitants' of the district, whose lineages were headed by *tendaanas*, and the descendants of immigrants, whose lineage leaders were called *na'ams*. The lineage head is custodian of the shrines of the lineage's ancestors. Fortes considered that religion played an important part in holding the lineage together and argued, in the Durkheimian tradition, that ancestor worship had a vital social function. A man's allegiance to the compound of his lineage segment was a sacred duty, and the lineage leader had authority because he was the living representative of the ancestors. According to Fortes, it would be a sin to sell the portion of the lineage's ancestral land to which a man inherited rights of use, because his ancestors' graves are built on that land. He wrote, 'the land that a man owns in his clan settlement is usually the land that has come down to him by inheritance from his father. It is hallowed land because it has come to him thus' (Fortes 1949b: 181–2). If a man has several sons, then some of the younger men will be obliged to move away, because land is scarce in long-established villages. Younger sons must clear areas of bush and start new farms. When their father reaches old age, however, such sons return. Fortes considered that they did so out of a sense of filial piety towards their father and the ancestors of the lineage. While economic necessity was undoubtedly the main reason for the family dispersing, 'the process of reintegration is as much or more the result of ritual and affective forces' (1949b: 185). There was an element of reconstruction in Fortes' analysis. Twenty-five years earlier, the Tallensi had been driven out of the hills at the heart of their territory after defeat by the British. They only returned in 1936.

Worseley pointed out that in Fortes' account of Tallensi clanship (Fortes 1945), he had written of ancestral graves being 'often treated very casually' (Fortes 1945: 219). Sometimes they were so neglected that only elders descended from that ancestor knew where to find his grave. Even if it was the ideal that a lineage should farm the land on which its ancestors' graves stood, this was not always so in practice. Changes in ownership of land took place after population movements, and frequently resulted in the land surrounding the ancestral graves passing into the hands of another segment of the lineage, or even another clan. Evidently the urge to look after the ancestors' shrines was not sufficient to ensure a lineage always worked the land of its ancestors. Worseley proposed a more practical reason for people's attachment to the land.

He showed that the Tallensi were living in conditions of scarcity, both of food and of land. The Tong Hills, at the heart of Tallensi country, had a population density of 171.6 inhabitants per square mile. Famine was common and children often had to search for waste scraps, or glean seed from harvested land to feed themselves. It was not surprising that rights to the most fertile land were carefully guarded, and the best land is that around the long-inhabited compounds, because this land has been tended and manured the longest. New farms opened in the bush depend on shallow, unmanured soil. Fortes admitted that there were strong economic elements in the individual's adherence to his lineage. 'As the Tallensi themselves often put it,' he wrote, 'it is all a question of manure, including human excrement. A home farm in one of the old settlements kept at a high level of fertility... is not lightly abandoned. This... puts a premium on the right to inherit them' (1949b: 263).* Worseley concluded that young men returned to their father's homestead when he reached old age, less out of filial piety than the desire to inherit the right to farm some of his land. To acquire such rights, a man must be present when the lineage land is reallocated, and he must remain there to work his portion. If one lineage segment decreases in size over several generations, while another grows, the larger segment will be able to appropriate unused land.

Worseley demonstrated how Marx's axiom, that control of the means of production conferred power, elucidated the economic basis of lineage organisation in small-scale societies. His study remained one of the few to apply Marxist theory to social anthropology for a decade and a half. It was not until the 1970s that the study of social process recaptured Marx's insights.

The theoretical and social context for the revival of Marxism

Marxist anthropology developed in response to dissatisfaction with several aspects of contemporary anthropological theory. Most importantly, perhaps, it questioned the validity of treating small-scale societies as isolates, suspended in time and space, rather than as elements in the colonial and post-colonial world. It also questioned

---

* Fortes is contradictory on this point. Elsewhere, in support of his argument that duty to protect the shrines of the ancestors was the determining factor in drawing the Tallensi back to the Tong Hills, Fortes wrote that they were economically better off where the British had resettled them, 'It was fertile land, won from the uncultivated bush. They were better off for food than they were in the hills' (Fortes 1949b: 185).

both the Functionalists' tendency to attribute equal force to all elements in the social system, and the Structuralists' claims that social life was driven by the structure of people's thought rather than the practical outcome of their actions. Structural Marxists sought a compromise position, arguing that the material conditions of existence cannot completely determine people's ideas. Alternative cognitive systems can be developed in the same environment, and can react back upon material conditions. Lineages, for example, are constituted through kinship. They enable the co-operative labour of kin, and the joint rights of kin to productive resources. Yet human social kinship is always partly fictive and does not completely coincide with biological relatedness. Kinship is thus simultaneously part of the infrastructure of material relationships, and the superstructure of ideology (e.g. Friedman 1975; Godelier 1977).

Marvin Harris, on the other hand, uncompromisingly rejected the theory that people's ideas can transform the material conditions of their existence. He dismissed the efforts of writers such as Sahlins, Godelier and Friedman to integrate Structuralism and Marxism as an unnecessary obscuring of the Marxist tenet that it is the material conditions of existence which determine consciousness, rather than the converse (Harris 1979: 219). During the 1960s, Harris developed the theory of Cultural Materialism, which attempts to purify Marxism of its ambiguity concerning the role of ideas in social process and placed primary emphasis on the role of technology and demography in determining the conditions of social life, leading Structural Marxists to dismiss him as a 'vulgar materialist' (Bloch 1983: 153). Harris relied on the distinction between people's own idea of the significance of their social action (the *emic* perspective) and the sociological observer's analysis (the *etic* perspective). 'Etic operations have as their hallmark the elevation of observers to the status of ultimate judges of the categories and concepts used in descriptions and analyses' (Harris 1979: 32). Harris followed Marx's dictum that people's ideas ('consciousness') are determined by their embeddedness in a mode of production, but adhered to the Enlightenment principle that the detached observer is exempt, and can objectively determine the true causes of events. For Harris, causes of social action always proceed from the material to the ideological, and never the other way around. The actual conditions in which people produce what they need for their subsistence, and reproduce the next generation, limit the possible forms that social relationships can take. The material conditions of social life, created by people acting through the medium of social relationships, in turn limit the possible forms that values and ideas can assume. Harris rejects the converse proposition, that people's ideas can have a determinative effect on their material or social condition (Harris 1979: 55ff.).

Marx had paid relatively little attention to non-Capitalist modes of production (see chapter 1). In the course of developing and refining Marx's theory, new modes of production were modelled, and old ones re-evaluated. The static models of Functionalism, in which every custom played an indispensable part in sustaining the delicate balance of social relationships, were replaced by processual models which interpreted inequalities of power as the consequence of unequal access to labour and productive resources. New insights were gained into how a social system might undergo a transformation from one mode of production to another. It was recognised that during a period of transformation, more than one mode of production might coexist within a single society, or 'social formation' (Bloch 1983: 155).

Asad's criticism of British Functionalism (1973, cited in the conclusion to chapter 2) was paralleled in the United States, where it was also noted that anthropology had developed with colonialism, and that anthropologists tended to dismiss studies of the impact of colonial powers on native people as 'not real anthropology' (Hymes 1974: 31, 50). As British anthropologists were accused of collusion with colonial governments in Africa, so American anthropologists were challenged for participating in CIA counter-insurgency campaigns during the Vietnam War (Berreman 1968; 1973). Berreman argued that neutrality in science is unachievable; to be uncommitted is to be committed to the status quo. Research must therefore become socially responsible and confront the realities of the West's post-colonial domination over other societies. In France, the student rebellion of 1968 against the academic establishment also promoted a wish to engage social science with contemporary political issues. In all three countries, therefore, Marx's analysis of the interconnection between power and the control of resources, and the predatory tendency of capitalism upon other modes of production, gained favour during the 1970s.

Primitive communalism reassessed

Until the 1960s anthropologists generally considered that hunter-gatherers lived a precarious life, barely escaping starvation by foraging

widely for scarce resources. The lack of political hierarchy characteristic of most recent hunter-gatherers was therefore seen to be a
natural consequence of their lack of material wealth and of the need to
be constantly on the move. In the 1960s, however, some startling data
were obtained which turned this view upside-down, leading to the
conclusion that (despite its Rousseauesque appearance of naturalness)
egalitarianism among hunter-gatherers was politically contrived.
Observation of three weeks' foraging at two Aboriginal camps in
northern Australia revealed that the average length of time each person
devoted per day to the acquisition and preparation of food was only
four to five hours. People stopped foraging when they had obtained
enough for the time being. It was what Sahlins called an economy of
limited objectives (Sahlins 1974: 17, citing McCarthy and McArthur
1960. See Altman 1987: 94–5 for a reassessment of McCarthy and
McArthur's data.). Woodburn (1968) reported that the Hadza hunter-
gatherers of Tanzania probably spent an average of less than two hours
a day obtaining food (Woodburn 1968: 27). In 1964 Richard Lee made
similar observations over a four-week period during lengthy fieldwork
among the Ju/'hoansi or Dobe !Kung. Lee found that each active adult
foraged for an average of two hours nine minutes per day. Lee did not
extend his observations to the amount of time spent preparing food,
but Sahlins concludes that one man's labour in hunting and gathering
could support between four and five people. Taken at face value, San
hunting and gathering seemed at least as efficient in supporting a given
number of people as French farming prior to the Second World War
(Sahlins 1974. 21).

Sahlins concluded that it was not only hunter-gatherers but also
many subsistence farmers in Africa and elsewhere, who did not fully
realise their own capacity for food production: 'labour power is under-
used, technological means are not fully engaged, natural resources are
left untapped' (Sahlins 1974: 41). Sahlins argued that the reason is to
be found in the control of exchange. While households everywhere
need to exchange goods, this is often merely to ensure subsistence, the
type of transaction Marx called non-mercantile exchange. Political
systems differed, however, in the incentives they offered to produce a
surplus above subsistence needs. The Kapauku of Papua-New Guinea
studied by Pospisil (Pospisil 1963), for instance, are horticulturalists
who intensify production to compete for status through ceremonial
feasting (Sahlins 1974: 115). Pospisil's detailed ethnography of the

Kapauku shows, as Sahlins points out, that members of aspiring 'big men's' households work much harder than members of other households because they seek political power through the construction of alliances based on exchange.

Sahlins coined the concept of the *domestic mode of production* to describe an economy in which production is entirely directed towards the household's internal requirements, a trait which Marx attributed to primitive communalism. Although collaboration with other households may regularly occur, such co-operation 'does not compromise the autonomy of the household or its economic purpose, [or] the domestic management of labour power' (Sahlins 1974: 78).

An alternative characterisation of the simplest form of social organisation is contained in Woodburn's theory of immediate and delayed return, which is also influenced by Marxist theory (Woodburn 1982). Whereas Sahlins regarded the autonomy of households as a determining characteristic of the domestic mode of production, Woodburn argued that egalitarian political systems among hunter-gatherers are deliberately preserved by means of levelling transactions which take place between domestic units in order to prevent particular households accumulating a surplus. Woodburn suggests that there are two types of hunter-gatherer political system, based on *immediate* or *delayed return*.

In an immediate return system, people forage daily for their immediate requirements, without storing food for the future. Technology is simple and everyone can quickly make what they need. Anyone is free to hunt and gather wherever they wish. The land and the animals and plants which live on it are unowned. Consequently social groupings are flexible and short-lived, and, while sharing is stressed, no one depends on anyone else for food or other essential resources. This has the consequence of subverting authority, and preventing the emergence of any basis for coercion or social differentiation on the basis of wealth. The Hadza, with whom Woodburn himself worked extensively, practise no form of territoriality. Woodburn claims that among the Hadza, children and young unmarried adults are in no way dependent on older people for the resources they need to survive. In delayed return systems, labour is invested in resources which become assets over which people hold rights. Such resources include the complex equipment (large boats and stone fish traps) of the Inuit, and the stored food and art objects exchanged by north-west coast Indians in the potlatch. Under these circumstances, differences of power can develop: between owners of equipment and non-owners, between rich and poor lineages, and between men and women. The transition out of immediate return resembles Marx's concept of movement away from primitive communalism.

Woodburn argues that farmers and herders cannot help but have delayed return systems, because they invest work in planting and tending their crops or raising their herds, but hunter-gatherers need not have delayed return systems. He does not consider hunter-gatherer political systems to be determined by the natural environment nor, in Woodburn's assessment, is individual self-interest sufficient to explain egalitarianism. The successful hunter is obliged by his community to distribute his catch, and the best hunters always give more than they receive. Anyone who is arrogant is ostracised. The Ju/'hoansi or !Kung San have an elaborate sharing network called *Hxaro*, through which personal possessions are exchanged. Bead necklaces, arrow heads and other personal possessions are given as gifts through *Hxaro*. If an animal is killed, it belongs to the owner of the arrow head, not the hunter who shot with it. People cultivate *Hxaro* partnerships with members of other bands, and most personal possessions are given to others as an expression of friendly intent, and to impose an obligation to return gifts at a later date. The Hadza, on the other hand, gamble with bark discs to redistribute personal possessions in a random fashion, achieving a similar levelling of access to belongings without developing long-term social relationships.

Wolf's 'kin-ordered mode of production without lineages', although based on the same ethnographies, places the emphasis differently again. Wolf regards the lack of ownership rights claimed over the land and, by extension, the animals and plants on which people depend, as crucial to egalitarianism (Wolf 1982: 91). Like Woodburn, Wolf considers that domestic units are not socially independent but Wolf regards kinship, rather than gambling or meat-sharing, as a way of establishing rights to people's labour.

The lineage mode of production

The 'lineage mode of production' was a concept introduced by Meillassoux in his analysis of the Guro of the Ivory Coast (Meillassoux 1964) and developed both by French Marxist anthropologists during the 1970s (see Godelier 1975; Lefébure 1979; and Terray 1972) and, later, by Eric Wolf (1982). Societies displaying this mode of production are characterised by coalitions made of a number of households, or domestic units, which are bound together by rights in property which they have jointly inherited and which they jointly manage. Over time, these develop into the corporate lineages identified by the Structural Functionalists. Kinship provides both the ideology by which group membership is justified, and the means by which labour is co-ordinated. Being bound by such mutual rights and activities has three political consequences. Members of the junior generation are subject to the political authority of elders, from whom (as the Tallensi example shows) they will inherit rights to the essential subsistence resources which belong to the group. Authority is therefore vested collectively in the elders of the group. Women are often used by senior men to create strategic marriages which maintain inter-lineage relationships in the absence of an over-arching, centralised government. Like the domestic mode of production, the lineage mode of production is a convenient analytical tool, which focuses attention on how political relationships are sustained by property rights and by exchange. The lineage mode of production provides a useful means for analysing the societies of many nomadic pastoralists and subsistence farmers which is more insightful than the static structural models of Radcliffe-Brown's Functionalism.

Nomadic pastoralists

Pastoral societies share with most hunter-gatherers the trait of mobility, but they differ from hunter-gatherers in having a narrow resource base. Instead of exploiting a wide range of wild food sources, they invest their effort in intensively husbanding their livestock: sometimes a single species like cattle or camels, or two related species such as sheep and goats. Nomadism is frequently associated with a lack of political hierarchy. Burnham, like Woodburn, argues this involves something more than simple ecological determinism (Burnham 1979). It is not simply the need to move which prevents the emergence of entrenched leadership, but a deliberate exploitation of nomads' ability to move, which enables them to escape coercion by would-be despots. When disputes can be resolved by one party leaving camp, there does not need to be elaborate machinery for intervention, to avoid the breakdown of social relationships in the community. As Sahlins argued with regard to the domestic mode of production, Burnham concludes that households therefore need not surrender their political autonomy. Burnham argues that pure nomads are inherently egalitarian and that political centralisation only occurs when some form of interaction with cultivators is taking place, as was the case in Central Asia from around AD 1000.

Goldschmidt argued that dependence on livestock for subsistence is itself inimical to the emergence of political inequality (Goldschmidt 1979). Under good conditions a herd can increase rapidly, but during drought or epidemics a herd is extremely vulnerable. The mobility of livestock renders herds also vulnerable to theft by raiding parties. There is a practical limit on the number of animals which can be herded as a unit, and large herds must be dispersed. As is the case with hunter-gatherers, the absence of political domination does not render the household a social isolate. Rather, risk can be reduced by spreading one's livestock as widely as possible through loans and bridewealth payments. Loans cement relationships based on reciprocal dependence within the lineage, and bridewealth cements alliances between groups. This analysis throws further light on the egalitarian, uncentralised social organisation of the Samburu (chapter 2) and the Nuer (chapter 4).

Cultivators

Investment of labour in cultivated land discourages regular movement. Cultivated land is a valuable resource, but it can be defended if the land-owning group is politically well-organised (see the example of the Yanomamö in chapter 3). Cultivation is characterised by irregular labour demands, especially for preparation of the land and the harvesting of crops which, Marxist anthropologists such as Terray argue, is met by long-term social relationships that exist between members of a lineage. Lineage leaders co-ordinate joint labour. Terray considered West African lineages were primarily held together by the need for co-operation in agricultural work. Terray took Meillassoux's study of the Gouro (Meillassoux 1964) and his own of the Dida as examples. He classified the labour demands of agriculture into two types. Preparing the land and seasonal harvesting required *extended co-operation*. Sowing, planting and day-to-day maintenance of the land only demanded *restricted co-operation* (Terray 1972: 117). The whole village united to carry out net hunting and, formerly, to go to war. Effective net hunting requires a very large party and 'helps to create cohesion among lineages with often distant origins' (Meillassoux 1964: 89, quoted in Terray 1972: 118). The disappearance of net hunting destabilized Gouro villages, causing them to break up into their constituent lineages. In villages where lineages were strong, extended co-operation in agriculture is carried out by whole lineages, while restricted co-operation occurred within lineage segments. If men out hunting with bows or guns found new land suitable for cultivation, they blazed the trees and informed the 'elder of their community', who arranged for it to be cleared by members of his lineage (Terray 1972: 126). The harvest, as the product of lineage co-operation, was stored in granaries controlled by the lineage elder. Most is redistributed to lineage members, but some is used to feed guests or relatives from neighbouring villages. Although this might allow the elder to acquire a following of personal dependants, Meillassoux considered that the power of the lineage elder was constrained by his physical dependence on younger members of the lineage for their labour, and by the fact that land is abundant in this part of West Africa. Elders' power was 'functional' in the sense that younger men depended on the elders' knowledge but, if in dispute with the elders, young men could withdraw their labour and force the elders' capitulation.

The Wahgi of highland New Guinea illustrate a similar political and economic system (O'Hanlon 1989). The defence of territory is central to Wahgi politics. A Marxist perspective focuses attention on the need to retain control over the lineage's land. People who lose in warfare are expelled from their land by the winners, and must begin new gardens elsewhere. Although the Wahgi had not been involved in war since the 1930s, there was warfare in progress nearby while O'Hanlon was in the field, and local warfare has broken out since (O'Hanlon 1995). In order to secure their territory against attack, the men of a Wahgi clan must demonstrate their unity and self-sufficiency to outsiders, so intimidating potential enemies. This is done at ceremonial dance displays. Both clans and subclans need leaders if they are to defend their interests. Internal disputes must be resolved, and external relationships managed. Leadership is not as formalised as it is among the Tallensi, but one or two men in each subclan are recognised as more prominent than others. As Sahlins pointed out, the 'Big Man's' lack of control over lineage land places severe limits on his power to coerce others (Sahlins 1963). His control is limited to persuading other households to work harder than they need to supply their own subsistence, in order to provide food for the feasts which accompany dance displays (Sahlins 1974: 115ff.).

Eric Wolf and the impact of colonialism

During the 1970s, various new modes of production were proposed, as anthropologists attempted to fill the gaps in Marx's analysis of non-Western societies. As the preceding section has indicated, these sometimes overlapped. Wolf identifies three modes of production – the capitalist, tributary and 'kin-ordered' modes – which, although not exhaustive of human social variability, provide a parsimonious way of classifying human societies for the purpose of analysing the impact of Europe on the rest of the world since the year AD 1400 (Wolf 1982). The following section will summarise Wolf's analysis and use case studies to exemplify the impact of capitalism on non-Western societies during and after the colonial period.

The kin-ordered mode of production

In the kin-ordered mode of production social kinship (that is, the cultural interpretation of biological relatedness) locates people from birth into social relationships which allow them to call upon each other's labour during subsistence activities. Wolf recognises two variants of the kin-ordered mode, one in which no exclusive rights are claimed by groups of kin within the community over productive resources (Woodburn's immediate return economy and Sahlins' domestic mode of production), and one in which access to productive resources in a certain area is restricted to those who are 'licensed by kinship' to claim membership of the resource-owning group (Meillassoux's lineage mode of production).

Wolf equates the first variant with food-collecting bands of hunter-gatherers who do not invest labour in modifying the land, but in my view this equation, although a long-standing myth in anthropology, is fallacious. The question of rights over land in hunter-gatherer societies will be reconsidered in chapter 6. Wolf links the second variant of the kin-ordered mode of production with the transformation of the land through collective labour by means of cultivation. Those who work the land together transmit rights to the land they have worked to their children, generating lineages such as those found among the Tallensi and Wahgi.

The inherent weakness of social systems governed by the kin-ordered mode, in Wolf's assessment, is their tendency to generate the segmentation of the community into opposed groups. Women lose status once they are used as pawns in marriage exchanges between lineages. The power of leaders derives from their rights to manage the land and labour of the lineage. No leader can develop authority over a wider community unless he can gain control over an independent source of power.

The tributary mode of production

An essential characteristic of many peasant agricultural economies is that producers can cultivate a surplus over the household's subsistence needs. Anyone with the power to oblige people to work longer, to produce such a surplus, can extract it as tribute. This trait is treated by Sahlins as the means by which the domestic mode of production is subverted by New Guinea Big Men who can persuade others of their ability to negotiate alliances. Such Big Men, however, lack the powers of coercion normally associated with tributary systems. Sahlins distinguished the voluntary dependency solicited by Big Men from the tributary systems of Polynesia (Sahlins 1963).

Wolf treats Marx's feudal and Asiatic modes of production as two extremes in a continuum which he characterises as the tributary mode of production (cf. Godelier 1974). The tributary mode is found in centralised states wherever political or military rulers extract surpluses from the primary producers. Although the producers, whether herdsmen or peasant farmers, have use rights over the land they exploit, their rulers claim a superior right, on which they base their authority to collect tribute. The rulers' power will be greatest where they control some strategic productive resource such as the water supply for irrigation, or long-distance trade, and can support a standing army as an agent for coercion. The relative power of local overlords and central rulers varies with the strength of their respective control over such resources.

Incipient tributary states in nineteenth-century Cameroon

Rowlands (1979) argues that the small states which existed in the grassfield (savannah) region of Cameroon (West Africa) during the nineteenth century demonstrate various stages in the transition from a lineage to a tributary mode of production. Rowlands' historical reconstruction captures the phase during which lineage-based societies of the same type as the Tiv and Tallensi become transformed into states resembling, on a smaller scale, the Asante. Local trade took place in subsistence commodities, and was conducted by household heads. Long-distance trade took place in prestige goods such as slaves, gold, ivory, kola nuts and guns, control of which enhanced the position of elites. Entry into the long-distance trade between the Sahara and European trading posts on the coast was crucial to the transformation in mode of production. Rowlands asks how certain households made the transition to trading in prestige goods. The ecology of Cameroon made it most efficient for farmers on the grassfields to specialise in the production of cereals, starch foods (yams, maize), the raising of live-stock (goats, pigs, poultry), and wood-carving and iron-smithing. The forest zone to the south provided the best environment for the produc-tion of palm oil, camwood and salt. Inhabitants of both zones required the others' products, which they obtained in exchange for their own produce. There was also some economic specialisation on the savan-nah plateau itself. The central kingdoms, with closest access to the palm oil-producing regions, found it cost-effective to trade in bulky dry foods, while those on the eastern margin found it more efficient to trade in high-value, low-bulk iron tools.

The unit of production was the compound, consisting of an extended family (i.e. a minimal lineage segment). Men produced livestock and craft goods suitable for trade, while women carried out the agricultural and domestic work which provided for subsistence. The compound head was responsible for storing and distributing dry foods produced by the women of the compound. He could divert surpluses directly into trade, or into provisioning trading expeditions carried out by his male dependants. Household heads in the central kingdoms were therefore well-placed to exploit the capacity of their dependants to engage in surplus labour, and expropriate this to increase their own wealth. Among households on the eastern edge of the plateau, men were the wood-carvers and iron-smiths. This left them little time to engage in trade and they relied on middlemen funded by central plateau compounds.

How did successful compound heads invest their profits from trade? Primarily by joining 'subscription societies', which were associations of patrilineal kin, age-mates and friends. To participate, a man had to have wealth in the form of brass rods (compare the example of similar associations among the Tiv, outlined in chapter 4). At regular intervals, all members of such a society contributed a set number of brass rods, and each member in turn took the 'pool' to use in a venture approved by his fellow members. Such ventures included amassing bridewealth for a son's marriage or financing a trading expedition. Heads of lineages or lineage segments could also use the 'pool' of brass rods allocated them to obtain a title or privileged status in a ritual association which gained higher status for their whole lineage or lineage segment (compare the Bwami association of the Lega, briefly mentioned in chapter 3, and described by Biebuyck 1973).

Bafut was the kingdom which had most successfully exploited the trade in subsistence goods. Here, the king had instituted palace associations. Every lineage in the kingdom was obliged to send a representative to join one of these associations, to represent its affairs at court. Lineages sought to increase their standing in the kingdom, by supporting the promotion of their representative. This was achieved by making payments of livestock, wine, brass rods and food to other members of the palace association and to the king. Several smaller kingdoms on the plateau went to war during the nineteenth century to protect their land against encroachment, and to protect their palm oil trading partners from domination by Bafut. Bafut, however, was actively expanding by raiding smaller chiefdoms to obtain slaves, and by dominating palm oil-producing villages in order to extract oil as tribute, rather than through trade. Rowlands deduces that the palace elite, who were the beneficiaries of slave trading, were in the process of detaching themselves from the support of their own lineages, and forming a separate class of title holders who held exclusive control over long-distance trade. Only they could afford the guns, gunpowder and cotton cloth reaching the area from European trading posts on the coast.

Bafut would eventually have achieved a centralised structure resembling that of the Asante, had this trend not been halted by the intervention of German colonists. Until the nineteenth century European traders in West Africa were confined to the coast, but they then began to move inland and conquer the kingdoms with whom they had formerly traded. The Germans both established palm oil plantations on the coast and obtained further palm oil by trade from the forest zone. The grassfields kingdoms became reduced to tributary states, supplying slaves to the southern forest zone, where they were put to work on plantations. Smaller kingdoms and northern forest villages were depopulated by slave raiding until the Germans finally conquered the region.

Slavery in Africa

During the seventeenth century, 1,341,000 Africans were enslaved and taken to work on plantations in the Caribbean (Wolf 1982: 195). In the eighteenth century, six million were reduced to slavery, four million of whom were put to work on sugar plantations. After 1850, the slave trade declined with the growth of mechanised production but between the seventeenth and nineteenth centuries slavery was part of a triangular trading pattern controlled from Europe. The British traded commodities manufactured in Britain for African slaves. British trade with Africa rose by 400 per cent between 1730 and 1775. The produce of the Caribbean plantations (coffee, sugar, cotton) obtained through slave labour was in turn shipped back to Britain.

West African political organisation was transformed by this unprecedented, predatory relationship. The rise of the Asante confederation coincides with the period when the Gold Coast (now Ghana) was the centre of slave supply. The Asante benefited from crops introduced from the New World which increased agricultural productivity and enabled specialist villages of craftsmen and gold-panners to be supported by chiefs. Rowlands' study of the Cameroon grassfields shows how, on a smaller scale, a lineage mode of production could become transformed into a centralised polity based on the slave trade. Societies such as the Tiv and Tallensi were vulnerable to the slave-raids of the kingdoms to their south. The Tallensi lineage heads called *na'am*s were formerly slave-takers supplying the Asante (Wolf 1982: 230). Although the *na'am* is elected, he owns the products of all the locust bean trees growing in his clan settlement's land, as well as the right to declare when certain stretches of river and bush can be opened for fishing and hunting. Until the British intervened to suppress slavery, vagrant human beings found on clan land were handed over to him, and he sold them as slaves. Then, and during the colonial period, stray dogs and cattle, and lost brass or copper, were handed to the *na'am* (Fortes 1940: 258–9).

Warfare was not the only means by which slaves were obtained for sale to Europeans on the coast. Under the lineage mode of production, people's labour is 'locked up' in kinship groups, to whom they owe their work (Wolf 1982: 205). However, traditional mechanisms existed for detaching people from their lineage. A person might be placed, or voluntarily put themselves, into pawnship, to settle debts, or obtain food during famine. If this occurred, they consigned the right to their labour and reproductive capacity, to someone else. A man who infringed the lineage's code of conduct could be expelled from his group becoming, in effect, an outlaw and vulnerable to leaders such as the na'ams of the Tallensi. Captives could be taken in warfare. Once trade with Europe provided the rulers of forest kingdoms such as the Asante with guns they stepped up wars of conquest. Both ordinary African compound heads and kings could increase their labour supply by acquiring rights over such people. Kings put pawns, criminals and captives to work in cultivation, gold mining or long-distance trade (Wolf 1982: 208).

A well-developed tributary state
In northern India a rather similar tributary mode to that of feudal Europe operated prior to British conquest. Northern India was ruled from 1527 by Turks from Turkestan, who introduced a ruling elite composed partly of Turks, partly of Persians, Uzbekis and other immigrants, and partly of local Rajputs (Wolf 1982: 241). In Kangra (part of Punjab), north of Delhi, the local raja claimed as tribute half the gross produce on good land, and between a third and a quarter of the produce from poorer land. 'The more avaricious, or perhaps simply the more powerful, rajas added to these basic rates a whole host of additional levies: an army tax and a war tax, for example, a weigh man's tax, a money-tester's tax or a tax to cover the cost of transporting the grains to the royal granaries; and – what must have been most galling of all – a tax to cover the cost of writing receipts' (Parry 1979: 22). The Functionalist model of a balance of power between ruler and ruled clearly fails to illuminate such an oppressive regime.

A characteristic of both Indian and African tributary states is that, as the case of the Asante showed, lineages played an important part in the political structure. The difference between the lineage and tributary modes of production is not that there are no lineages in the latter, but that lineages are not politically autonomous; rather, their leaders are coerced into acting as agents of the central authority. Fox reconstructs the position of Rajput clans in the state of Uttar Pradesh under Moghul and British rule. The Rajputs were landowners and peasant farmers. Each lineage was led by a raja who received tribute from other members of the lineage, and recruited soldiers from the lineage to defend its land or conquer new territory. The raja was responsible for passing a portion of his tribute up to the emperor. Each segment of the lineage occupied a village, and constituted its farmers, whose members had client relationships with craftsmen, agricultural labourers and other resident occupational groups. According to Fox, each power stratum in the state took a share of the farmers' grain heap, and the balance of power between centre and village 'was reflected in the distribution of the peasant's productivity' (Fox 1971: 54). The Moghul Empire had sufficient military power to extract a greater or lesser quantity of tribute from the Rajas, but remained dependent on them to carry out local government.

Lineages are destroyed by the transformation of land into a commodity which becomes the private property of individuals under capitalism (Fox 1971: 15). In 1690, the Mogul province in which Calcutta lay was governed by the Navab of Bengal. The Navab relied on Indian merchant bankers to manage his enormous wealth. Huge loans were advanced to the British, which enabled them to develop weaving contracts with local craftsmen, in order to supply cloth to China (through British traders). At this time, Rajput lineage segments were still expanding into new land, and often refusing to pass on tribute to their rulers. The British sought to undermine the Navab's position by supporting the dissident Rajput. Matters came to a head in 1757, when the British defeated the Navab. They plundered his treasury, stealing five million pounds. Such enormous wealth enabled them to oust the merchant bankers on whom they had formerly depended and take control of the province (Wolf 1982: 242–6).

Like the merchant seigneurs of late pre-Revolutionary France, the British sought to increase their revenue from taxation, which they doubled between 1756 and 1776. Many farmers and craftsmen were ruined. Local agriculture was transformed from subsistence production to the production of cash crops such as cotton and opium for sale in China. Even though major famines occurred in 1770 and 1783, the cultivation of cash crops such as sugar, tobacco, spices, cotton, jute and indigo at the expense of subsistence crops continued, contributing to the Indian Mutiny of 1857.

Cash crops and labour migration
The traditional states of India had monetised economies for 2,000 years. In East Africa, a largely subsistence economy was rapidly transformed during the early twentieth century by the simple step of demanding taxes in cash, and providing Africans with the opportunity

to earn such cash by cultivating new market crops or by working in the newly opened copper mines (Elliott 1974; Watson 1958). The effect of these changes varied according to the local subsistence economy and organisation of labour, and were studied by several anthropologists from Manchester University under Gluckman's direction. A.L. Epstein studied the transformation of social relationships that took place in Luansha, in a copper-belt town then located in the colony of Northern Rhodesia (now Zambia) (Epstein 1958). The British colonial authorities intended that the African migrants would only reside in the town for a short period and remain oriented to their rural, 'tribal' community of origin. In 1931 the British introduced the elected office of 'tribal elder'. Each elder was intended to act as an intermediary between the colonial authorities and members of his 'tribe' working in the mines. Yet urban society did not reproduce rural social relationships. The son of a chief might find himself in a work team led by a commoner. Inter-tribal differences were less important than the common predicament of wage labour in the mines. When an announcement was made in 1935 that taxes were to be increased the African workforce rioted, and the so-called 'tribal elders' fled when their fellow-tribesmen accused them of being in league with the British (Epstein 1958: 32). Other groupings emerged to take their place. One originated as a library association which had been formed to promote literacy in English. It repudiated ethnic divisions and campaigned successfully to improve the quality of maize sold to African workers, and to abolish the application of traditional, 'tribal' law in urban courts.

Capitalism in the rural economy
The changes in urban social organisation which Epstein documented follow the predictions of a Marxist model, but many studies of social change in rural areas made during the colonial era implied that rural societies could absorb the effects of capitalism and return to an equilibrium. Duffield's more recent study of a town in the Sudan shows how corrosive the effects of capitalism can be upon rural social life. In capitalist farming, those who own the land and equipment do not provide the labour. Agricultural labourers sell their labour to the owners of these resources, who oblige the workers to labour for longer than they would need to, if they had only to meet the costs of their own subsistence. The labourers' surplus produce provides the capitalist with his profit, which he reinvests in expanding his capital. These character-

istics contrast with peasant farming, in which members of the household or lineage, the productive unit, share ownership of land and
equipment and the primary goal of the labour is to provide for their
own subsistence, even when they have to yield a greater or lesser
proportion as tribute to a higher political authority. For peasants cash
crops are a subsidiary activity, grown on spare land and in spare time.

Maiurno (Duffield 1981) is a small town on the bank of the Blue Nile
established in 1906 by the son of the last independent Khalif of Sokoto,
now part of northern Nigeria, after his father's defeat by the British.
Farm land around the settlement is of two types: *riverain* land, flooded
annually by the Nile, and *rain* land, further from the river banks, which
depends on rain for water and is therefore less productive (Figure 5.1).
Riverain land is owned by the richest peasants and worked largely by
migrant labour, often provided by Nigerian pilgrims to Mecca who
have run out of money and cannot afford to get home. It is a very
exploitative relationship. Large privately owned irrigation schemes

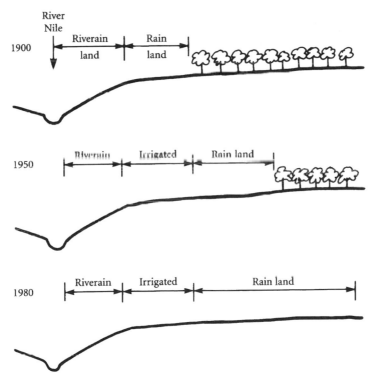

Figure 5.1 Changing patterns of land use in Maiurno

outside the immediate area also employ wage labour. Rain land, on the other hand, is worked by peasant households who rely substantially on ties of friendship or kinship to recruit labour through reciprocal work parties.

Cash crops were introduced by the British colonial authorities in the 1920s, as a source of income to enable people to pay the taxes the British had imposed. Since almost all the cash income from crop sales was appropriated in taxation, growing cash crops could not, at that stage, allow local capital accumulation. Mai Wurno, founder of the village, based his power in part on his control over the rain land, and in part on his possession of slaves. Slavery was quickly outlawed by the colonial government of the Sudan, but the British legitimated his control of rain land by granting him ownership of and hereditary title to five square miles of the rain land nearest the town.

In the Korean War of the 1950s a high price could be obtained for cotton. An irrigation scheme was introduced by the colonial government to supply pumped water to the rain lands nearest the river, to increase cotton production for sale overseas. Mai Wurno's son was one of four men granted leases to cultivate irrigated cotton, as he was already one of the largest owners of suitable land. He may also have had the means to bribe officials (Duffield 1981: 71). Most of those who had previously been cultivating the land which was to be irrigated were displaced to more distant, unirrigated land. The capital to set up the scheme came from local commercial enterprises operated by Mai Wurno's son and other local entrepreneurs, who had profited from ownership of shops, or the lorries used for road transport. While some profits were invested in the expansion of commercial activities, other capital was dedicated to the intensification of irrigated farming, relying on hired labour. Thus a division arose in the peasantry, between those who could afford to hire labour, and those who could not. Those who could afford to hire labour withdrew from, and ridiculed, the traditional, reciprocal work parties.

In the early 1960s, the productivity of the original irrigated land began to decline, and the price of cotton also fell. The wealthy responded by clearing further unirrigated rain land on which to grow guinea corn, an alternative cash crop. This was facilitated by the introduction of tractors, replacing some manual labour. Tractors were bought by people living in town who had made a profit through shops, transport, or cotton sales. Mai Wurno's son was first to buy one. The increased production of cash crops made possible by using tractors has allowed the further expansion of farms belonging to the wealthy, consuming all the accessible, uncleared land. Poorer farmers can no longer allow their land to revert to bush by clearing virgin soil, because there is none left.

The shortage of land is exacerbated by the way in which cash crops are produced. The desire to increase cash earnings has led richer farmers to abandon a fallow phase in the crop cycle. While the annually flooded riverain land can withstand this for some time, it leads to rapid impoverishment of rain land. The rich, however, see farming primarily as a short-term means of raising cash to invest in commerce. The long-term fate of the land is not of interest to them because it is not their main form of capital. They are, in fact, treating it as a consumable resource.

The strategy of the richer, who concentrate on cash crop production, has thus increasingly diverged from that of peasants who produce primarily for their own subsistence. Poorer peasant households rely to a greater extent on hoes rather than tractors. They grow a greater variety of crops on rain land, and by rotating crops can preserve the fertility of the soil for twenty to thirty years. Because they depend on the land for their subsistence it is in their interests to maintain its fertility. Even among the peasantry, two economic strata have emerged. The prosperous peasantry have introduced a new form of co-operative labour to replace the traditional work parties. This has become known as the *jitu* system, in which two or more households related by kinship work the land together, occupy a single compound and keep a single grain store to provide for their subsistence. In some cases, sons of such households have set up successful small-scale businesses in town. If they can invest their profits in a tractor, they will allow their fathers to use it.

By 1980, cotton yields were so small that only the poorest peasants, and the elderly, were attracted to the original irrigated land. Farmers working land irrigated by the local pump scheme are advanced loans intended to enable them to buy cotton seeds and fertiliser, and to hire the labour to weed, plough and harvest the cotton. Now, however, they often need the cash advance to pay for their immediate subsistence, and may not be able to afford to grow grain for their own food. They depend on the unpaid labour of their own or relatives' children. In effect, they constitute a third social class, below the self-sufficient peasantry, and are in the process of being eliminated from agriculture.

Duffield poses the question, why haven't the poor peasantry set up *jitu* arrangements? He concludes that without grain to store there is no mutual benefit from co-operation. Sons who continue to live with their fathers, who might thus in time develop into an extended family, would inherit their fathers' debts, whereas migration will give them access to cash as apprentices or farm labourers and allow them to marry. Hence the poor who cannot provide for their sons' needs (helping them to get married, for example) are deprived of their family's labour.

Capitalism and the 'Third World'

Chapter 1 summarised Marx's theory of capitalism in the West, and noted that, although Marx devoted little attention to analysing non-capitalist modes of production, he did draw attention to the way in which capitalism was engulfing and transforming other modes in Asia, Africa and the Americas. One of the principal insights of Marxist anthropology was its revelation that Functionalist 'tribal' studies had depended on the entirely artificial device of analysing small-scale societies in isolation from their colonial context.

The peasant household's primary goal is to meet the subsistence needs of its members. Participation in market exchange is subordinated to self-sufficiency. Cash crops are grown on soil not needed for subsistence. Peasant farming is unmechanised. Labour is principally provided by members of the household. Peasants tend to have large numbers of children, because they will provide the next generation of labourers. Since the labour demands of the agricultural cycle fluctuate, goods can be produced for the market during slack periods in the subsistence agricultural cycle. Scott (1976) argues that peasants have two principal strategies for reducing risk. One is to rely on traditional crops which have been long-used in the district and are known to give a reliable yield, even though alternative varieties may give better yields under favourable conditions. The second strategy is to institute social arrangements such as the reciprocal beer parties of the Fur (see chapter 4), which ensure that each household can call upon the labour of others. Scott calls these social arrangements the 'moral economy of the peasant'.

The capitalist mode of production instituted by colonial regimes is inimical to both strategies. The aim of a colonial regime is not to 'bring civilisation to the native', it is to obtain primary resources such as minerals and food as cheaply as possible for the industries and workers of the metropolitan power, and to create overseas markets where goods manufactured in the metropolitan country can be sold at a profit. The colonising power also attempts to finance government of the colony from local taxation (Figure 5.2). To do so successfully

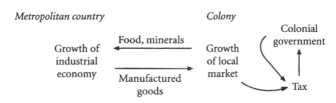

Figure 5.2 Relations between the metropolis and colony

depends on 'unlocking' resources from non-market spheres of exchange regulated by inheritance, tributary obligations or reciprocity. Where land is vested in lineages, it must be transformed into private property which can be bought and sold. Where redistribution takes place through a tributary mode of production it must be converted into cash taxation collected directly by the central government. Reciprocal labour exchanges must be replaced by hiring labour for cash.

The greatest contribution of Wolf's *Europe and the People Without History* (1982) is probably his demonstration that the traditional societies of Africa, Asia and the Americas have never been the isolated, timeless units implied by Functionalist analysis and that, by the time they *were* studied by the Functionalists, they had become incorporated into the world capitalist economy. Following Marx, two phases can be identified in the growth of capitalism. In the first phase, wealth accrues through mercantile exchange, but production remains unmechanised. Human labour is commoditised through slavery. In the second phase, mechanisation of industry reduces the demand for human labour, but increases both the demand for raw materials from the colonies, and the incentive to create markets for manufactured goods within the colonies.

'African Socialism'

It was shown earlier in this chapter that the traditional organisation of pastoralism and subsistence farming in Africa could be analysed according to the model of the 'lineage mode of production'. 'African Socialism' is a term used to describe a number of political platforms

devised by pro-Independence politicians towards the end of the colonial era in East Africa and implemented, to a greater or lesser extent, in
countries such as Kenya and Tanzania. The basic tenet of African
Socialism was that the capitalist regimes of the colonial era, which had
promoted individualism and social division, would be replaced by
collective, socially unifying policies that would build on the collective
institutions which existed in rural Africa prior to colonial conquest.
Jomo Kenyatta, for example, declared one year before Kenyan independence in 1963:

> We are not the slaves of Western Capitalism or Eastern European
> socialism. We must develop our own standards and ideals, based on
> our own culture and the inherent African socialist philosophy, in
> which every man accepts his duty to his neighbours, and the com-
> munity in turn is the source of his security.
> (Kenyatta 1968: 187, quoted by Grillo 1991: 2).

In light of the recent collapse of Communist regimes in Eastern
Europe, it is particularly apposite to ask how successful these attempts
to implement Socialist policies in East Africa have proved, and why
they have been by no means completely realised. In Kenya, it is
arguable, much of the traditional social order was destroyed during the
colonial period (Grillo 1993: 68). Dinham and Hines describe how
imposition of hut and poll taxes forced Africans to become wage
labourers. By 1924, 20 per cent of the best land had been reserved for
European settlers. Both pastoralists such as Maasai and Kikuyu farmers lost land to colonists; in 1924 1,715 settlers employed 87,000
African labourers (Dinham and Hines 1983). After Independence, the
government of Kenya took steps to control the profits accruing to
foreign companies. State Coffee and Tea Marketing Boards were set up
to set the prices paid to growers. Smallholders' coffee co-operatives
provided almost 57 per cent of the crop in 1978. Brooke Bond was paid
to advise smallholders growing tea on how to harvest their crop.

Unfortunately, Kenya was now so deeply embedded in the capitalist
economic system introduced during the colonial period that it was
impossible to reconstruct the pre-colonial order. The Commonwealth
Development Corporation and World Bank helped Africans to buy
European-owned farms, and Africans now own 72 per cent of the
country's large coffee plantations, but many were acquired by the

wealthy, creating a class of Kenyans with a vested interest in maintaining large farms earning income from exports. By 1980, there were 3,200 large farms in Kenya, but 1.5 million smallholdings (Dinham and Hines 1983: 92–7). Eighty-eight per cent of smallholders farm only for their own subsistence, and must sell part of their maize crop to buy essential items such as matches, tea, salt and schooling for their children. The poorest 30 per cent of Kenya's population earn 6.4 per cent of the country's total income while the richest 2 per cent earn almost one-third. On this measure, which of course neglects the scale of non-market production, Kenya was the fifth socially most unequal country in the world during the 1980s (Dinham and Hines 1983: 111). There are more landless people than there were at Independence, and poor smallholders are being forced to sell their land to pay for children's schooling, to repay loans or buy essential subsistence goods. Foreign corporations such as Brooke Bond and Del Monte have taken over good land for growing ornamental plants and pineapples for export. Although self-sufficient in food until 1980, that was the first year in which maize, the staple, had to be imported. Kenya does not appear to have averted the processes that took place on a smaller scale in the Sudanese village studied by Duffield.

In Tanzania, a far more radical policy was adopted after Independence. Tanzania has prevented foreign private investment, although relying on loans for development. Foreign companies established before Independence were either wholly nationalised, or the state acquired shares in them. The peasantry has been seen to a larger extent as the producer of export crops such as coffee, cotton and cashew nuts (Dinham and Hines 1983: 113). The strategy for harnessing peasant production was *Ujamaa* (collective effort), introduced in 1967. Scattered peasant hamlets were grouped into villages. The government undertook to provide villages with schools, health and water supplies. Each extended family was to keep its own field (*shamba*), but in return for government services, each village was to farm one collective field planted with crops intended for export. In 1972 central government administration was devolved to regions to bring planners closer to the problems of production. However, food production has still fallen. A drought in 1982 compelled the government to seek 300,000 tonnes of food aid (Dinham and Hines 1983: 125).

Dinham and Hines conclude that the Tanzanian government has not put enough effort into providing appropriate technology, since most of its investment in agriculture goes into large farms. There is, in consequence, insufficient labour available to work family and village fields. Prices for peasant-produced crops have not been protected. Transport is expensive. Most importantly, perhaps, the rules for distributing the proceeds of work on the village field have not been clearly specified, so that work on the fields is subject to a form of the so-called 'tragedy of the commons' in which anyone who labours on the field is deprived of a fair return when others claim a share without having worked for it.*

Was the notion of African Socialism a myth? Ironically, one of the concept's roots is the description of traditional forms of government in the Structural Functionalist book *African Political Systems* (Fortes and Evans-Pritchard 1940). Some of the earliest work on the subject was written by a British Communist expatriate George Padmore who, in the 1940s, identified communal ownership of land and the dependence of traditional chiefs' authority upon popular support, as the essential qualities of the pre-colonial mode of production. Even though it might be argued that Socialism is an alien, Western, construct imposed on African culture, contemporary African writers advanced similar views (Grillo 1993: 71–3). Dinham and Hines argue that although co-operative effort at the level of the extended family was traditional in Tanzania, this was not the case at the village level (Dinham and Hines 1983: 116). In a study of a Tanzanian village, Caplan found that the extra workload fell upon women, yet the local government official exhorting them to raise production of cash crops was a man from another part of the country (Caplan 1993). The cash crop to be planted on the village field was cotton, yet the peak labour period clashed with that for local food crops. Collective labour was being directed to an inappropriate resource. The introduction of cassava and coconut trees was so much more successful that many men withdrew their labour from subsistence production to grow these new cash crops individually. Men's wealth was increasing as women bore a greater responsibility for providing household subsistence. Co-operation within the extended family was in consequence declining.

Despite these intrinsic problems with Tanzanian policy, foreign capitalist agencies must take a large part of the blame. In 1976 the World Bank declared itself alarmed 'at the threat of [Tanzanian] peas-

---

* Ostrom has published an excellent analysis of the conditions under which producer co-operatives are most likely to succeed (Ostrom 1990).

ants returning to food production on too large a scale', and funded a project to reduce peasant farming by concentrating it in specified villages. Although 40 per cent of World Bank investment in Tanzania is in agriculture, none has been designed to increase production of basic foodstuffs. Consequently subsistence crops such as maize have been pushed on to marginal land, while cash crops such as tobacco, more vulnerable to drought, have displaced them (Dinham and Hines 1983: 125).

Is there an evolutionary progression in modes of production?

Marxist anthropology escaped from the static models of Functionalism and Structuralism, and encouraged a convergence between anthropology and history (Godelier 1972; Wolf 1982). It did not lose sight, as Interactionism sometimes had, of the fact that interaction always takes place within an existing system generated by cumulative social processes.

Although a typological sequence can be constructed, based on the degree of political domination, which places kin-ordered hunter-gatherers at one end of a continuum and tributary states at the other, Wolf repudiates the evolutionism implicit in Marx and explicit in previous American writers such as Sahlins (1963) and Service (1962). Wolf shows how the traditional states of Asia characterised by tributary modes of production were intimately connected with the uncentralised nomadic pastoralists around them, who displayed a lineage mode of production. The nomads were flexible and mobile, rendering them difficult to subjugate, even though the states depended on trade routes across the desert and semi-desert that separated Constantinople from Peking, Kashgar from Delhi. States prospered or declined according to their influence over the nomads. The nomads were good at attacking the states, but bad at consolidating their victories, because that demanded assimilation to a different mode of production. Genghis Khan's successor is said to have been told, 'The empire was created on horseback, but it cannot be governed on horseback' (Wolf 1982: 33).

There remains, none the less, a sense in which Marxist analyses treat egalitarian hunter-gatherers who, it is supposed, make no claims of ownership over land, as representative of the original human condition. Self-interest is regarded as the preserve of liberal, market economics. Marxism explains how differences of power develop when property rights are instituted, but does not explain what specific conditions will promote the sharing of productive resources. The failure of the Tanzanian government to re-establish common fields was no doubt due in part to the international economic and political environment, but it was also due to the assumption that African farmers would tend naturally to pool their labour, if given the opportunity. Socioecology explores the conditions under which co-operation and reciprocity serve the individual's interests, and this theory forms the subject of the next chapter.

CHAPTER SIX

Socioecology

Socioecology was developed in response to the discovery that animal behaviour was not, as many Victorians had imagined, 'red in tooth and claw'. A war of all against all was not the inevitable outcome of the struggle for survival. Bees co-operate in the hive, as do chimpanzees within their troop. Enlightenment thinkers, in their search for a rational social order, had speculated about the origin of social life. Hobbes had deduced that individuals would only surrender their freedom of action if a leader could guarantee others would do likewise. Rousseau inferred that social behaviour originated when people formed coalitions to defend their property. Socioecology attempts to explain the evolution of behaviour within a Darwinian framework and offers answers to some of the issues raised by Hobbes and Rousseau.

Although Darwin recognised that the evolution of social behaviour among insects should be explicable in terms of natural selection, he was unable to find such an explanation (Maynard Smith 1982: 167). Neo-Darwinian theory translates the notion of 'the survival of the fittest' into that of 'reproductive success'. If bodily form and behaviour are genetically determined, then natural selection will result in those genes which produce the most adaptive forms and patterns of behaviour being transmitted during reproduction more frequently than the alternative genes which prove less adaptive. Starting with Hamilton in the late 1950s, biologists developed theories to explain how social interaction can contribute to an animal's reproductive success, assuming at first that social traits were under direct genetic control. Two questions were asked:

1 Under what conditions may it be advantageous, in evolutionary terms, for animals to co-operate with other members of the same species, or to engage in reciprocal exchanges? Forms of interaction were defined as 'strategies', drawing (as interactionism had done) on games theory.

2 What mechanisms favour the spread of such behaviour through natural selection?

The seemingly obvious answer to the second question, that it is 'better for the species' (an answer analogous to the Structural Functionalist arguments of Durkheim and Radcliffe-Brown), was rejected. Wynne-Edwards studied the behaviour of red grouse on moorland, and found that in any year some grouse did not breed. He argued that, because there was insufficient food available for all to raise offspring, some remained celibate to enable the others to breed successfully. The problem with this explanation is that, if the behaviour of the celibate grouse is determined by a gene for 'altruism', this gene is not going to be transmitted to the next generation. An alternative gene for 'selfishness' will quickly displace it (see Trivers 1985: 79–85).

Sociobiology attempts to explain variation in patterns of human behaviour in terms of the consequences of behaviour in particular environments. These environments may be natural or social. Sociobiology follows the Darwinian rather than the Marxist or Spencerian paradigm. It is not concerned with the idea of evolution as a cumulative process that causes societies or cultures to pass through certain stages. There is no directionality in Darwinian evolution.

In order to make the individual rather than the population their unit of study, sociobiologists looked at the behavioural strategies followed by individual animals and considered the consequence for the individual when their strategy was played against other individuals pursuing the same, or different strategies. The method was taken from games theory, but using different aspects of the theory to those relied upon by Barth in his analysis of social process in the Swat valley (see chapter 4). Games theory, as originally applied to human economic behaviour by von Neumann and Morgenstern, assumed that players acted rationally, and in their self-interest. When applied to the Darwinian evolution of behaviour the criterion of rationality (that is, deliberately seeking the strategy that will be best for the individual) is replaced by the unintended outcome of acting according to certain genetically determined strategies. The criterion of self-interest, that is, the utility of the goal to the actor (which, in human cultures, might range from honour to financial gain), is replaced by the single criterion of Darwinian fitness: reproductive success or inclusive fitness (Maynard Smith 1982: vii, 2).

Interactionist theories brought about a return to the study of society in terms of interacting individuals, rather than treating society as a supra-organic system in the tradition of Durkheim and Radcliffe-Brown. Sociobiology offered a way of explaining patterns of interpersonal interaction within a Darwinian framework, accounting for the appearance not only of competition, but also co-operation and reciprocity in human social interaction. Some anthropologists have applied sociobiology to human societies. The claim that a significant proportion of customary human behaviour is under direct genetic control has been convincingly rebutted by Harris, Sahlins and Durham (Harris 1979, chapter 5; Sahlins 1976b; Durham 1991; see also Layton 1989a). In the remainder of this chapter the term *Socioecology* is used in preference to *Sociobiology*, to denote the application of adaptationist models to the explanation of human social behaviour, without the inference that such behaviour is under direct genetic control. Despite his uncompromising attack on Sociobiology, Harris' 'cultural materialist' approach is consistent with Socioecology. Harris argues that the uniquely large amount of variability in human behaviour shows '*Homo sapiens* has been selected to acquire and modify cultural repertoires independently of genetic feedback' (Harris 1979: 123, my emphasis). The premise of Socioecology is that learned behaviour makes a large contribution to the reproductive success of human individuals. It is the capacity for learning to construct social strategies that is selected for. Harris further argues that, just as a species does not struggle to survive collectively but persists as a result of adaptive changes in individual organisms, so men and women respond opportunistically as individuals to 'cost-benefit options' in ways which have consequences for patterns of social interaction (Harris 1979: 61). Harris, moreover, draws attention to a point overlooked in simplistic adaptationist models: the greater the imbalance of power in a society, the more likely it is that the weak will be forced to behave in ways which favour the survival of the powerful.

Whereas Durkheim and Radcliffe-Brown took the 'function' of a custom to be its contribution to the persistence of the social system, for Socioecologists the function of patterns of behaviour is their contribution to the reproductive success of the individual. While Durkheim and Radcliffe-Brown regarded individual behaviour as the expression of norms, deviation from which was punished by society, Socioecologists regard variation in the behaviour of individuals as the source of new strategies whose success or failure will be determined by their effect on the individuals who use them. Socioecology returns to issues raised by Malinowski's Functionalism. It asks how individuals pursuing their own interests can benefit from living in society, but tries to explain the variability of human behaviour in adaptive terms, and thus to overcome the weakness of Malinowski's appeal to universal human needs. The theories of Socioecology make it possible to put forward hypotheses about the adaptive qualities of social behaviour which can be tested by comparing behaviour in different societies, or changes in behaviour over time within a single community.

Socioecology finally dismisses the premise of evolution as progress which lingers implicitly in Marxist anthropology. Recent hunter-gatherers can no longer be interpreted as survivors of the original human condition. If they can throw light on the earlier evolution of social behaviour, it is merely because they are living under similar ecological pressures to those which are inferred to have impinged on early modern human populations in East Africa or Western Asia. Even the 'original human condition' is, moreover, an adaptation to a specific set of circumstances and is therefore no more 'natural' than any other human condition. It does not matter how long modern hunter-gatherers have been living under those conditions. Populations whose ancestors were herders or cultivators will be as informative as those whose ancestors have always lived by hunting and gathering. Socioecology offers a new approach to the sociological questions posed during the Enlightenment.

Julian Steward

Julian Steward first applied an adaptive model to hunter-gatherer social groupings in the 1930s. Steward was a severe critic of the culture and personality school, and reacted against the historical particularism of Boas and his pupils by searching for cross-culturally valid social laws (Murphy 1977: 4). Sanderson has characterised Steward's approach as a compromise between the very general and highly abstract formulations of Leslie White and the nineteenth-century evolutionists and the historical particularism of the Boasians (Sanderson 1990: 92).

Steward criticised the culture and personality school for emphasising normative patterns (Steward 1977a [1960]: 72) and, in Murphy's assessment, Steward's most important break with the Boasian tradition was to turn from the study of cultural traits to the actual behaviour of individuals (Murphy 1977: 24–5). Steward appears to have developed his adaptive model of hunter-gatherer band structures over a long period. His earliest paper on the subject identified three types of band – patrilineal, matrilineal and composite – distinguished according to whether membership was inherited from the father, the mother, or whether both parents belonged to the same band (Steward 1936). In this preliminary formulation, Steward attributed the prevalence of the patrilineal band to innate male dominance and the greater importance of the male as the hunter! Composite bands, however, occurred under specific conditions such as those in which people relied on migratory herds of game (Steward 1936: 334). Some Inuit communities, for example, congregate in large bands at the time of the twice-yearly caribou migrations but disperse during the remainder of the year. By 1960, Steward also attributed occurrence of the patrilineal band to particular ecological circumstances, those which demanded the co-operative hunting of fairly sparse but *non*-migratory game. He justified this on the grounds that it was advantageous for men to remain in their father's territory, whose geography they were familiar with (Steward 1977a [1960]: 77). In 1968 Steward developed this model further, writing 'the factors that explain the patrilineal band are more environmental than technological. . . large, highly mobile animals that do not migrate long distances, where hunting exceeds collecting in effort and sometimes in quantity, where population is sparse, and where transportation is limited to human carriers' (Steward 1977b [1968]: 123).

Steward's interest in the patrilineal band stemmed from his failure to find such an institution among the Shoshoni, with whom he had worked in an attempt to reconstruct their pre-colonial social life. Traditionally, the Shoshoni had no organised social groupings larger than the family. In 1938 Steward argued this was due to scarcity of game in the Basin Plateau of the south-west United States. The reliance of the Shoshoni on gathering sparsely distributed wild seeds during the pre-colonial period caused each family to wander alone across over-lapping ranges. In winter several families camped together at Pinyon pine groves but each grove bore fruit irregularly and different sets of families assembled at different groves in successive years (Steward 1938). He noted that the Owens valley Paiute, who lived on the eastern scarp of the Sierra Nevada, occupied a better-watered environment. Patrilineal bands not only existed, but their members co-operated to defend the band's resources against outsiders.* Steward recognised that resources could be created through the social environment. Compar-ing the Shoshoni with the Carrier Indians of British Columbia, Steward found that the introduction of the fur trade had created a sufficient material surplus for the Carrier to transform their simple lineage system into a status-based system sustained by the potlatch, even though their natural environment was unchanged (Steward 1977a: 74).

The selection of learned behaviour

Although Socioecological theories do not assume the actual strategies people follow are in any direct way genetically programmed, it is assumed that learned behaviour will be subject to selection in an anal-ogous way to genetic behaviour. Successful strategies will tend to spread through a population at the expense of alternative strategies which do not contribute so much to the individual's reproductive success. The origin of a strategy in learned behaviour (culture), rather than direct genetic determination, is relevant to the processes of natural selection if it facilitates the survival and spread of that strategy at the expense of alternative ones. Learned strategies have two advan-tages over those which are directly programmed genetically. They are not dependent on parent-child links for their transmission. 'Lateral' transmission occurs where individuals learn from people other than their parents. Further, strategies can be adopted and discarded in less than one generation, which is the minimal time required for a new transmissible genetic trait to be expressed (see Smith 1988; Dawkins 1980; Durham 1991; and Odling-Smee 1995).

This chapter will exemplify the application of Socioecological theory to human behaviour in three areas of research: optimal foraging (which does not entail use of games theory and is an example of

---

* In later papers, Steward modified this interpretation, and concluded that only 'proto-bands' had existed in the Owens valley: see Steward 1977c [1970]: 393.

'behavioural ecology'), reciprocity and territoriality. There are other applications, such as Irons' and Borgerhoff Mulder's work on marriage strategies which will not be considered (but see Irons 1979; and Borgerhoff Mulder 1987).

Optimal foraging theory

The theory

Optimal foraging theory was developed to explain the foraging behaviour of animals, although it borrows from the formulae devised in micro-economics to enable shopkeepers to calculate how many products they should stock on their shelves. Having been found to predict animal feeding behaviour quite accurately (see Krebs and Davis 1984: 91–112), the theory was then reapplied to the study of human hunter-gatherers by several anthropologists (e.g. Hames and Vickers 1982; Hawkes *et al.* 1982; Jones 1980; O'Connell and Hawkes 1981). Imagine a hunter-gatherer setting out for the day across a landscape he or she knows well, in which a variety of potential foods will be encountered, although the forager cannot tell when or where each will be found (a so-called 'fine-grained' environment). Optimal foraging theory sets out to predict which potential foods the forager should stop to exploit, if (s)he is to make the best use of the available time and energy, and which ones should be disregarded because exploiting them would take up time that could better be used in obtaining other foods.

The extent to which human reproductive success is affected by alternative strategies is often difficult to measure within the time-span of anthropological field observation. Socioecologists such as Borgerhoff Mulder and Smith have argued that the goals of behaviour studied by Marxists, such as the search for wealth and power, are 'proxy goals' which help achieve the ultimate goal of enhancing the individual's reproductive success (Borgerhoff Mulder 1987; Smith 1988). Foraging behaviour is assessed on the premise that those who obtain food most efficiently will enhance their reproductive success.

In a Spanish provincial town studied by two friends of mine there was a railway station. Several taxi drivers would wait for the arrival of passengers on the trains. Most of the drivers were kept busy driving people into town, or out to the surrounding villages, but one always turned customers away. My friends once asked him why. He replied that he was waiting for the customer who would ask to be driven to

Madrid and was unwilling to risk losing this customer while taking someone else to a local destination. Unfortunately for him, the customer for Madrid was a rare, if not mythical creature, and he would have done better to accept the many small fares he was offered (Mike and Nanneke Redclift, personal communication). The problem for the hunter-gatherer is similar. Should (s)he continue in the hope of encountering a giraffe, or red kangaroo, or should (s)he divert some time by stopping to pick berries? In order to find out the best solution, the costs and benefits of exploiting each potential food must be calculated. Optimal foraging theory does not assume that the forager actually *makes* these calculations; the extent to which they do so is an open question. The theory merely predicts the best (i.e. optimal) solution and then investigates actual behaviour to discover whether behaviour matches the prediction. If it does not, either the theory is inadequate, or the individual is not making the most effective use of his or her environment.

While acknowledging that there may be numerous other qualities such as vitamins, the benefits of each potential food are usually measured in calories. Calories are the *currency* within which costs and benefits are measured. The rate at which the forager *profits* by selecting a particular food is measured in terms of the time taken to chase it (if it is mobile), then to prepare it. Nuts must be cracked open, meat must be butchered and cooked. The overall rate of profit to be gained from including a certain food species in the diet will depend on how often it is encountered. Despite the potential profit from driving someone to Madrid, it was the taxi driver's failure to encounter customers for the capital often enough that made his strategy so unsuccessful. If one food species which gives a high yield is often encountered the human forager, like some animal predators, may find it best to specialise wholly in hunting that one resource, somewhat as the Native Americans of the great plains did with the buffalo. Usually, however, the *search time* required to locate a high-ranking resource, or the rate at which it is randomly encountered, make it more profitable to include other foods in the diet as well. Each can be ranked according to its relative costs and benefits. If the rate at which higher-ranking resources are encountered goes up, lower-ranking resources can be dropped from the diet. The highest-ranked resources will always be exploited when they are encountered.

The Ache provide one of the best examples of the application of the theory to hunter-gatherers (Hawkes *et al.* 1982). Table 6.1 gives a selec-

Table 6.1 Ranking of foods in the Ache optimal diet

Resource	Yield cals/kg	Pursuit hrs/kg	Processing hrs/kg	Profitability cals/hr	Rank
Collared peccary	1,950	0.01	0.02	65,000	1
Oranges	355	-	0.07	5,071	4
Honey	3,037	-	0.93	3,266	6
White-lipped peccary	1,950	0.69	0.02	2,746	7
Monkey	1,300	0.97	0.10	1.215	11
Palm fruit	350	-	0.37	946	12

Source: from Hawkes *et al.* 1982: table 3.

tion of the calculations made by Hawkes and her fellow researchers on foods which the Ache were seen to hunt or gather. Several interesting points can be noted from these calculations. Although oranges give a lower yield in calories/kilo than monkeys, the shorter processing time makes them a more profitable food to exploit (and, since they don't run away, the pursuit time is zero). The collared peccary gives an equal yield in calories/kilo to the white-lipped peccary but the latter is harder to catch and therefore ranks lower in the hierarchy, because more time must be devoted to its pursuit. Palm fruit is the lowest-ranked item in the observed Ache diet. Although the Ache were not asked to rank their various foods, they were observed to make the kind of decisions optimal foraging calculations predict. Several discussions on the merits of hunting monkeys took place in the presence of the anthropologists. It was generally said that monkeys were not worth hunting because they were not fat enough. When encountered, however, monkeys were usually hunted. They never disregarded reports from other Ache of nearby orange groves in fruit, but only turned to the exploitation of palm groves late in the day.

One of the best tests of optimal foraging theory is to study how hunter-gatherers alter their strategies when circumstances change. The Ju/'hoansi of the Kalahari gave Lee a long list of 'famine foods' which they would only eat when higher-ranking foods become scarce (Lee 1968: 34). In high latitudes, many foods are only available seasonally, and during lean months additional items such as shellfish must be added to the diet. Winterhalder found that the Cree of the North American woodlands changed their hunting patterns once they were able to buy guns and traps from the Hudson Bay Company. These greatly reduced pursuit time, and made it profitable to hunt species that otherwise would have taken too long to catch (Winterhalder 1981: 87). When large, migratory game were virtually extinguished by over-hunting in the woodlands during the later nineteenth century, how-ever, the Ojibwa had to rely entirely on smaller animals such as fish and hare (Rogers and Black 1976). The introduction of guns and motor cars to central Australia made kangaroo hunting more efficient and hunting remains a popular activity despite the fact that beef can be bought. On the other hand, low-ranking foods such as grass seeds which, although common, are time-consuming to process, dropped out of the diet once imported, milled white flour became available (O'Connell and Hawkes 1981).

Most real environments are not fine-grained but more or less patchy. Resources are concentrated in certain areas. In a highly seasonal en-vironment, foragers know this in advance and can move camp to exploit seasonally available patches. Many Inuit (Eskimo) traditionally moved between coast and interior, exploiting seal, freshwater fish, birds and berries according to the season. Even if a high-ranking patch is encountered unexpectedly, as is more likely in tropical forest, it will pay the forager to stop searching for other foods and stay in the patch for a while. Optimal foraging theory predicts that (s)he should do so until the rate of return drops to the aggregate rate already being achieved. Hawkes *et al.* (1982) calculate that the average return from Ache hunting is 1,115 kilocalories per hour, per person. Upon entering a grove of orange trees in fruit, the individual's return rate rises to 4,438 kilocalories per hour. The best strategy for members of the band will therefore be to stay in the orange patch until there are so few oranges left, and those which remain are so hard to reach, that the return rate for each member has dropped to 1,115 kilocalories per hour. A palm grove, on the other hand, will only yield 810 kilocalories per hour. It would therefore be best for the Ache to ignore palm patches except on a bad day, when their average return has dropped to around 800 calories per hour. This may be why Ache rarely turn to palm patches except late in the day, when the chances of improving their return rate from higher-ranking foods have diminished.

An interesting outcome of research into hunter-gatherer optimal foraging is the realisation that the foods upon which cultivators rely are generally low in a hunter-gatherer's optimal diet, consisting of grass seeds such as wheat or rice, tubers or the pith of palms such as sago.

This implies that cultivation originated not as a blinding insight into the benefits to be gained from planting seeds, as nineteenth-century progressive evolutionism contended, but as an adaptive response to a decline in the availability of higher-ranked foods. Many recent hunter-gatherers in fact practise what can be termed 'low-level' husbandry. Grass is regularly burned to promote new growth, the ends of tubers are replanted so that they will regenerate (see Jones and Meehan 1989; Layton *et al.* 1991; Winterhalder and Goland 1993). Hunting and gathering tends to be practised in environments where it is more efficient than the competing strategies of herding or cultivation, not because hunter-gatherers have miraculously survived, untouched, from the early period of human evolution.

The shortcomings

Those who use optimal foraging theory are well-aware that it simplifies actual situations. Food qualities other than calories are disregarded and no account is taken of the fact that, in the case of humans, items such as leaves and grasses may be obtained entirely as non-food resources to make, for example, baskets or nets. Simplicity is, however, considered a strength of the theory, as long as it is effective in predicting hunter-gatherer foraging behaviour.

The theory does not make any assumptions about the source of the cognitive skills that enable foragers to operate efficiently. There is no reason to suppose they are genetically determined in any simple way and they are probably to a large extent learned. It is possible we have developed cultural skills which mimic the more direct genetic determination of other species' behaviour. Smith points out that, since optimal foraging theory has its origin in micro-economics, it 'humanises' animals rather than 'animalises' humans (Smith 1983: 637–40). The grocer should clear his shelves of low-selling lines (analogous to the Ache's palm pith), to make more room for lines which have a better rate of profit. There is, however, a risk of developing a circular argument. Evolutionary processes are first modelled on economics, but economic behaviour is in turn explained through evolutionary models.

Sahlins and Douglas claimed, in their arguments against Marxist determinism, that human dietary preferences are culturally determined. Totemic food avoidances are a good example. According to Australian Aboriginal legend, each local group was endowed with a territory containing the spirits of unborn children, given them by a heroic, ancestral being who was at once human- and animal-like. People avoid eating the animal species associated with their ancestral being, because this would be tantamount to eating one's own kin. Such prohibitions are instances of Lévi-Strauss' 'totemic operators', which translate structured thought into action (see chapter 3). Like Lévi-Strauss, Douglas (1966: 53–7) and Sahlins (1976a: 169–77) argue that food avoidances are entirely predicated on the symbolic, rather than the economic value of the species. Douglas proposes the Structuralist argument that the Jewish food prohibitions specified in the Old Testament apply to animals which do not fit neatly within the cognitive categories of Jewish culture. Animals which have front feet that resemble hands, but do not walk upright; creatures such as eels and worms which crawl without limbs; cloven-hoofed animals which are not ruminants, such as the camel and pig, are forbidden because they challenge the structure of ancient Jewish thought (see chapter 3). Although Sahlins is critical of Douglas (Sahlins 1976a: 118–19), he puts forward a similar argument for food avoidances in the United States today. Horse and dog are not eaten because they are treated as sentient creatures, named and loved by their owners, and conceived of as semi-human. Eating them would be almost cannibalism.

As a criticism of optimal foraging theory, the argument is based to some extent on a misapprehension. Horse-breeding is a less efficient means of generating protein than cattle-ranching. The inefficient stomach of the horse requires it to eat approximately four times the quantity of grass required by a cow. Harris argues that the rise of beef as the favoured meat of United States consumers is entirely explicable in economic terms: it was caused by the development of long-distance railways providing refrigerated transport between the great plains and the east coast (Harris 1979: 254–7; cf. Ross 1980). If present-day Americans can readily satisfy their hunger without resorting to horse or dog, then they can allow themselves to be sentimental. Hunger changes people's values. The Australian explorer Leichhardt was driven, on different occasions, to eat a raw baby kangaroo and the leather binding of his plant press. Many Australian totemic prohibitions prove, in practice, to be less comprehensive than they seem. People can eat their totemic animal if someone from another clan has caught it, or they can eat certain parts but must avoid the tail, the neck, or some other part. In practice, the system of signification operates within the limits imposed by the material conditions of existence.

Optimal foraging assesses the immediate costs and benefits of individuals' behaviour to themselves. Each organism is assumed to be acting in isolation. Dwyer cites the case of a hunt organised by a man ('M2') from the New Guinea village of Bobole, to show how misleading such an approach may be (Dwyer 1985). The man's half-sister had recently married into Namosado, a community several kilometres away. He was indebted to another Bobole resident, who had given him meat in the past. A third man, who helped bring back bridewealth from Namosado, had slipped and injured himself as the party returned. Although M2 subsequently paid compensation for the injury, ill-will continued and he wanted to dispel the tension within the community. He therefore went hunting with four other men who, between them, returned with thirty game mammals and forty-nine fruit bats. Despite their extraordinary success, M2 kept none of the catch for himself. The meat was distributed widely through Bobole and Namosado, and not just to those with whom M2 shared demonstrable genetic kinship.

Although Dwyer contends that his data can be used to question the applicability of Socioecology to human behaviour, in doing so he draws attention to ways in which the individual's survival (and therefore reproductive success) is conditioned by interaction with other people. In the New Guinea highlands, people need to preserve unity of purpose within their own community and they need allies in other communities (see the Wahgi example in chapter 5). Optimal foraging is what Maynard Smith calls a 'game against nature' (Maynard Smith 1982: 2). The behaviour of predator and prey will influence each other's reproductive success, but their strategies are drawn from different 'gene pools'. Dwyer's case study shows the importance of considering the adaptive consequences of interaction with other members of one's own species.

The evolution of social behaviour

The evolution of social behaviour has been explored through the application of games theory to evolution. The aim of the evolutionary theory of games is to show what will happen if particular strategies are played against themselves and others, in order to measure the costs and benefits for the reproductive success of the players. The theory does not try to explain how particular strategies come into existence (they are assumed to appear at random, like mutations), and their genetic basis may be unclear. Unlike some varieties of interaction theory discussed in chapter 4, strategies are taken to exist within an ongoing pattern of social interaction, but the theory does develop aspects of Interactionism, particularly those formulated by Blau. Maynard Smith termed the strategy that wins against itself and all other existing strategies being played in that field of interaction an *evolutionarily stable strategy* (Maynard Smith 1982: 10). Strategies may be evolutionarily stable in one environment, but not in another. In some environments none of the strategies being 'played' by members of a population against one another will be evolutionarily stable.

Hawk and dove

One of the simplest models of a game applied to the evolution of social behaviour is the 'hawk-dove' game. Although it is most immediately applicable to territoriality, the game is not supposed to represent any specific animal example, but to reveal the logical possibilities inherent in all contests (Maynard Smith 1982: 6, 10ff.). The model supposes there are two contestants to each encounter. It also supposes there is a fixed set of alternative strategies, namely *hawk* and *dove*. Neither contestant knows in advance which strategy the other will adopt, or who will win if they both opt to fight. A hawk escalates the contest and continues fighting for the resource both want until it is injured, or the opponent retreats. Hawks are assumed to be evenly matched and each therefore wins 50 per cent of their contests. Doves signal their willingness to fight, but retreat as soon as their opponent escalates the contest.

Imagine two animals are competing for a resource such as a territory which, if won, will increase the winner's reproductive success. The loser may have to contend with a less good territory, which will lower their reproductive success. These, together with the frequency of injury, are the costs and benefits of the encounter. There are three possible forms the contest can take. If it is between two hawks, each has a 50 per cent chance of winning, but a 50 per cent chance of being injured and losing. If hawk and dove compete, the hawk always wins. If dove plays dove, the resource is shared between the two contestants and each gains half as much as a successful hawk.

The dove strategy is not a stable one, because as soon as it is challenged by a hawk it will be defeated. Hawk is a stable strategy if the resource is so valuable that it is worth risking injury to obtain it. If the resource is not that valuable, and the cost of injury is high relative to the benefits of winning, then the stable strategy may be to play hawk on some occasions and dove on others. Maynard Smith considers other strategies which may 'invade' the field of play. The *bourgeois* strategy is to play hawk if the individual is on its own territory, but dove if it intrudes upon another's territory. Whenever two bourgeois strategists meet one will therefore always play hawk and the other dove. Maynard Smith shows that the cumulative cost of this strategy is less than that of invariably adopting hawk or dove, regardless of the opponent's strategy (Maynard Smith 1982: 22). It wins more often than dove and is injured less often than hawk. It is therefore an evolutionarily stable strategy because it does best when played against itself and against the other two.

The Prisoner's Dilemma

The 'Prisoner's Dilemma' is a more complex game which provides a model for the evolution of co-operation, particularly in the sense of reciprocity, in which players make their moves alternately. The Prisoner's Dilemma is based on the situation in which two suspects have been arrested by the police and are being interrogated in different rooms (an alternative is to imagine two resistance fighters captured by an invading army). Each prisoner is told that, if they alone implicate the other in the crime, they will be given a token sentence. If both confess, both will receive a moderate sentence, since their confession helped the police solve the crime even though they admitted guilt. If they refuse to confess (that is, to 'defect'), even though the other has done so, the sentence will be heavier. Each prisoner knows that, if the other has remained silent, the best strategy is to remain silent too, because both will then be released without charge. If, on the other hand, the other prisoner is suspected of having confessed, it will be better to take the same course oneself (Trivers 1985: 389–90). It is a non-zero sum game, because the scale of gain (or loss) to the players depends on which strategies they adopt. At first sight, defection appears to be the evolutionarily stable strategy, because it draws against itself, and wins against remaining silent. Defection is, however, a more costly strategy than mutual co-operation, because it still earns a small sentence.

The costs can be represented numerically as follows: if I defect and the other remains silent, it costs me 1 and him 4. If both defect, it costs each of us 2. If I remain silent and he defects, it costs me 4 (the so-called 'sucker's pay-off'). If both remain silent, the cost to each of us is 0. The cost of me defecting is therefore 1 or 2, while the cost of remaining silent is 0 or 4. The model will only be applicable to real-life situations when the costs of the alternative strategies are ranked in this order.

Each prisoner faces the dilemma that, although 'defection' is less risky than co-operation, if both defect they will both do worse than if they had co-operated with each other. Axelrod points out that, whereas Hobbes' theory of the origin of co-operation supposed a sovereign had to intervene to uphold co-operation, the Prisoner's Dilemma can explain how co-operation could evolve by direct interaction between equal players (Axelrod 1990: 6). It is true that, in the model, the captors play a role rather like Hobbes' Sovereign but in reality this role is played by the blind forces of natural selection. Axelrod realised that co-operation can only develop if the prisoners can anticipate each other's intentions. Since they are secluded from one another in the cells, this must derive from prior knowledge. When the game is played repeatedly by the same players the stable strategy may be to co-operate, but if it is played once the stable strategy will be to defect.

Axelrod devised a computer program to test the most effective strategy for players to adopt if the game is played repeatedly, inviting people to submit strategies which could be played on the computer against their own, and competing strategies to discover which gave the best long-term outcome. He discovered that the most stable long-term strategy is one called 'Tit for Tat'. In this strategy, each player begins by anticipating the other will co-operate (that is, they do not confess) and then, on subsequent moves, do what the other player did in their previous move. In this way other players who co-operate are rewarded, but those who defect are punished. Axelrod asks how such a strategy could 'invade' a field of play in which everyone else adopts the Hobbesian, selfish strategy of defecting. He argues that a single 'Tit for Tat' player cannot win but, if pairs or small groups enter the field playing this strategy, their success against each other will result in them doing better in the long run than the perennial defectors (Axelrod 1990: 50–1). There is, however, one more element to be taken into account. If the players know they are playing for the last time, and do not depend on each other for further co-operation, the best strategy becomes, once more, to defect. Their 'game plan' will therefore have to include an assessment of the probability they will meet again. The higher they estimate this probability to be, the more they are likely to co-operate (Axelrod 1990: 10–13; see also Ridley 1996).

Adaptation and social behaviour

Socioecologists recognise four types of social interaction: co-operation, reciprocity, competition and spite (Trivers 1985: 41–65). The following paragraphs consider the evolution of co-operation and reciprocity in humans.

In *co-operation*, both parties benefit immediately.
In *reciprocity*, I give to you, so that you benefit and
I lose, but in the expectation you will return the favour.
In *competition*, only one party can gain, at the other's
expense.
In *spite*, I hurt you, to hurt myself. Both parties lose.

Since the benefits of co-operation are immediate, and the other players' strategies are apparent, it is relatively easy to appreciate how co-operation may evolve. Such co-operation has evolved in the hunting strategies of species such as wild dogs and lionesses. The Mbuti depend on the co-operation of about thirty men and women to hunt successfully with nets in the Ituri forest of central Africa and net-hunting communities will only form smaller camps during the season when wild honey can be collected (Turnbull 1965: 106–7). The Tiwi of northern Australia need fifteen men to conduct a fire drive in the savannah grassland, with women and children acting as beaters (Hart and Pilling 1966: 42). The Netsilik Inuit camp on the Arctic coast in winter. Seal meat is a vital part of the winter diet. Seals are speared when they rise to the surface to breath through holes in the ice. Seals have, however, evolved a way of reducing the risk of getting air. Each seal keeps several blow holes open and moves between them. Hunters must co-operate to ensure each of the seal's breathing holes is guarded, and thereby guarantee hunting success. Balikci estimates that a Netsilik winter seal-hunting camp needs fifteen hunters to operate effectively, and notes that when a man is successful his wife divides the seal into fourteen portions, giving one to each of his hunting partners (Balikci 1970: 58, 75). Smith, who calculates in detail the benefits of co-operation among the Inujjuamiut, found the optimum size for parties hunting at seal breathing holes to be as low as three (Smith 1991: 323–7). None the less, in all three examples a single hunter will do less well than someone who co-operates and co-operation is therefore an evolutionarily stable strategy.

Altruism

The strategy of forgoing a resource to benefit others, observed after the New Guinea hunt reported by Dwyer, is harder to explain. Similar behaviour, such as a hunter sharing his game with other members of the camp, or members of a band allowing other bands to forage on their territory, has nevertheless been widely observed among hunter-gatherers. Such behaviour is known as *altruism*. Marxist anthropologists identified the lack of exclusive claims to territory as the basis for egalitarianism among hunter-gatherers. Assuming it was the natural, or original human condition they considered that it did not need to be accounted for.

The first neo-Darwinian explanation for altruism was put forward by Hamilton (1964; Hamilton's theory is summarised in Trivers 1985: 45–7, 126–7). Hamilton showed that individuals who are closely related genetically can benefit from altruism. In a bee or ant nest, all the 'workers' are children of the same queen. If, therefore, a few sacrifice their lives to save the colony, the survivors are likely to carry the same 'altruistic' gene, or gene complex. This extension of the concept of reproductive success is known as 'inclusive fitness': sacrificing one's life for the colony does not increase one's personal fitness, but it does ensure one's genes are transmitted to the next generation. Trivers cites the case of Belding's ground squirrel, a small North American mammal which frequently suffers from predation, in support of Hamilton's theory. Individual ground squirrels sometimes give an alarm cry when they see a predator approaching but, if they do so, they draw attention to themselves and are more likely to become the prey. Female ground squirrels stay near their place of birth, but males move further away on reaching sexual maturity. Once they have dispersed, males rarely give alarm cries and they are unlikely to be feeding next to close kin. Adult females were more likely to give an alarm call on those occasions close kin *were* feeding nearby (Sherman 1980, summarised in Trivers 1985: 110–14). The gene(s) determining the inclination to give the alarm cry will therefore be favoured by selection.

Hamilton's theory has been applied to altruism in humans. Chagnon argued that cross-cousin marriage among the Yanomamö (see chapter 3) results in members of allied lineages becoming increasingly genetically related. Death in defence of the settlement would therefore have the same effect as sacrifices among soldier ants or bees, perpetuating the genes responsible for the behaviour through related individuals

(Chagnon 1982). The Sarakatsani are behaving as this theory of altruism predicts, by refusing to behave altruistically to anyone more distant than a second cousin (see chapter two). Beyond the level of second cousin, the probability of sharing the same gene is too low to compensate for the risk of sacrificing oneself.

Altruism and reciprocity

Sometimes, even among non-human species, altruism also occurs between individuals who are not closely related. Trivers devised the concept of reciprocal altruism to explain such behaviour. The best non-human instance is found among vampire bats (Wilkinson 1984, summarised in Trivers 1985: 363–6). Vampire bats live in colonies, and fly out every night to suck blood from cattle. Each bat must feed at least once every three days to survive, but the cattle often brush the bats off. A well-fed bat will regurgitate part of its meal and share it with one which has been unsuccessful. Trivers argues that reciprocal altruism will become an evolutionarily stable strategy where there is a risk of death, such as from starvation, and where it is impossible to predict which individual will be successful on any one occasion, yet those who are successful in obtaining food get more than their immediate need. When the once-successful individual is unsuccessful on another occasion, the debt can be repaid. Both partners will therefore survive whereas, on their own, both would probably sooner or later have died. This pattern of behaviour can be construed as a version of the Prisoner's Dilemma because when each participant co-operates by sharing its food, it does not know for certain what the other player's intentions are. Sharing benefits both players in the long term, even though the best short-term strategy would be the selfish one of not sharing. Axelrod's finding that co-operation will only develop when there is an indefinite series of exchanges is supported by this study: bats regurgitate blood most readily for those with whom they have been in contact for longest (Trivers 1985: 364).

The best example of such behaviour among hunter-gatherers is that of meat-sharing. It is characteristic of hunter-gatherer bands that they share the meat of large game animals throughout the camp while vegetable foods are regarded as the property of the household whose members obtained them. Vegetable foods are found regularly and predictably. Although high in the optimal ranking of foods, large game animals are only occasionally caught, yet when obtained they come in large chunks with more meat than the hunter's household can consume. Even if some hunters are better than others, no one can be sure who will be successful on any given occasion. The !Kung of southern Africa, the Gidjingali of northern Australia and the Ache of Paraguay all share the meat of large game animals throughout the camp, but each woman's foraging efforts normally go towards feeding her own family (Altman and Peterson 1988; Kaplan and Hill 1985; Marshall 1976).

Reciprocal altruism is not confined to hunters and gatherers. Far from treating it as symptomatic of a stage in human social evolution, Darwinian theory predicts that such behaviour will be adaptive wherever the appropriate conditions are found. Reciprocal aid between households, such as the reciprocal beer parties of the Fur, is very widespread in peasant societies. It is also found in shanty towns such as Los Peloteros (see chapter 2). Every household needs to call on neighbours for help when a member falls ill, or crops fail through accident, but none can anticipate when it will need help in future (Erasmus 1955; Scott 1976; Panter-Brick 1993). The same considerations encouraged people to participate in the 'friendly societies' established during the Industrial Revolution, only here the pattern of contribution is reversed. As in the 'subscription societies' of Cameroon (see chapter 5), each member contributes regular small sums in the expectation that all will need to call to a larger extent on the society's funds sooner or later. Axelrod applies the model of the 'Prisoner's Dilemma' to the resolution of international conflict, where the players (nation states) must anticipate each other's intentions (Axelrod 1990: 186–91).

Weiner's ethnography, based on fieldwork close to where Malinowski had worked fifty years earlier, suggests the Trobrianders act exactly as they should if playing the 'Prisoner's Dilemma'. People construct *keyawa* exchange partnerships so that they can get help to build up resources when they need them most and, in return, must reciprocate when any of their *keyawa* partners are in need (Weiner 1976: 57, 125).

> Villagers read exchange events by treating the objects and styles of exchange as evidences of attitudes and expectations . . . The transaction usually states an accomplished fact while allowing each participant to subvert that fact. Exchange. . . gives scope to an ongoing process wherein the donor and the recipient may continually re-evaluate the other's and their own current condition or states of being in the system (Weiner 1976: 213)

The 'Tit for Tat' strategy which solves the Prisoner's Dilemma explains why reciprocity is, as Mauss and Polanyi had noted, embedded in social relationships. Although earlier writers tended to assume that reciprocal exchanges were undertaken because people needed social relationships, the model of the Prisoner's Dilemma suggests people need social relationships to guarantee reciprocity. It is, however, common for people to exchange small gifts as tokens of their continuing goodwill.

Reciprocity is a stable strategy under the conditions of uncertainty outlined above but, under other circumstances, it may be 'invaded' by alternative strategies. Smith considers several alternatives (Smith 1988: 233), one of which is storage. In a highly seasonal environment, such as the Arctic, the timing of food surpluses is highly predictable. The Nunamiut, for example, obtain 80 per cent of their annual meat supply during the fifteen days of the autumn and spring caribou migrations (Binford 1979). All households who co-operate in a caribou drive immediately receive a share of the meat, but it is more effective for each household then to store surplus resources obtained during the seasonal glut and eat their own stored food during leaner periods, particularly since storage is easier in the Arctic than the tropics. The heavy reliance of the native Americans of the north-west coast on storage was outlined in chapter 4. It is probable that money's capacity to function as a store of value accounts for the decline of reciprocity, and the social relationships it requires, in Western society. If so, Polanyi's analysis of the destructive effects of the market on social relationships is supported by Socioecological theory.

Territoriality

A *territory* is an area occupied more or less exclusively by an individual or a group, who use some means to announce their ownership and, if necessary, physically to defend it. Socioecologists recognise three forms of territoriality:

1 Defence of a small area in which an essential resource is located, such as a bird's nest site or, among humans, a waterhole in the desert.

2 Asserting a superior right to all food resources over a wider area.

3 Patrolling the boundary of the territory to prevent outsiders from entering at all.

A *home range* is an area within which an individual or group habitually move in search of food. A home range is not a territory if the individual or group do not assert any rights over it against others.

Contrary to Rousseau and the Marxists, hunter-gatherers do generally claim rights over land. They do so most often by asserting a primary right to all the resources within an area, even if neighbouring bands are generally given permission to enter the area. One of the few societies who seem to fit the image created by Rousseau and Marx are the Batek De, who live in the forest of Malaysia. The Batek De consider that land was created for all to use. While individuals may have a sentimental association with the area in which they were born, this does not give them any rights of ownership over it (Endicott 1988: 113). There are no lineages, bands or other semi-permanent groups larger than the conjugal family (Endicott 1979: 10).

Hunter-gatherers living in both the tropics and the Arctic generally allow neighbouring bands to forage over each other's territories, at the cost of allowing the current hosts reciprocal rights to enter the guests' territory on future occasions (see Smith 1991: 110–13, for an Arctic case study). Like the participants in the *kula* studied by Malinowski, the value of owning something is the right which ownership brings to give it to others. However, the kind of territoriality which hunter-gatherers practise varies according to the type of environment they live in, and it is possible to study the circumstances in which reciprocal access appears most adaptive. Casual boundary-crossing is tolerated by the forest-dwelling Mbuti, but rights of mutual access are more highly formalised among the desert hunter-gatherers of Australia and southern Africa. Both procedures differ from that which traditionally existed on the north-west coast of North America, where territorial boundaries were forcefully defended, even to the extent of killing trespassers.

The Ituri forest in which the Mbuti live is a relatively fine-grained environment in which game and vegetable foods are quite evenly distributed. Most game animals only move over short distances (Turnbull 1965: 173; Harako 1981: 503). Cashdan argued that groups living in the richest areas of the Kalahari are least tolerant of visitors from other groups entering their territory (Cashdan 1980) although she later also described how those communities living in the harshest part of the Kalahari could control access to resources by insisting that visitors gain permission to camp with the host band (Cashdan 1983). The Ju/'hoansi or Dobe !Kung live in a much patchier environment than the Mbuti. Regional drought occurs during three to four years every decade and, in any one year, rainfall can vary by a factor of ten over a few miles. Each band lives in a *n!ore* (territory) centred on a semi-permanent waterhole and none could expect to survive indefinitely on the resources within its *n!ore*. Access across the boundary of such territories is not defended, but visitors must approach the owners for permission to camp at a waterhole or forage in the surrounding country. Footprints are easy to spot in the desert and it is virtually impossible to hunt or gather without being discovered. Visitors usually accompany residents when foraging. Bands from two or more waterholes often join forces to exploit a 'major' resource such as tsin beans or mongongo nuts (Lee 1979: 351). Lee was told, 'It's when they eat alone and you come along later and you find them there, that's when the fight starts' (Lee 1979: 336).

The Yankunytjatjara of the Australian Western Desert occupy a patchy environment somewhat similar to that of the Dobe region of the Kalahari. According to traditional procedures which pre-date colonial contact in the 1930s, visitors must seek consent to forage in another group's *ngura* (territory), but such consent is rarely, if ever, withheld. Totemic avoidances express the special relationship with the ancestral being who allocated each group the rights to its territory (Layton 1986; cf. Myers 1986). Foraging parties traditionally lit regular small fires to indicate their line of travel and parties encountered unexpectedly were suspected of having malevolent intentions, either wishing to steal food, or to make a revenge killing. Radcliffe-Brown's failure to study traditional daily life in Australia caused him to miss this whole dimension of Aboriginal society and to assume, wrongly, that each band claimed exclusive rights to the resources in its territory (see chapter 2).

Contrary to the 'hawk' strategy of boundary defence practised on the north-west coast of North America, low-latitude hunter-gatherers are playing a genteel version of Maynard Smith's 'bourgeois' territorial strategy. In the desert, rain can be seen falling many miles away. No one can conceal the temporary abundance of plant foods which follows rain. If that abundance yields more than the local band need for their immediate subsistence they can gain more, in the long run, by sharing it with members of neighbouring bands than by overeating, thereby gaining the right to share in others' unpredictable abundances in future.

The strategy of reciprocity will be 'invaded' by that of boundary defence when variation in the abundance of resources becomes synchronised over a wide area. In such an environment there is no longer any need to insure against future shortage by allowing others to share one's good fortune. A model which predicts when it will pay animals to defend territories was devised thirty years ago by Brown (1964). As with optimal foraging theory, to which it is closely related, the 'economic defendability' model of territoriality assesses the costs and benefits of defending a territory, and predicts the conditions in which it will increase the individual's reproductive success to practise territoriality. There are said to be three main costs in defending a territory. There is a physical risk in patrolling the territory, if it results in challenges from other individuals, as represented in the hawk-dove game. Patrolling a territory also takes time and energy which could be spent in alternative ways such as foraging or raising young. Finally, there is a risk that the resources within the territory might fail. The principal benefit gained from preserving rights over a territory is the elimination of competition for its resources from other members of the species. Not all individuals in the population may succeed in gaining a territory, or some may gain larger ones than others.

Claiming exclusive access over territories is most profitable when resources are densely and evenly distributed, but in sufficiently short supply to make it worthwhile competing for them. As resources become more scarce, an increasingly large territory would be needed to guarantee self-sufficiency and the costs of patrolling its boundary would therefore increase until eventually they outweighed the benefits. As resources become more unpredictable, it becomes increasingly less certain that the individual will be repaid for defending the territory and, again, defence eventually becomes uneconomic. Cashdan was the first to point out that low-latitude hunter-gatherers adapt to this constraint by allowing the kind of inter-access described above rather than abandoning territoriality altogether (Cashdan 1983).

Inspired by Steward's original work with the Shoshoni and other basin plateau groups, Dyson-Hudson and Smith applied Brown's model to several hunter-gatherer communities and one pastoral society, the Karimojong of East Africa (Dyson-Hudson and Smith 1978). The Native Americans of the north-west coast such as the Tsimshian (chapter 2) are the best example among recent hunter-gatherers of groups who defended the boundaries of their territories against trespass. Territories were held by ambilineal or matrilineal descent groups, who obtained all their food within the territory (Richardson 1986). Any hunter who found another man trespassing on his group's territory would challenge him and often one was killed (Boas 1966: 36). The Western Shoshoni of the Californian basin plateau lived in a much harsher environment. Steward established that, during the summer, small families foraged independently, living on wild grass seeds and small game. Because the game animals do not live in herds there was no advantage to the Shoshoni from co-operating in the hunt. During the winter the Shoshoni lived on the nuts of the pinyon pine. Although several families camped together, each pinyon grove fruited unpredictably. No consistent group of families would amalgamate into a corporate lineage because there was no benefit from defending particular groves (Dyson-Hudson and Smith 1978: 28).

Among cultivators such as the Yanomamö and Wahgi, the lineage has a clear territorial function in co-ordinating defence of gardens and their crops against raids. Rousseau's hypothesis that warfare originated with the appearance of cultivation is to some extent supported by the prevalence of warfare among horticulturalists. Three levels of territoriality can be recognised among East African peoples such as the Nuer and Karimojong. Like the Nuer, the Karimojong combine cultivation with cattle herding. Dyson-Hudson and Smith found that households defend their patches of crops against trespass and theft both because they have invested time and effort in cultivation and because the patches are small, concentrated and therefore easy to defend. Rights to cattle are shared by the members of lineages. Their defence by the warriors was described in the example of the Samburu (chapter 2). The most scarce and unpredictable resources are pasture and pools of water. These are so thinly spread and unpredictable it would be physically impossible for a lineage, let alone a household, to defend the area its members would need to support its livestock. Lefébure argues that by sharing rights to pasture throughout a tribal community, households are guaranteed access to the resources on which their herds depend wherever they camp within the community's territory (Lefébure 1979). It is entirely consistent with Socioecological theory for different strategies to be adopted towards different resources.

Socioecological theory replaces the formalism of Structural Functionalism and the implicit progressive evolutionism of some Marxism with models which predict when both social networks built

on reciprocal exchange and corporate lineages will become evolutionarily stable strategies.

Signalling social intent

One of the most interesting of Axelrod's discoveries was that reciprocity will only become a stable strategy when players anticipate continuing to interact for an indefinite period. Reciprocal exchange of
subsistence resources in human communities is accompanied by
frequent exchange of tokens which signal the individual's willingness
to continue recognising reciprocal obligations. The constant flow of
gifts in many hunter-gatherer societies is striking. When Europeans,
even anthropologists, first encounter it they often mistake what is
really an invitation to enter into reciprocal relationships for begging.
Jean Briggs, speaking at the Association of Social Anthropologists'
1990 annual conference, described how she returned to an Inuit community wearing a new anorak. An Inuit friend promptly asked for it.
Jean refused, intending the anorak would help her survive the Arctic
conditions. Her friend fell silent for a while, then remarked: 'I don't
want to be thinking, when will Jean die, so that I can inherit her anorak.'
Not surprisingly, the anorak promptly changed hands (for other
examples, see Briggs 1970: 209–11). In the Western Desert of Australia,
no one should seek to belittle anyone else by making them feel indebted.
Myers writes that the immediate use-value of the tools, clothing and
even food exchanged among the Pintupi of central Australia is not
great. Anyone can easily obtain or make them. Exchange is important
because it expresses the moral basis for continuing to live together and
co-operate within the camp (Myers 1988). Among the Yankunytjatjara,
one never says 'thank-you' effusively. A simple '*uwa, palya* (yes, good)'
is sufficient and people should not look each other in the eye when
giving or receiving gifts in case that is construed as domination. The
!Kung have an exchange system called *Hxaro* (see chapter 5), which
maintains an extensive network of friendships between people both
within the same band and in different bands (Wiessner 1982). When
partners live far apart, it is important to keep up a balanced flow of gifts
to let each partner know the other still values the relationship. Women
play the main part in maintaining these partnerships, going on long
journeys to visit *Hxaro* partners and giving them ostrich-shell necklaces, water carriers etc. This form of gift-giving is very different to the
competitive exchanges of the potlatch, which aggressively assert the

rights of the giver rather than the receiver. It guarantees the right to visit exchange partners when one's own *n!ore* is stricken by drought.

Like baboons, chimpanzees signal mutual support by grooming each other. Chimpanzees have gone further than baboons in developing rituals of embracing and kissing to reconcile relationships after a dispute (de Waal 1982: 41). It takes time to groom another individual, time which could be spent on other activities such as looking for food. Dunbar argues that, as group size increased during human evolution, language evolved to provide a less time-consuming way of signalling positive intent, which could be used to communicate to several people at once. For Dunbar the original function of language was akin to greetings in the street, where one rarely waits to find out the answer to one's question, 'how are you?' He also notes that, among hunter-gatherers, the community rarely all meets in one place (Dunbar 1993: 865). It is possible that language was favoured as an adaptation because of its unique capacity to express ideas about the past and future, and people far away in space as well as time, such as *Hxaro* partners in other camps, on whom one may depend in future, and who have been indebted in the past.

Socioecology thus offers exciting opportunities for explaining variation in human behaviour. Unlike Marxism, however, it tends to disregard the long-term consequences of interaction, which result in differences in wealth or power. The Achilles' heel of Socioecology is its explicit reliance on models derived from market economics when, as shown in chapter 4, a pervasive market is unique to industrial society. How valid is the analogical process that explains animal behaviour through models designed to elucidate the policies of shopkeepers, and then reapplies these models to non-Western human populations (cf. Maynard Smith 1982: 172)? Is the approach truly universal, or does it merely recreate other societies in our own image? This puzzle has been taken up by the Postmodernists, who have used it to cast doubt upon the validity of general theories about human society. Postmodernist anthropology is assessed in the final chapter.

CHAPTER SEVEN

Postmodernism and anthropology

In chapter 4, interactionist theories were shown to have laid the grounds for two divergent trends in anthropological thinking. One, provoked by the model of social life as a game in which the moves consist of transactions in goods and services, was developed by the Marxist anthropology which dominated the 1970s and taken up in different ways by Socioecology. Both argue that the outcome of such games can be explained in terms of general laws which operate independently of the participants' intentions. The second trend, prompted by the model of cultural interaction as a language, is the subject of this chapter. Social life is interpreted as transactions in meaning, rather than in substance.

This approach has its roots in a German tradition of interpretive sociology which influenced both Boas and Weber. Boas, although by training a natural scientist, had come to favour a historical/interpretive approach to cross-cultural studies. As early as 1887, he wrote, 'civilisation is not something absolute but... relative, and our ideas and conceptions are true only so far as our civilisation goes' (Boas 1887: 589, quoted by Stocking 1982: 13). The German sociologist Weber, drawing on the same philosophical tradition, distinguished between *explanation* and *understanding*. In his book *Wirtschaft und Gesellschaft* (*The Theory of Social and Economic Organisation*), Weber contrasted causal explanation and interpretive understanding (Weber 1947 [1925]: 79ff.). Explanation depended on recording statistical regularities in human behaviour which could then be explained in terms of sociological laws. Understanding depended on observation of meaningful interaction, in order to discover the meanings specific to that time and place which actors attributed to their own and others' behaviour. When we *explain* other people's behaviour it is not necessary for our intentions to coincide with theirs. We can explain why a car skidded off the road at a bend, without needing to understand why the driver was travelling too fast, in the rain. Our explanation can be put forward by applying general laws: the centrifugal force of the turning car, the friction of the tyres on the road and the lubricating effect of water. When we try to *understand* other people's behaviour, the test of our success is whether the meanings we attribute to their actions correspond to the meanings they intend. Have we successfully intuited why the driver was travelling too fast? Was he late for an appointment? Had he felt slighted by another driver? It is the subject community, not the observer, that sets the criteria for successful understanding. The same objects and actions mean quite different things when interpreted in the idiom of different cultures. It was this distinction Evans-Pritchard hinted at in his 1950 Marrett lecture (see chapter 4), and recent trends such as Feminist Anthropology belong to the broader Interpretive tradition than, narrowly, to the Postmodernism which draws upon it.

Postmodernism means different things to different people. This is, in fact, the central irony of a word which is used to dispute the possibility of any grand theory of human behaviour. This chapter will outline four strands in the writing of Postmodernists and trace their relation to the broader tradition of interpretive sociology.

1 The arrogance of the Enlightenment, or modernist conceit that the white, European male can detach himself from his culture and take a comprehensive, objective stand in his study of the world.
2 The error of supposing that theories enable knowledge of the world 'as it really is'.
3 If meanings are constructed through interaction, there can be no pre-existing Durkheimian 'collective consciousness'.
4 There is no ivory tower for the scientist to retreat into; all theories are inherently political and must be judged by their practical effects on people's lives.

The modernism to which Postmodernism opposes itself is the tradition of objective knowledge created during the Enlightenment, when acceptance of divinely revealed truth and a divinely ordained social order was replaced by the idea that we can discover the truth of how the world works for ourselves by empirical investigation, and construct a better society for ourselves. Comte divided the evolution of human thought into three stages of increasing objectivity. At first, humans explained events as the outcome of the arbitrary actions of gods, then they became sophisticated enough to formulate metaphysical abstractions. Finally, human thought achieved a third stage in which the world was explained in terms of scientific truth. Western Europe was unique in its success in attaining the third phase. Although nineteenth-century theorists such as Marx and Durkheim recognised that cognition is generally shaped by culture, they had always 'privileged' their own perspective as if it were exempt from such constraints. Durkheim, for example, envisaged the progressive evolution of human systems of thought from what he supposed to be the wholly socially determined structure of the original totemic system, through the relatively rational philosophies of ancient China to the totally objective thought of his own time and place. Postmodernist anthropologists reject Marvin Harris' claim that there is difference in kind between native ideas and the objective knowledge of the scientist. 'Only by recognising the difference between emic and etic definitions... can a demystified... strategy avoid the sterile relativism of the Boasian programme' (Harris 1979: 238). Postmodernist anthropology draws upon Boas' theoretical position, seeing Western thought as itself culturally relative.

Contemporary Postmodernists can, for convenience, be divided into two schools. 'Hard', or extreme Postmodernists such as the French philosopher Derrida claim that structures of meaning can never be translated in their entirety and are not anchored by reference to the outside world. All cultures, including our own, have constructed autonomous, self-contained worlds of meaning. The 'soft', or moderate Postmodernism of Derrida's contemporary, Foucault, owes more to the interpretive tradition, arguing that there are communities who share a common 'discourse' but that, while each discourse has its own rules, reference can none the less be made to things that exist independently of that discourse and can affect its form.

The arrogance of the white, European male

Situating the anthropologist
In 1973 Cree and Inuit hunter-gatherers living around James Bay, at the southern end of Hudson Bay, obtained a court injunction to halt the construction of a dam to feed a hydro-electric generator until their rights to the land had been recognised (Feit 1983). During the ensuing hearings, an Inuit witness refused to take the oath when asked to swear to tell 'the truth, the whole truth and nothing but the truth' because, he said (after a whispered conversation with the interpreter), he could 'only say what he knows' (Harvey Feit, personal communication; cf. Clifford 1986: 8). Postmodernist anthropologists commend the Inuit witness' caution.

Feminist anthropology
One of the most important challenges to the conceit of the European male observer's comprehensive objectivity is posed by feminist anthropology.

In the English-speaking world, reappraisal of Malinowski's field-work had a seminal impact. When his diary was posthumously published (Malinowski 1967), it became clear that the emotions he had experienced in the field were often different to those he had admitted in his published work. This was particularly damaging because it was Malinowski, foremost among the Functionalists, who had set out to write himself into the ethnographic account, describing his emotions and frustrations, and providing an eye-witness account of his observations (Malinowski 1922: especially 4–8, and see above, chapter 2). Weiner's fieldwork further demonstrated the incompleteness of Malinowski's account.

During 1971 and 1972, Annette Weiner carried out ten months' research in a Trobriand village close to where Malinowski had worked half a century earlier. Almost as soon as she had begun fieldwork, Weiner was invited to attend a mortuary ceremony. She walked to the ceremony with local women who were carrying bundles of dried banana leaves and grass skirts. Once at their destination, she found them, and many women from other villages, engaged in complicated transactions which involved piling thousands of such bundles in the central clearing of the hamlet. On her return home that evening, she looked in vain for any reference to this custom in Malinowski's work. Weiner's subsequent fieldwork confirmed many of the details of Malinowski's account of Trobriand funerals but she also found that her emotional response to these rituals differed markedly from his. Malinowski's diary revealed that he was revolted by the way that death was handled and this, in Weiner's assessment, accounts for his emphasis on 'the bizarre and "primitive" quality of rituals surrounding death . . . [whereas she] was left with a sense of beauty: a feeling that to die in Kiriwina is much more humane than to die in a sterile hospital room' (Weiner 1976: 63).

Unlike Western money, Trobriand exchange goods are embedded in social relationships. Trobriand men control property which they use to gain power. They do so through the chains of transactions studied by Malinowski which link named individuals over several generations such as, for example, in the transmission of ownership of a particular plot of land. Weiner concludes that men's power is situated in historical time and space. In Trobriand ideology, however, men have no part to play in procreation. Women are wholly responsible for conceiving and bearing children and play a critical role at funerals, ensuring that the dead person's spirit returns to the timeless land of the dead. Women's power is therefore situated in an ahistorical continuum through which the permanence of the matrilineal group is constantly recapitulated, a dimension which Malinowski had neglected (Weiner 1976: 20, 231). Weiner did not intend her work to challenge the quality of Malinowski's data or insights, so far as they went. As Diane Bell argues (Bell 1993: 29), the strength of feminist anthropology derives not from arguing for the complete relativism of all viewpoints, because that would weaken the force of the feminist insight. Understanding is made more profound when the role of emotion in perception is admitted. Weiner wished both to highlight the role of women and to reveal where Malinowski's interpretations had been limited by the feelings and assumptions he had taken to the field from his own European gender and culture. 'Our assumptions of the social construction of reality are bound to follow a male-dominated path when we deny, for example, the significance of objects labelled women's things' (Weiner 1976: 12). Like the Inuit witness, Malinowski could only say what he knew.

Henrietta Moore shows how a male anthropologist working with the Marakwet of Kenya would have gained a very partial view of male domination. The organisation of space in Marakwet society is an objectification of the male view of the world. Men's livestock is valued more highly than women's crops. Men should be buried near the dung heap outside the compound, women near the heap of chaff from threshing. Rhetorical ability and responsibility confer prestige on men and husbands should speak for their wives during public disputes. Women may contribute but men say that, like children, women talk before they think. Knowledge is regarded as a body of tradition held in common by men. Men inherit property as of right, but women must negotiate with their husbands to obtain property. This cultural model, however, misrepresents actual relationships of production so as to trivialise women's real contribution. Although women subscribe to the male view when with men, they say different things when they are on their own. Women's initiation ceremonies are held almost every year, bringing together women from numerous villages. A distinct body of ritual knowledge is passed on between the generations of women while the initiates are in seclusion. It is learned gradually over many years. Although obedience to husbands is stressed, girls are also taught about the power of female sexuality and the strength of female solidarity. They are taught that they can put pressure on their husbands by with-holding the opportunity for intercourse. They are told how, when a man mistreats his wife, she can call on other women to bind and beat him until he promises to give them livestock. 'The open expression of things which should never be said in public is an important part of the ritual' (Moore 1986: 174). As the girls' initiation proceeds, older women stand outside the house where they are secluded and shout abuse at men. Although the phrases used were often highly metaphori-cal, they were all obscene, and the women enjoyed shouting them out. If men passed close by, the women reinforced the message with obscene gestures.

Kamala Ganesh, who had grown up in northern India, studied a small group in the south who had gained notoriety for living in a mud-walled fortress in the town of Tirunelveli which the women were never allowed to leave. Ganesh was surprised to find, having worked at length with women inside the fortress that, far from considering themselves trapped and underprivileged, the women were proud to carry the primary responsibility for perpetuating their group. Although this meant suffering some deprivation and hardship, 'they saw themselves as bearers of the tradition of classical womanhood celebrated in myth and literature' (Ganesh 1993: 137).

Neither Western nor Third World cultures are uniform. The extent to which gendered cultural experiences are closed to members of the opposite sex will vary from culture to culture. Both Western and Third World anthropologists come to the field with sympathies and insights that derive in part from their personal histories. None the less, the lesson that no fieldworker can ever achieve a total, bird's-eye objectivity has been advanced forcefully by indigenous anthropologists, who argue that they are likely to be more sensitive to the adverse impact of colonialism than are Western writers (Amadiume 1993: 196–7; Raharijoana 1989: 193). The very indigenous social structures which western anthropologists purport to study may in fact be artefacts of the colonial era. Pancrace Twagiramutara is one of those who have argued that the terms *Hutu, Tutsi* and *Twa* were formerly used to identify modes of subsistence shared by people of heterogeneous origin in the region of central Africa colonised by the Belgians (Twagiramutara 1989). Alex de Waal similarly concludes that the colonial powers both invented the idea that the three categories were distinct racial groups and subsequently formalised the division by issuing identity cards specifying which group a person belonged to (de Waal 1994).

Action or reflection?
Realisation that anthropology had been implicated both in sustaining colonial regimes in Africa, and in the United States' aggression in Southeast Asia prompted Marxist anthropologists to call for a conscious engagement with the oppressive effect of Western relationships with the Third World. Although motivated by the same developments in international relations, Postmodernists have tended to argue the contrary view, that the West's claim to be able to present a unified account of humanity has been irrevocably called into question by the inescapable involvement of academics in oppression. 'There is no master narrative that can reconcile the tragic and comic plots of global cultural history' (Clifford 1988: 15). Postmodern anthropologists are suspicious of uses of theory to promote social change.

Participant observation, the basic research technique of social anthropology, depends on the anthropologist interacting with the people whom (s)he is studying. Postmodernism draws upon the interpretive insight that complete objectivity is rendered impossible by the fact that the anthropologist must *situate* themselves within the community. Men will tend to obtain the male point of view; members of a dominant European culture will sometimes find it harder to hear dissenting or revolutionary voices. The anthropologist arrives in the community, moreover, already *situated* within their own previous experiences, largely obtained within their own culture. The Austrian sociologist Alfred Schutz developed this interpretive approach in his critique of Weber's prescription for interpretive understanding (Schutz 1972 [1932]). Meaning, Schutz argued, is that which individuals attach to their own acts. Awareness and meaning are obtained by 'reflecting' back, or casting a retrospective glance upon lived experience (*Erlebnisse*) as it carries us forward. For the anthropologist, such reflection will inevitably reach back to experiences gained before starting fieldwork. The particular meanings we attribute to past experiences will change according to when we reflect back upon them. There will always be many interpretive schemes we could draw on and we choose whichever is appropriate to the project in hand. Such subjective activity differs even between individuals who frequently come into contact, but more so between people separated in time or space. Schutz used the term 'intersubjectivity' to describe the condition in which we experience the world as something whose significance we share with others (Schutz 1972: 139). To intuit the subjective meanings another person attributes to the world, we try to imagine the 'project' in which the other is engaged yet, to the extent that our previous experiences differ, we can never fully achieve intersubjective understanding. 'I ascribe to you an environment which has already been interpreted from my subjective standpoint' (Schutz 1972: 105).

Rather than assuming they are gifted with a uniquely Western skill for objectivity, anthropologists have had to learn to be reflexive, to ask themselves what past experiences they are relying upon to interpret an event and how their presence is subjectively interpreted by those they are working with. Reflexivity enabled a new form of ethnographic discourse. It became acceptable for anthropologists to write themselves into the account, to describe their anxieties in the field and their struggles with informants. It also enabled debates with informants to be presented, so that the people with whom one worked were transformed from objects of research into active subjects who participate in an inter-cultural discourse with the anthropologist.

An engaging example of this approach is Paul Rabinow's *Reflections on Fieldwork in Morocco* (1977). Rabinow describes his introduction to a café owner in the old quarter of the city where he began fieldwork. He admits that 'as a New Yorker and a devotee of street life' he felt more at ease in the café than in the expatriate Europeans' quarter. Soussi, the owner of a store opposite the café and Ali, a healer, became Rabinow's main points of entry into the life of the community. Ali's healing had no obvious parallel in Rabinow's previous experience and, as he questioned Ali about his practices, Rabinow's 'common sense world' was changed. Equally Ali, asked to reflect on what he normally did as a matter of habit, had to learn to present his practices to an outsider. 'There began to emerge a mutually constructed ground of experience and understanding, a realm of tenuous common sense which was constantly breaking down, being patched up, and re-examined' (Rabinow 1977: 39). Rabinow is honest about the worry of arguing with Ali, of feeling he had to assert his own feelings in order to avoid becoming a non-person and reflects upon why he felt challenged by Ali's behaviour. As Ali introduced Rabinow to local culture, he comes to seem as much a hindrance as a help. When Rabinow moves to the village in which he hopes to discover the real culture of the region, he finds his motives subjected to wildly unexpected interpretations. He was interpreted as a Christian missionary who had come to subvert Islam. Ali's family belong to one faction in the village. One man from another faction asserted that the interview to which Rabinow was subjected by the local gendarme was a warning that anyone who spoke to the anthropologist would be thrown into jail (whereas the gendarme was simply asking Rabinow whether his car was properly registered).

Theories must also be situated. The nineteenth-century evolutionism of Herbert Spencer can all too easily be shown to legitimate colonial expansion, by presenting the free market economy of Western Europe as the inevitable outcome of an unfolding process of development, earlier stages of which had survived in isolated corners of the world. Functionalism can be seen to deny the effects of colonial domination and to facilitate the British colonial policy of indirect rule by reconstructing the mechanisms of pre-colonial government. Edward Said's *Orientalism* (1978) is an extended exercise in situating Western understandings of the 'other'. The structure and orientation of the present volume is itself undeniably situated by my own vicarious experiences as a student in 1968, the more recent collapse of Communism in Eastern Europe, work on Australian Aboriginal land claims, and employment in England during a prolonged period of government by a party committed to free market policies.

Theories do not enable knowledge of the world 'as it really is'

Language has a fundamental property which was recognised by Rousseau and emphasised by Saussure: the connection between sounds or written forms and ideas is *conventional*. The sounds we use to denote ideas, only 'mean' something because our cultural tradition agrees they should. It is arbitrary whether we use the sound *horse*, *cheval* or *equus* to denote the four-legged animal that neighs. At a more fundamental but contentious level, it has been claimed that the way language structures our experience of the world is also arbitrary. According to this theory, our concepts of time and space are imposed on the world by language. The view was cogently argued in the 1930s by Benjamin Whorf. Whereas English represents time in terms of three basic categories, past, present and future, Hopi represents time in terms of two categories. Whorf could not translate these exactly but attempted to match them against the most 'consonant' concepts in English (Whorf 1956 [c.1936]: 58). Hopi divided time into the *manifest* or objective, and the *manifesting*, or subjective. According to Whorf, what we call the present and past were, without distinction, treated as manifest, while the future was treated as manifesting. However, manifesting included not only the future, but all striving of purposeful desire, by people, or growing plants, or gathering rain clouds. The very distant past, which has been forgotten, shades into manifesting time. The moment of transition between manifesting and manifest time was called 'becoming true'. Hence, Whorf argued, Hopi put much more effort than an English-speaker might consider appropriate into preparing for future events. Earnest hope and good intentions affect the way in which the growth of plants, as well as the performance of human plans, become manifest. Whorf gives some convincing examples of how the everyday behaviour of English speakers is also determined by the categories of our language (Whorf 1956: 135–7).

Steven Pinker draws attention to the fact that the linguist Edward Sapir, whose ideas influenced Whorf, was himself a student of Boas. While regarding Sapir's analysis of the way that different languages demand attention to different aspects of reality as interesting, Pinker has subjected Whorf's theory to a biting critique. Pinker points out that the Hopi have a sophisticated calendar and recorded days and seasons with knotted strings and notched sticks (Pinker 1994: 59–67). Pinker's argument is that any language is adequate to describe the world and the examples he uses to challenge Whorf mainly concern what Quine (1960) called 'observation sentences', a point to which this chapter will later return. This does not necessarily affect the argument that different languages embody different theories of causality.

A more extreme argument than Whorf's has been put forward by the French Postmodernist Derrida. Although it was argued in chapter 6 that the human capacity for language was an essential element in the development of the unique scale and complexity of human society, this event can be reinterpreted as a ironic myth of origin in which, from the moment humans first represent the world through arbitrary signs, they cease to know it as it really is (cf. Derrida 1976 [1967]: 145; 1978: 292). Derrida argued that the impossibility of exact translation between languages demonstrates there is no meaning which exists outside language. As he put it, there is no 'transcendental signified'. Since we can only know the world in terms of its meaning for us, knowledge is an artefact of language and as arbitrary as language itself (Derrida 1976 [1967]: 49–50). As language changes, so it becomes impossible to recover the meanings that people intended in the past.

Derrida points out that terms like culture, rationality and progress only make sense because they are opposed to other terms: nature, superstition, stagnation. The virtue of anthropology has been to call the familiar into question by showing that it is not self-evident or meaningful in itself (Derrida 1978: 282). Hobbes and Rousseau questioned the divine validation of contemporary European society by opposing it to another condition, the anarchy or nobility of the supposed original human condition. Previous chapters have shown how Functionalism and Socioecology in turn questioned the self-evident, given character of the 'natural human condition' by showing that it, too, was contrived. Even as anthropology enabled this understanding, however, it was compelled to use the existing categories of Western discourse. The Socioecological theory of territoriality appears to have elucidated one of the weaknesses of Marxism, by showing that the collective ownership of property within small-scale societies is not given in nature but is the outcome of rational self-interest, yet it does so through the culturally specific model of market values. The 'violence' of anthropology occurs at the moment that the cultural space of an exotic culture is 'shaped and reoriented by the glance of the foreigner' (Derrida 1976 [1967]: 113). Derrida follows Lévi-Strauss in regarding writing as a form of oppression, in which the exotic is appropriated, and reconstituted within our own system of cognitive oppositions. In this view, the history of anthropology is nothing better than a history of misrepresenting others in a word-play on the shortcomings of our own culture.

Azande 'witchcraft'

Evans-Pritchard's vivid account (1976 [1937]) of what he terms Azande 'witchcraft' repeatedly raises issues of appropriate translation which exemplify Derrida's argument. The Azande live around the area where the modern borders of the Sudan, the Congo and the Central African Republic meet.

Evans-Pritchard was told that certain Azande inherit a substance, *mangu*, which is embedded in their bodies and can be found during post-mortem examination. The substance gives one the capacity to cause harm to others. To realise its potential one must actively wish ill of someone else, becoming a *boro mangu*, which Evans-Pritchard translated as 'witch'. A witch sends the power of their witchcraft out at night, when it can be seen travelling as a white light, slowly to steal the vital organs from the victim's body. Evans-Pritchard once saw such a light travelling past near his hut to settle on a neighbour's roof and, 'curiously enough' the neighbour was ill the next morning (Evans-Pritchard 1976: 11).

Evans-Pritchard found that the Azande did not consider witchcraft miraculous. Anyone can be a witch; you might be one yourself without knowing it. Evans-Pritchard concluded that witchcraft is an *idiom* in which most misfortunes are explained. Craftsmen know that to fire pots successfully they must eliminate air bubbles and pebbles from the clay; carvers know they must use well-seasoned wood if their work is not to crack. Malinowski had similarly pointed out that Trobrianders 'understand that magic, however efficient, will not make up for bad workmanship' (Malinowski 1922: 115). If all these precautions have been taken and the pot or carving still breaks, the Zande craftsman will blame witchcraft. Others may continue to insist poor craftsmanship was responsible.

Evans-Pritchard's most famous example of the Azande use of witchcraft as an idiom for the explanation of misfortune is the case of the collapsing granary. During the heat of midday, people sometimes take shelter in the shade of a grain store. Such stores are built on wooden posts to stop rats from eating the grain. Termites eat the supports and sometimes cause a granary to collapse. If a man is killed by a collapsing granary, people know his death was caused by the need to shelter from the sun, and by the actions of termites. Witchcraft explains why that man took shelter under that granary on the day it collapsed (Evans-Pritchard 1976: 22). The nub of the problem is that witchcraft explains what Western scientific thought would regard as a coincidence, that is, unworthy or incapable of explanation. It was therefore very difficult to find a suitable translation.

If you suspect you are the victim of witchcraft the first move is often to convene a gathering of the men Evans-Pritchard terms 'witch-doctors': a loaded term, especially in the context of Christian mission-ising. The Azande witch-doctors' power derives from eating the right substances in the right manner. Evans-Pritchard terms a gathering of witch-doctors a 'seance'. A seance is a spectacular entertainment for the onlookers, but the divinations of witch-doctors have no validity in Azande law. A legal determination requires use of the so-called 'poison oracle', which will be outlined below.

Evans-Pritchard suggests that a seance has three advantages over the poison oracle. It increases the prestige of the man who convenes it. Witches can be frightened away by the witch-doctors' activities, elimi-nating the need to take more serious steps against them. A seance provides a public forum for expressing grievances against neighbours and spouses. When performing before an audience of commoners, the witch-doctor adopts a boastful, bullying tone not allowable in normal daily conduct but accepted because he is in a trance-like state of height-ened consciousness. His manner is taken in good part by the audience because they know his acts and words are imbued with the power of the substances he has eaten. Perhaps the behaviour of television presen-ters, when they subject members of the public to humiliation in front of a studio audience, is a better parallel than the notion of a 'witch-doctor'! When the witch-doctor accuses someone of witchcraft his claims have an authority denied to other commoners.

Evans-Pritchard talked in detail with a number of witch-doctors to discover how they determined who was responsible for acts of witch-craft. He found that the witch-doctor must, from the outset, be aware of local antagonisms and quarrels within the village. The witch-doctor knows, like a good sociologist, that there are a number of typical enmities in Zande life, such as those between co-wives or richer and poorer neighbours. Before the seance begins, the witch-doctor asks his client to name, in public, his wives and neighbours. He then uses his magic to determine who is responsible for the witchcraft, dancing until exhausted as he does so. Evans-Pritchard points out that the very fact of inviting the client to advance such names allows the client, consciously or otherwise, to select those most likely to wish him ill. The witch-doctor dances to each name in turn, progressively eliminating those whom he believes not to be responsible, using both his state of heightened consciousness and his intuition of local interpersonal relationships to divine who it is that, at that time, harbours destructive feelings of malice towards the witch-doctor's client. Evans-Pritchard was satisfied that witch-doctors were not charlatans, and believed as strongly as any other Zande in the procedures used.

When he finally identifies the culprit, the witch-doctor often reveals his identity through innuendo rather than by name so that only the client, who best knows his or her personal situation, can be certain who has been singled out. The client again provides some of the necessary links in the process of identification. One might compare it to horoscopes in our popular press which declare that 'romantic situations in the office will take a new turn', although this would trivialise what, for the Azande, is a serious procedure. The process of bringing latent conflicts into the open by coaxing the client to talk through their concerns has also been compared with psychotherapy.

If the client decides to put the witch-doctor's intuition to the test, he must consult the poison oracle. To consult the oracle, a man must wait until the cool of the day, then take some chickens and go to a quiet spot with some friends, preferably including an impartial witness. Here *benge* is prepared from the stem of a particular forest creeper and administered to each chicken in turn. When some of the *benge* has been fed to the first fowl it is addressed inside the chicken. Although Evans-Pritchard translated *benge* as 'poison', the Azande regard it as a sentient agency which can engage in communication. The questioner must make sure the *benge* knows the relevant facts concerning the victim of witchcraft and understands the question. Then the *benge* is given two alternatives:

If x is the case, kill the chicken.

If x is not the case, spare the chicken.

The *benge* answers, but its response must be tested by putting the contrary question after it has been fed to the next chicken. Thus, on the second occasion, the proposition will be:

If x is the case, spare the chicken.

If x is not the case, kill the chicken.

Once the outcome of the enquiry has been verified, the wing of the diagnostic chicken is taken to the local prince or governor, with a request that the witch be asked to desist. A gentleman, even if certain of his innocence, will always apologise. To respond angrily would only provide further evidence of one's malice.

Evans-Pritchard felt obliged to conclude that although the Azande reasoned logically within the limits of their culture, they could not step outside of that culture and perceive the illogicality of their procedures. 'One cannot well express in its language objections not formulated by a culture' (Evans-Pritchard 1976: 150).

Ahern has neatly shown how Evans-Pritchard was himself victim of the same constraints (Ahern 1982). In translating *benge* as 'poison' Evans-Pritchard based his analysis on the premise that it was a lethal chemical. He tried, many times, to force the Azande to confront this 'truth', but they regarded his questions as silly. When he asked what would happen if you went on feeding more and more *benge* to a chicken Evans-Pritchard intended them to concede that it would eventually die of an overdose but the Azande replied that, if you did so without asking a question, they supposed the chicken would eventually burst. When he pointed out that they removed the stomach and neck before eating a chicken that had been killed by the oracle, the Azande said that was done in case the *benge* went on answering the question after you had eaten it. Contrary to Evans-Pritchard's expectation, the Azande did not seem distressed by such questions, nor did they feel their position was being undermined. They found such questions silly, and told Evans-Pritchard, 'you do not understand such matters' (see Ahern 1982: 308–9). Ahern borrows from linguistics the concept of regulative and constitutive rules (see Searle 1969), and compares the Azande oracle to a game (a concept which was originated by Wittgenstein; see Baker and Hacker 1980). The regulative rules of tennis, for example, define the etiquette (wearing white clothes, not arguing with the umpire's decision on disputed points). The constitutive rules are what make it tennis. If an alien anthropologist appeared at Wimbledon and asked the players, 'Why don't you hit two balls over the net? One of them would be sure to get past your opponent', the players would reply, 'Don't be silly, that wouldn't be tennis.' Evans-Pritchard's questions were inviting the Azande to disregard the constitutive rules of oracular consultation, and these must be followed in order to communicate with the oracle.

The philosopher Quine, working within the interpretive tradition, imagines an anthropologist or linguist arriving in an unfamiliar community and seeking to understand its language. Quine argued that a distinction can be made between words which refer to objects and those which do not. Words like 'rabbit', which refer to objects, can be learned through 'ostension', that is, by pointing to one of the class of objects to which they refer (Quine 1960: 17). Their meaning is unambiguously anchored in the environment. Quine recognised that many words are only partly explicated by ostension. A term such as 'bachelor' can only partly be explicated by pointing to an unmarried man; 'collateral information', that is, knowledge of the cognitive structure of the culture, is required to provide a full understanding of the status of bachelor. Causal theories belong to the cultural structure and a sentence such as 'neutrinos lack mass' (or 'witches send out their witchcraft substance to harm others') lie at the opposite pole to 'rabbit' (Quine 1960: 76). Experience is never adequate to determine which of many possible theories is correct: 'alternatives emerge: experiences call for changing a theory, but do not indicate just where and how' (Quine 1960: 64); 'countless alternative theories would be tied for first place' (Quine 1960: 23). Quine's argument supports to some extent the subsequent claims of Postmodernists that cultural meanings are not determined by an external world but, like Foucault, considers references to the world can provide a bridge between otherwise closed cultures.

There is no collective consciousness

Just as interactionists had replaced Radcliffe-Brown's idea of social structure with the study of social process so, as anthropologists began to investigate cultural symbolism in daily life, they became dissatisfied with Lévi-Strauss' holistic models of the structure of culture. In his models of totemism and caste, or his analysis of myth, Lévi-Strauss assumed culture had an independent existence as a kind of collective consciousness. Everyone in a 'primitive culture' learnt exactly the same set of symbolic equations as they grew up, because these were imposed on them from outside by the collectivity, and people were incapable of individual reflection outside this collective representation. Any element of individualism would necessarily undermine this collective understanding, and destroy the capacity of symbols to communicate

(Lévi-Strauss 1960: 66, and see chapter 3, above). The trend within Interactionism to interpret cultural life as a process of negotiating meaning led towards a Postmodern anthropology.

Pierre Bourdieu wrote one of the earliest critiques of the Structuralist theory of culture in 1972, constructed around his fieldwork with the Kabyle, a Berber community of Algeria (Bourdieu 1977). Bourdieu criticises a number of aspects of the structural anthropology prevalent in the early 1970s. The anthropologist, an outsider, seems to regard understanding a foreign culture as an exercise in code-breaking, seeking to find familiar meanings, or sense, behind outwardly bizarre customs. It is as if the anthropologist were listening for a radio message transmitted by an enemy submarine which, even though it is in a secret code can, if the code is broken, be revealed to say something as readily understood as 'surfacing to disembark spy at 0800 hours' (see chapter 3). In the same way, anthropologists reduce exotic behaviour to familiar categories such as gift-giving, feuding, familial kinship. How appropriate are such renderings of meaningful behaviour to the way social activities are understood by the participants?

The anthropologist's account, moreover, sets out the structure of the culture explicitly, whereas those within it accept its premises unreflectively. The difference is like the difference between learning a foreign language from a textbook which sets out the rules of grammar, the form of regular and irregular verbs, and learning a language by hearing it spoken. In the latter situation it is difficult, if not impossible (unless one is specially trained), to formulate the implicit rules we rely upon. The meaningful behaviour of people in other cultures can only be understood by themselves within the implicit, unarticulated assumptions on which their behaviour is based. Bourdieu referred to this body of implicit knowledge as *habitus* (compare Malinowski's 'imponderabilia of daily life', in chapter 2). Participants have what Bourdieu termed a *practical mastery* of tact and appropriate behaviour. Elaborate rituals which explicitly spell out people's status, although loved by anthropologists, are actually rare. It is misleading for anthropologists to devote too much space to such exotic rituals in their ethnographies and they should rather concentrate on the implicit routines of daily life.

Culture as text

As was shown above, Derrida followed Lévi-Strauss in regarding ethnographic writing as intrinsically oppressive, appropriating the exotic and reconstituting it within our own system of cognitive opposi-tions. If Derrida were correct, even Bourdieu's efforts to escape from the straitjacket of Structuralism would be futile, since he is obliged to render Kabyle practice in Western terms.

Derrida argued that writing, not speech, is the primary manifesta-tion of language. He criticised Rousseau and Saussure for regarding writing as a secondary medium, a mere representation of speech. Both had deplored the tendency for writing to cause people to mis-pronounce words through reading them phonetically. In part, Derrida's argument is based on the fact that science and literature are essentially written traditions (Derrida 1976 [1967]: 27). In this respect, Derrida's argument is similar to that of Goody and Ong, who claim that certain types of knowledge are only attainable in a literate tradition (Goody 1977; 1987; Ong 1982). The claim that writing literally has primacy over speech cannot apply to oral cultures, but this is not Derrida's prin-cipal line of argument. Saussure recognised that science and literature have a special relationship to writing, and Derrida does not wish to question 'the truth of what Saussure says' (Derrida 1976: 39), an ironic concession, since what Saussure actually said is doubtful (see chapter 3)!

Instead, by a sleight of hand, Derrida redefines writing to mean any manifestation of language that leaves a trace or inscription (Derrida 1976: 46–8). In this sense, speech itself is a form of 'writing', albeit infi-nitely more transitory than writing, in the narrow sense of the word. Derrida rejected the notion that meaning exists outside of language. He follows Saussure in arguing that meaning is created by a chain of *differences*: sounds or letters (signifiers) are differentiated from each other and each is associated with a signified, or mental construct. The meaning of each construct is, in turn, determined by its place in the system, in which it is differentiated from other constructs (see chapter 3). The absence of 'transcendental' meaning outside language has two consequences. First, it is only through the practice of language that differences are established. A language cannot exist only in the present, but is the outcome of practice through which the 'trace' of opposed signs can be detected. Second, if no external constraints are imposed on this practice, meanings will constantly change, through the random 'play' of linguistic differentiation (see Derrida 1976: 50–60). A text persists while language changes, but can only be read in terms of the current state of play within the language (Derrida 1976: 102).

Geertz (1988) argued in a similar, but less radical fashion, that we cannot go back and check the events which an ethnographer described. Trobriand life is changing and we will never experience it as Malinowski did. We must therefore read ethnographies as texts and ask what it is *within the text* which makes it convincing to the reader. If all cultures are self-contained systems of values and meanings, with no relationship to an empirical world we and the Trobrianders, Azande or Nuer might both experience, then how is it that anthropologists seem to describe other cultures so well? Geertz claims it is through rhetoric, through the persuasive style of writing. Ethnographies are exercises in literary talent rather than the presentation of verifiable evidence. Geertz subjects several famous anthropologists' writing to literary criticism, stating, 'the question here is not the truth of such statements' (Geertz 1988: 63), but how are they made believable (Geertz 1988: 64). Geertz seeks to deconstruct Evans-Pritchard's 'maddening brilliance': how does he trick us into thinking we have directly encountered the world of the Nuer or the Azande? Evans-Pritchard is notorious for not citing references in his work. Instead, the reader recognises his allusions to Weber or Comte and is flattered that they have been admitted to an intellectual club in which everyone shares the same values and accepts the same authorities. Vivid examples are skilfully chosen and presented, as if one were sitting in a comfortable slide show witnessing slices of the exotic brought fresh from the field, such as 'those hapless Zande forever taking refuge from the sun under a store house precisely at the moment when the termites have finally eaten their way through its supports' (Geertz 1988: 64–5). Evans-Pritchard writes in the same relaxed, confident tone whether describing the hazards of walking through long grass, or those of facing enemy rifle fire. The reader follows him as unquestioningly as a soldier might follow an inspiring officer into battle.

Geertz's book is based on lectures he gave one year before the 'Writing Culture' conference which had a seminal effect in confronting anthropology with the challenge of Postmodernism. Rosaldo, contributing to the conference, develops many of Geertz's arguments, and takes Evans-Pritchard further to task for presenting Nuer culture as a unified, timeless whole, rather than an emergent phenomenon, negotiated by living actors. Evans-Pritchard depicts the Nuer as exemplars of an anthropological archetype, the proud but democratic nomad (Rosaldo 1986). Crapanzano, in the same volume, points out how vulnerable Geertz's own writing is to a literary critique (Crapanzano 1986: 68–76).

If the Postmodernist's claim is true, the meaning of his text would be at risk as soon as he sent his manuscript to the printers. If his argument has been correctly transmitted to us, then it must be false. But Tylor, in his contribution to *Writing Culture*, justifies his characterisation of Postmodern ethnography by citing other authorities (Tylor 1986: 132). Derrida likewise claims to be able to 'read' Saussure with confidence; he cites Pierce as an authority. The irony of this process was noted by Umberto Eco: 'If Derrida assumes that his interpretation is the good one, he should also assume that Pierce's text had a *privileged* meaning to be isolated, recognised as such and spelled out unambiguously' (Eco 1990: 35).

The writings of Herodotus and Tacitus have been called into question on the grounds that they reveal the construction of systems of difference, and therefore have no validity as accounts of fact external to the mental constructs of their authors. Tacitus' Germans are constructed as egalitarian, limited in their material desires, chaste, and generally opposed to the values of Tacitus' own culture. The Scythians figure in Herodotus' account as a mirror image of the Egyptians. The Egyptians are the oldest of peoples, the Scythians claim to be the newest. Egypt is dominated by monumental architecture, the Scythian landscape lacks cities, temples and even agriculture (see Gould 1989: 100–9 for an interesting assessment of this argument, and compare Whitehead 1995). It might equally be claimed that Rousseau and Hobbes reopened a classical debate in which the construction of the 'natural' or 'original' human condition underwent a series of transformations unfettered by any empirical observation of small-scale societies. It is less plausible to make such a claim of the Functionalists, even though they undoubtedly relied on some of the conceptual structures they had inherited from the nineteenth century.

Derrida's theory of meaning remains strictly Saussurian in the sense that signs are said only to gain meaning from their position in a system of other signs. It differs from Saussure in denying that linguistic signs make any reference to objects which exist outside language itself. This is a 'dictionary' theory of meaning, in which the dictionary can only define words in terms of other words, or previous meanings of the same word (i.e. it is 'self-referential'). The system is closed and can only refer to itself.

In order to unravel the source of Derrida's paradoxical claims, I shall argue that there are two distinct issues which need to be addressed:

intersubjective understanding in the field and subsequent communication through ethnographic texts.

Culture as drama or narrative

The constructed character of cultural meanings is unquestionable. Bourdieu argued that, at any moment, the significance of what people are doing as they interact depends on what has previously happened: meaningful behaviour is, as Derrida argued with regard to language, constructed through time. It has a narrative structure. I give you a gift because at an appropriately distant time in the past you gave me one. What will happen next always remains uncertain: there will be a number of possibilities. Habitus is improvisation, not a set of predetermined rules. People may value this uncertainty precisely because it enables them to resolve an ambiguous situation in their favour. Far from individuality being inimical to cultural life, it is integral to the way that meaningful behaviour is actualised. The Kabyle say that 'a man who has no enemies is a donkey' (in other words he is unduly passive). Although the proverb seems paradoxical to us, the Kabyle regard a challenge to one's honour as 'a high point in a man's life'. It is a chance to realise one's potential as a person of honour (compare the Sarakatsani code of honour outlined in chapter 2). The anthropologist who analyses social life as a fixed structure of relationships will miss this dimension. Bourdieu's concept of the construction of meaningful life through action is very similar to Giddens' theory of Structuration (see chapter 4). Giddens drew attention to the processes by which usage feeds back on to the structure of a cultural system. While Saussure recognised agency in a way that Durkheim did not, by introducing the concept of *making selections* from the system, Saussure still regarded individuals primarily as users of a system which existed independently of them, rather than as the modifiers and embodiers of a system which only exists through usage. For Bourdieu and Giddens, however, there is a constant interplay, or negotiation, between existing and new usages.

This is well illustrated by the changing meaning of the expression 'Band Aid'. 'Band Aid' is the trademark of a company which manufactures small sticking plasters to protect cuts and scratches while they heal. Some years ago, it was common to use the term 'a band-aid solution' to denigrate an inadequate and short-term response to a problem. When the popular musician Bob Geldof launched the idea of raising money to help relieve famine in the Third World by inviting bands to play at charity concerts in Britain and the United States, he called the initiative 'Band Aid'. Geldof's Band Aid was immediately successful, and the connotations of the term were transformed. This is not unlike Derrida's theory of 'free play' in which words gain their current meaning through usages which set themselves in opposition to previous usages. Each usage leaves a 'trace' which, in time, is eradicated by successive transformations of meaning.

Victor Turner took a view which is similar, but different from Bourdieu's in one important aspect. Turner adopted the philosophers Schutz and Dilthey's concept of *Erlebnisse* or 'living through', in which life takes on meaning as present problems are related to the past celebrated by the culture (Turner 1990). For Turner, however, the most creative spaces are not in everyday routines but at the margins of social life, in play and joking. Art and life each inform and transform each other, through repeated performances. 'Liminal' moments, such as those van Gennep identified in initiation rites, are eminently suitable for transforming people's perception or 'reading' of social life. It can, in the same vein, be argued that the performance of myth and the production or creation of works of art are moments when the artist/narrator *makes a claim* about the interpretation of cultural events. This is what the Lega ritual expert is doing when he draws on the indefinite possibilities provided by the objects in the Bwami basket to commend or ridicule the initiate (see chapter 3). Kirin Narayan gives a good example of this creative process in her account of how an Indian teacher gives new meaning to a traditional story by identifying the characters of the story with listeners in his audience (Narayan 1993). A more radical process took place as Narritjin and other artists among the Yolngu of northern Australia renegotiated the content and display of their art as they attempted to explain their values and affiliation to the land, to a Euro-Australian audience (Morphy 1991). The process by which anthropologists develop theoretical insights in their ethnographic writing is perhaps comparable.

Within the community under study, people may disagree over the interpretation of events. If people agree on the meaning of a simple gesture or an elaborate ritual, we should try to discover how such consensus is achieved rather than take it for granted as the product of a 'collective consciousness'. Stephen Tylor regards the description of such processes as the defining feature of Postmodern ethnography:

'Post-modern ethnography attempts to recreate textually this spiral of poetic and ritual performance... [as] one of co-operative story making... none of whose participants would have the final word in the form of a framing story or encompassing synthesis' (Tylor 1986: 126).

Culture as performance

If 'writing' can be presented, following Derrida, as the primary form of linguistic expression, then anthropological fieldwork can be construed as an exercise in reading texts. Postmodern anthropologists have claimed this to be so (Geertz 1973b: 443–5; Crapanzano 1986: 51). I believe their stance glosses over an important distinction; the fieldworker is not studying texts which were constructed in the past, but present performances, coming into being at that moment which, according to Whorf, the Hopi termed 'becoming true'. 'The fieldwork experience itself (unlike its representation in text) is unambiguously two-way' (Ganesh 1993: 139). The process of fieldwork should not be confused with the production of an ethnographic account.

Schutz argued that each community participates in a distinctive 'world of experience' (Schutz 1972: 136). Although we are separated by the divergence of our past experience, where we participate in that 'world of experience', the listener is present as the speaker engages in meaningful discourse, and the listener responds. If we read a book, on the other hand, interpretation is vicarious; 'the reader relives the author's choice of words as if the choice were made before his very eyes' (Schutz 1972: 134). Derrida sought to deny this distinction by redefining writing as anything which separated language from the immediacy of unmediated perception (Derrida 1976: 24). Ricoeur, however, showed that it remains a valuable distinction (Ricoeur 1979). Ricoeur argued that social interactions, as they are carried out, are performances in which the participants have some access to each other's fleeting, subjective intentions. If the listener responds inappropriately, the speaker can try again to convey their subjective intention. This can be illustrated with two examples from fieldwork in central Australia. The Yankunytjatjara word *punganyi* can be translated either as 'hit' or 'kill'. Like many English words, the circumstantial meaning can only be intuited from the context. When Yankunytjatjara speak in English, they generally translate *punganyi* as 'kill'. I was once talking with a Yankunytjatjara friend when he spotted his favourite dog trying to steal meat hanging in a tree. 'Kill that dog!' he shouted. I would quickly have discovered if I had misconstrued the instruction. On another occasion, the same man and his dog climbed into our four-wheel drive vehicle to set off on a journey through the bush. We had learned that *kapi palya* is translated as 'good' (i.e. drinkable) water, and were familiar with the Yankunytjatjara acceptance of obligation, *uwa, palya* ('yes', good'). Roz, my wife, patted the dog on the head and said '*papa palya*'. Paddy Uluru pursed his lips and corrected her: '*papa wiru* ['likeable dog']; *papa palya* got no teeth'. Thus, we began to intuit, *palya* is better equated with 'sweet' than 'good'. Derrida regarded language as a self-referential system in which words are defined only with reference to other words. During fieldwork, however, we interact with people in an environment that has meaning for them, to which they can point. Words are used to make ostensive references. Language is used to do practical things (cf. Sarup 1989: 59, 61). When someone says, 'That man is my father' (but genealogy shows him to be what we term an uncle) or when they say '*mangu* caused that granary to collapse' it is true that we, and those we work with, can only apprehend the man or fallen granary in terms of their respective meanings for us, yet at that moment the man and the granary form *in themselves* bridgeheads between otherwise closed worlds. Spoken words walk a tightrope between signification and reference. Carrithers has argued that human emotions provide a similar bridgehead. We can recognise that a Tikopean is angry and upset, even though the reasons for his emotions may be peculiar to the construction of Tikopean culture (Carrithers 1992).

Quine proposed a distinction between 'observation sentences' and 'theoretical sentences' (Quine 1960: 17). Like Frake's study of the Subanam classification of disease (chapter 3), many ethno-biological studies have been based on the access to culture provided by observation sentences, producing lists of indigenous names for animal and plant species, ecological zones and so forth (e.g. Williams and Baines 1993; Reid *et al.* 1993). Puttnam, however, questioned whether Quine's distinction could ever be complete (Puttnam 1995: 17, 61). In practice, even an object such as a rabbit is comprehended within a body of knowledge (Baker *et al.* 1993). We were once driving along a bush track in central Australia when two kangaroos bounded across the path. A Yankunytjatjara girl in the vehicle leapt to her feet shouting (in English), 'Look, Mummy, meat!' (Yankunytjatjara *kuka* can be translated as game animal, or meat.) On another occasion, when some Yankunytjatjara men were hunting rabbits, we encountered one which refused to run away, yet could not be hit. After a few attempts, one said, 'Leave him, might be *mamu*', and we returned to the vehicle. This, and similar events, led me to infer that *mamu* are malevolent agencies which can possess both people and animals. Puttnam suggested that the problem with Quine's distinction was that a term like *bosorkanyok* might equally well mean 'ugly old woman with wart on nose', or 'witch'. The latter is embedded within a theory of being, the former apparently is not. I suggest that terms such as witch can be elucidated by describing the way in which objects and events are connected. '*Mamu* cause animals to behave unnaturally'; 'a "witch" makes people ill by travelling at night as a white light'. Confronted with statements like this in the field, we realise how different the logical connections which people construct between referents may be. Yet, if representations are underdetermined by experience, we can only make the best match to constructs in our own culture – translation will inevitably be incomplete. The crux of the anthropological dilemma is the aptness of terms such as 'witch' or 'malevolent agency' (why not 'devil'?).

There is no ivory tower: the politics of writing

The term *fabrication* has two meanings. Steel boxes and buildings are fabricated, but so too are false alibis. A similar ambiguity is exploited in the idea of ethnography as fiction, associated with *Writing Culture* (Clifford and Marcus 1986). Contributors drew on Derrida's theory to challenge the transparency of ethnographic texts, highlighting ethnographers' use of various literary styles to argue that ethnography is something constructed by the writer.

The apparent naturalness of factual ethnography is usefully called into question by redefining it as a form of fiction, just as Derrida questioned the apparent transparency of speech by redefining it as a form of writing. Both reformulations highlight unexpected qualities of the seemingly natural categories (speech, description), but at the cost of importing inappropriate qualities of the seemingly artificial terms to which they are opposed (writing, fiction). As Eco wrote, 'Derrida – in order to stress non obvious truths – disregards very obvious truths that nobody can reasonably pass over in silence' (Eco 1990: 36). The process of mutual accommodation that occurs during the interpretation of meanings in the field ends once the ethnography is written, but the people described continue to exist.

Geertz was the first to put forward the idea of ethnography as fiction when he said of his own writing that constructing actor-oriented descriptions of Berber chieftains, Jewish merchants and French soldiers in Morocco was not all that different to constructing novels about nineteenth-century life in provincial France (Geertz 1973a: 15). I argue, to the contrary, that by treating ethnography as a self-referential system, Geertz glosses over the crucial distinction between Madame Bovary's hypothetical trajectory through provincial French culture and the real (albeit recollected) trajectories of the characters in Geertz's own case study. Clifford justifies the concept of ethnography as fiction by recalling the definition of art as the fashioning of useful artefacts (Clifford 1986: 6), yet he concedes 'we cannot refer to Samoans as "Meadian" or call Tikopea a "Firthian" culture as freely as we speak of Dickensian or Flaubertian worlds' (Clifford 1986: 13). Unlike Oliver Twist and Fagin, the Samoans and Tikopeans exist independently of what is written about them, and the ethnography makes reference to their existence.

Foucault argues for the existence of a community of knowers who share a common 'discourse' and contends that, while such discourses radically influence the way we talk about the world, they can none the less be said to make reference to things that exist outside of the discourse (Foucault 1972 [1969]). Foucault therefore positions himself somewhere between complete relativity and absolute objectivity. Each discipline, in Foucault's assessment, is characterised by a particular way of writing (or speaking). A mathematician would not describe, within the body of his text on calculus, how an idea came to him as he prepared to leave his house, because expressions such as 'two quantities both equal to a third quantity are also equal to each other' are held to be true regardless of the circumstances in which the mathematician is writing. This is a premise of mathematical *discourse*. Disciplines such as natural science, psychiatry and economics each recognise certain 'objects' around which discourse takes place: natural selection, madness or the market. For Foucault, unlike Quine, there can be no pure 'observation sentences'. The rules of a discourse determine which statements about such 'objects' make sense and which are considered irrelevant, marginal or unscientific. Foucault's interest is in how such rules direct the course of debate. One might, for example, point to the way in which the discourse of the free market makes consumer choice an 'object' but, when talking of the 'consumer's right to choose', marginalises the effect of unequal ownership of the means of production by refusing to concede its relevance. Foucault recognises that factors outside discourse can shape it. Such factors include the role of discourse in the decisions of government and in political struggles, and the appropriation of discourse by people who claim an exclusive right to use it. These external relations define a cultural space within which several possible discourses can be practised. Foucault is not himself interested in studying such a 'space' because this would 'neutralise' the internal relationships within a discourse by making them 'a sign of' (i.e. refer to) something else. It would be possible to discover what the term neurosis *refers to*, 'such a history of the referent would no doubt be possible' (Foucault 1972: 47), this is what makes Foucault less radical a Postmodernist than Derrida, but observation of the referent would not explain how, at a certain time, medical expertise was able to claim the authority to diagnose madness as a crime.

Gombrich's analysis of style and illusion in art made many of the points Foucault later made with regard to written discourse, yet highlights the referential quality of representational art. Gombrich argued that it makes no sense to try and interpret an artistic motif unless one has learnt how to classify and locate it within its stylistic tradition (Gombrich 1960: 63). Gombrich's concept of style corresponds quite closely to Foucault's concept of discourse. A 'correct' painting is not, for Gombrich, a faithful record of a visual experience but the faithful construction of a relational model (Gombrich 1960: 78); Foucault wrote similarly that 'a discourse is not a mere intersection of words and things, but a practice which systematically forms the objects of which it speaks' (Foucault 1972: 49). Whereas, however, Foucault put 'the history of the referent' to one side (Foucault 1972: 47), Gombrich was interested in how the artist solved the difficulty that 'the amount of information reaching us from the visible world is incalculably large, and the artist's medium is inevitably restricted and granular' (Gombrich 1960: 182). He concluded that it is not simply a matter of trying to supply as much visual information as possible, but rather that styles are devised to convey particular messages about the world: 'to say of a drawing that it is a correct view of Tivoli... means that those who understand the notation will derive *no false information* from the drawing' (Gombrich 1960: 78, his emphasis). A writer can no more be blamed for using a style than can an artist. Just as an artistic style tends to reduce the innumerable details of visual perception to regular forms, so written styles tend to reduce the richness of experience to categorical distinctions. The question, 'Is this a correct view of the Nuer?' remains as valid as 'Is this a correct view of Tivoli?', and can only be answered with reference to the Nuer themselves.

Since, however, all styles are chosen for a purpose, it is also legitimate to ask whether the writer has been honest about their purpose. If theories, policies and emotions mediate knowledge, they should be made explicit. The 'trick' which Postmodernist critics have accurately identified is to make one's style look 'natural'. If naturalism is impossible, the writer should make his or her style apparent, just as the Postmodern artist makes the paint visible on the canvas, rather than attempting to seduce the eye through the canvas to the world 'beyond'.

Evans-Pritchard's style of writing in *The Nuer* is guided by Radcliffe-Brown's theory of Structural Functionalism. Radcliffe-Brown contended that 'the actual relations of Tom, Dick and Harry may go down in our field notebooks. . . but what we need for scientific purposes is an account of the form of the structure' (Radcliffe-Brown 1952: 192). The reasons why Radcliffe-Brown took this approach are outlined in chapter 2. They explain why Evans-Pritchard's ethnographic style leaves no room for the lively case studies that characterise the ethnography of Malinowski and Firth. As Rosaldo concedes, 'Evans-Pritchard's object of scientific knowledge is social structure rather than historical contingencies and political action' (Rosaldo 1986: 93). Classical ethnography sought to separate the writer from the people about whom (s)he was writing, to separate the subjective experiences of the anthropologist from the 'objective referent of the text'. Postmodernist ethnography puts the anthropologist back into the ethnographic account, 'situating' them in their text. This is a different style of ethnography and attention can usefully be drawn to the stylistic techniques used, as Crapanzano does in his analysis of texts by Catlin, Goethe and Geertz (Crapanzano 1986). Socioecology, by focusing on the cost and benefit to participants of the transactions in which they are immediately engaged, demands a more fine-grained account of social life than does Marxism, but at the cost of leaving the long-term consequences of shifts in the control of productive resources, highlighted by Marx, out of focus.

Conclusion

Linnaeus believed species were little changed since their creation by God. Variation within a species was considered to be nothing more than evidence for the effect of soil and climate on a predetermined 'type'. Darwin's theory of natural selection refocused scientists' attention on variation within populations. Variation now provided crucial evidence for the almost imperceptibly slow process which led to the origin of new species. The two theories could be said to demand different styles of writing, but each continues to be useful in the biological sciences. In the same way, theories in the social sciences demand a style of writing appropriate to the particular perspective they bring to bear on the complexity of social life, and more than one theory may be useful to the analyst. Sometimes one theory provides a more detailed insight into phenomena previously studied according to an earlier theory. Socioecology and Marxism both extended the insights provided by Functionalism, while interpretive sociology has provided a more fine-grained understanding of the processes by which meaning is constructed than did Structuralism. At other times, theories lead to conflicting conclusions, as seems to be the case with Structuralism and Socioecology.

While it seems inadequate to dismiss the Linnaean approach as nothing more than an exercise in political domination, it has an inescapable political dimension. His classification remains invaluable as a means of studying biological variation at any moment in time, yet the view that human populations are a manifestation of a given 'type' also justifies racism. The same distinction can be made with regard to Functionalism or Socioecology. Any theory that is capable of practical application will have political implications and we must be conscious of the practical consequences of choosing to use particular theories.

In his contribution to *Writing Culture,* Stephen Tylor claims that science sought to present perception unmediated by concepts and failed, because such a goal was unattainable (Tylor 1986: 123). Tylor follows Derrida is arguing that writing can only be self-referential (Tylor 1986: 138–9). He concludes that Postmodern ethnography can take any form, because 'every attempt will be incomplete' (Tylor 1986: 136). This is a counsel of despair. It does not follow that theories are necessarily nothing but political ideologies (see Layton 1989b). Style is used to depict material brought into focus by theory and theories make reference to a world of objects. As Carrithers has pointed out, the Postmodernist attack on science depends upon an impoverished notion of how science is practised (Carrithers 1992: 152–4). Even paragons of the Enlightenment were aware that our perception of the world is mediated by our theories. Richard Watson has shown that seventeenth-century scientists also regarded the results of their experiments as 'provisional knowledge' and debated scientific method with sceptics who contended that 'it is impossible to know whether representations and interpretations of the world are true of it or even whether there is a world outside sensory impressions and imaginations at all' (Watson 1991: 275; cf. Gower 1997). Watson argues that one need only look at the practical results of taking science seriously to see that it has become increasingly effective. While this partly answers the Postmodern criticism, it does not address the question of how we decide on the criteria by which such judgements will be made.

Anthropological translation of indigenous ideas confronts the same problem. If representations are under-determined by experience, no complete translation will ever be possible. The best the anthropologist can do is to match indigenous ideas as closely as possible to constructs in his or her own culture. This is why Malinowski compared *kula* valuables to the crown jewels and to sporting trophies, despite noting that neither parallel was exact. But why does the anthropologist choose one translation rather than another? Ethnography has usually been written by the dominant about the weak, and the practice of translation confers power. When the anthropologist chooses what to render meaningful or rational about another culture, (s)he is using that power. If Quine was right to claim that experience is never sufficient to determine which of countless alternative theories is correct, on what grounds do we favour one theory over another?

Belief in witchcraft does not prevent the Azande from discovering that to make pots successfully you must get rid of stones and air bubbles in the clay. The Azande utilise at least two theories of causality, enabling them to debate whether bad workmanship or witchcraft has caused a run of breakages during successive firings. When he was in the field Evans-Pritchard found it most convenient to assume witches existed and organise his daily life accordingly. The problem he encountered once he began to write his ethnography was that Azande 'witchcraft' explains what members of Evans-Pritchard's scientific subculture regard as bad luck. He therefore chose to translate it in terms of a discredited, historically situated theory of causality. In retrospect the political dimension of his translation is evident. If he had translated the 'witch-doctor's seance' as psychotherapy, we would evaluate the Azande differently.

Now the weak have made their own voice heard, what justification is there for the anthropologist's practice of translating culture (Clifford 1986: 8–10)? How would the Azande write a comparative anthropology? Would they assess the degree to which a society had developed according to its ability to recognise witchcraft? Worth and Adair's work with Navaho film-makers suggests how unexpectedly the Navaho might write their own ethnographic narratives (Worth and Adair 1972). Henry Reynolds has reconstructed the way in which indigenous Australians interpreted the first European colonists they encountered. Reynolds shows how they found it incredible that settlers should hoard great quantities of tobacco, livestock etc. which they could not possibly need in the next few days (Reynolds 1982: 68). What extraordinary greed and meanness prevented them from distributing these goods so that they could enter into social relationships with indigenous people? Reynolds cites the case of an Aboriginal party who killed a bullock and offered the kidney fat to the frightened white owner, saying 'they were not like the whites themselves – greedy'. Women were regarded by Aboriginal men as an important political resource: bestowing women in marriage was probably the principal source of secular power (Reynolds 1982: 70). White pioneers, in an area bereft of white women, often took advantages of offers of Aboriginal women, failing to realise that in doing so the Aborigines were offering them the opportunity to enter into a web of reciprocal obligations and instead construing it as a market transaction, prostitution. Records show that the women were frequently soon turned out without even the meagre payments of food, clothing or axes that had originally been promised. Such behaviour was justified at the time in terms of the current Spencerian scientific orthodoxy that indigenous Australians were survivors of an early stage in human evolution and doomed to die out in the face of a superior race; that they were irrational in their thought and, as hunter-gatherers, innocent of any concept of rights over property. Does the use of Socioecological theory do equal injustice to Aboriginal society?

While the political implications of Spencer's theory provide adequate grounds for questioning it, there are further reasons why it now seems unsatisfactory. As anthropological theories have multiplied over time, we can see how each brings a different focus to bear on our experiences in the field. Theories developed since Spencer's time put our own prior assumptions about human nature more thoroughly into question, and give us a more fine-grained vision of the processes of social life.

It also becomes possible to see that ethnography, or writing about peoples, is impossible without some theory to guide our choice of events to describe, and the style by which we represent those events. Theories are not neutral. They are chosen for a purpose, to draw our own attention, and that of our readers, to aspects of social life and to propose causal connections between events. While our desire may simply be to give as complete an account as we can of social life, we write with a purpose that, to a greater or lesser extent, stems from the problems of our own time and place, our own lived experience. We must never forget that what we write may guide or justify others' actions in future. Theory is inextricably bound up with politics. The better we understand the role of theory in anthropology, the better we appreciate both its dangers and its usefulness.

References

Abegglan, J. C. and Shack, G. (eds.) 1985 *Kaisha, the Japanese corporation*, New York: Basic Books.

Ahern, E. M. 1982 'Rules in oracles and games', *Man*, NS, 17: 302–12.

Ahmed, A. S. 1976 *Millenium and charisma among Pathans*, London: Routledge.

Altman, J. C. 1987 *Hunter-gatherers today. An Aboriginal economy in north Australia*, Canberra: Aboriginal Studies Press.

Altman, J. and Peterson, N. 1988 'Rights to Game and Rights to Cash among Contemporary Hunter-Gatherers', in T. Ingold, D. Riches and J. Woodburn (eds.), *Hunters and gatherers: property, power and ideology*, Oxford: Berg, pp. 75–94.

Amadiume, I. 1993 'The mouth that spoke a falsehood will later speak the truth: going home to the field in Eastern Nigeria', in D. Bell, P. Caplan and W. J. Karim (eds.), *Gendered fields: women, men and ethnography*, London: Routledge, pp. 182–98.

Ardener, E. 1971 'Introductory essay: social anthropology and language', in E. Ardener (ed.), *Social anthropology and language*, London: Tavistock, pp. ix–cii.

Asad, T. 1972 'Market model, class-structure and consent', *Man*, 7: 74–94.

Asad, T. (ed.) 1973 *Anthropology and the Colonial encounter*, London: Ithaca Press.

Axelrod, R. 1990 *The evolution of co-operation*, Harmondsworth: Penguin (first published 1984, New York: Basic Books).

Baker, G. P and Hacker, P. M. S. 1980 *Wittgenstein: understanding and meaning*, Oxford: Blackwell.

Baker, L., Woenne-Green, S. and the Muṭitjulu community 1993 'Aṉangu knowledge of vertebrates and the environment', in J. Reid, J. Kerle and S. Norton (eds.) 1993, *Uḷuru fauna: the distribution and abundance of vertebrate fauna of Uḷuru (Ayers Rock-Mount Olga) National Park*, pp. 79–132.

Balikci, A. 1970 *The Netsilik Eskimo*, New York: Garden City.

Barnard, A. 1989 'Nharo kinship in social and cosmological perspective: comparisons between southern African and Australian hunter-gatherers', *Mankind*, 19: 198–214.

Barnes, J. 1954 'Class and committee in a Norwegian island parish', *Human Relations*, 7: 39–58.

Barth, F. 1959a *Political leadership among Swat Pathans*, London: Athlone.

1959b 'Segmentary opposition and the theory of games', *Journal of the Royal Anthropological Institute*, 89: 5–21.

1967a 'On the study of social change', *American Anthropologist*, 69: 661–9.

1967b 'Economic spheres in Darfur', in R. Firth (ed.), *Themes in economic anthropology*, London: Tavistock, pp. 149–74.

Barthes, R. 1967 *Elements of semiology*, trans. A. Lavers and C. Smith, London: Cape.

Bell, D. 1993 'Yes Virginia, there is a feminist ethnography: reflections from three Australian fields', in D. Bell, P. Caplan and W. J. Karim (eds.), *Gendered fields: women, men and ethnography*, London: Routledge, pp. 28–43.

Benedict, R. 1934 *Patterns of culture*, Boston: Houghton Mifflin.

Berger, P. L. and Luckmann, T. 1966 *The social construction of reality*, Harmondsworth: Penguin.

Berreman, G. 1968 'Is anthropology alive? Social responsibility in social anthropology', *Current Anthropology*, 9: 391–6.

1973 'The social responsibility of the anthropologist', in T. Weaver (ed.), *To see ourselves: anthropology and modern social issues*, Glenview: Scott Foresman, pp. 8–10.

Bertalanffy, L. von 1951 'Problems of general systems theory', *Human Biology*, 23: 301–12.

Biebuyck, D. 1973 *The Lega: art, initiation and moral philosophy*, Berkeley: University of California Press.

Binford, L. 1979 'Organisation and formation processes: looking at curated technologies', *Journal of Anthropological Research*, 35: 255–73.

Blau, P. 1964 *Exchange and power in social life*, New York: Wiley.

Bloch, M. 1983 *Marxism and anthropology: the history of a relationship*, Oxford: Clarendon.

Boas, F. 1887 'Museums of ethnology and their classification', *Science*, 9: 587–9.

1940a 'The limitations of the comparative method of anthropology', in F. Boas, *Race, language and culture*, New York: Macmillan, pp. 270–80.

1940b 'The study of geography', in F. Boas, *Race, language and culture*, New York: Macmillan, pp. 639–47.

1966 *Kwaliutl ethnography*, ed. H. Codere, Chicago: University of Chicago Press.

Bohannan, P. 1963 *Social Anthropology*, New York: Holt Rinehart.

Borgerhoff Mulder, M. 1987 'Adaptation and evolutionary approaches to anthropology', *Man*, NS, 22: 25–41.

Bourdieu, P. 1977 *Outline of a Theory of Practice*, trans. R. Nice, Cambridge: Cambridge University Press.

Briggs, J. L. 1970 *Never in anger: portrait of an eskimo family*, Cambridge, Mass.: Harvard University Press.

Brown, J. L. 1964 'The evolution of diversity in avian territorial systems', *Wilson Bulletin*, 76: 160–9.

Buckley, W. 1967 *Sociology and modern systems theory*, Englewood Cliffs, New Jersey: Prentice-Hall.

Burnham, P. 1979 'Spatial mobility and political centralisation in pastoral societies', in *Equipe Ecologique* (ed.), *Pastoral production and society*, Cambridge: Cambridge University Press, pp. 349–60.

Burrow, J. W. 1981 *A liberal descent: Victorian historians and the English past*, Cambridge: Cambridge University Press.

Campbell, J. K. 1964 *Honour, family and patronage*, London: Oxford University Press.

Caplan, P. 1993 'Socialism from above in Tanzania: the view from below', in C. Hann (ed.), *Socialism: Ideas, ideologies and local practice*, London: Routledge, pp. 77–91.

Carrithers, M. 1992 *Why humans have cultures: explaining anthropology and social diversity*, Oxford: Oxford University Press.

Cashdan, E. 1980 'Egalitarianism among hunters and gatherers', *American Anthropologist*, 82: 116–20.

1983 'Territoriality among human foragers: ecological models and an application to four bushman groups', *Current Anthropology*, 24: 47–66.

Chagnon, N. 1968 *Yanomamö, the fierce people*, New York: Holt, Rinehart and Winston.

1982 'Sociodemographic attributes of nepotism in tribal populations: man the rule-breaker', in King's College Sociobiology Group (eds.), *Current problems in sociobiology*, Cambridge: Cambridge University Press, pp. 291–318.

Clark, R. C. 1979 *The Japanese company*, Tokyo: C. E. Tuttle.

Clifford, J. 1986 'Introduction', in J. Clifford and G. Marcus (eds.), *Writing culture: the poetics and politics of ethnography*, Berkeley: University of California Press, pp. 1–26.

1988 *The predicament of culture: twentieth-century ethnography, literature and art*, Cambridge, Mass.: Harvard University Press.

Crapanzano, V. 1986 'Hermes' dilemma: the masking of subversion in ethnographic description', in J. Clifford and G. E. Marcus (eds.), *Writing culture: the poetics and politics of ethnography*, Berkeley: University of California Press, pp. 51–76.

D'Andrade, R. 1995 *The development of cognitive anthropology*, Cambridge: Cambridge University Press.

Dawkins, R. 1980 'Good strategy or evolutionarily stable strategy?' in G. W. Barlow and J. Silverberg (eds.), *Socio-biology: beyond nature/nurture*, Boulder: Westview, pp. 331–67.

Derrida, J. 1976 *Of grammatology*, trans. G. C. Spivak, Baltimore: Johns Hopkins University Press.

1978 *Writing and difference*, trans. A. Bass, London: Routledge.

Dinham, B. and Hines, C. 1983 *Agribusiness in Africa*, London: Earth Resources Research.

Douglas, M. 1966 *Purity and danger*, London: Routledge.

Douglas, M. and Isherwood, B. 1979 *The world of goods: towards an anthropology of consumption*, London: Alan Lane.

Drucker, P. and Heizer, R. F. 1967 *To make my name good: a re-examination of the southern Kwakiutl potlatch*, Berkeley: University of California Press.

Duffield, M. 1981 *Maiurno: capitalism and rural life in Sudan*, London: Ithica Press, Sudan Studies No. 5.

Dunbar, R. 1993 'Coevolution of neocortical size, group size and language in humans', *Behavioural and Brain Sciences Evolution*, 16: 681–735.

Durham, W. H. 1991 *Coevolution: genes culture and human diversity*, Stanford, Calif.: Stanford University Press.

Durkheim, E. 1915 *The elementary forms of the religious life*, trans. J. W. Swain, London: Unwin.

1933 *The division of labour in society*, trans. G. Simpson, London: Macmillan.

1938 *The rules of sociological method*, trans. S. A. Solovay and J. H. Mueller, London: Macmillan.

Durkheim, E. and Mauss, M. 1963 *Primitive classification*, trans. Rodney Needham, London: Cohen and West.

Dwyer, P. D. 1985 'A hunt in New Guinea: some difficulties for optimal foraging theory', *Man*, 20: 243–53.

Dyson-Hudson, R. and Smith, E. A. 1978 'Human territoriality: an ecological reassessment', *American Anthropologist*, 80: 21–41.

Eco, U. 1990 *The limits of interpretation*, Bloomington: Indiana University Press.

Elliott, C. M. 1974 'Agriculture and economic development in Africa: theory and experience 1880–1914', in E. L. Jones and S. J. Woolf (eds.), *Agrarian change and economic development: the historical problems*, London: Methuen, pp. 123–50.

Endicott, K. 1979 *Batek negrito religion: the world view and rituals of a hunting and gathering people*, Oxford: Clarendon.

1988 'Property, power and conflict among the Batek of Malaysia', in T. Ingold, D. Riches and J. Woodburn (eds.), *Hunters and gatherers: property, power and ideology*, London: Berg, pp. 110–27.

Epstein, A. L. 1958 *Politics in an urban African community*, Manchester: Manchester University Press, for the Rhodes-Livingstone Institute.

Erasmus, C. J. 1955 'Culture, structure and process: the occurrence and disappearance of reciprocal farm labour', *Southwestern Journal of Anthropology*, 12: 444–69.

Evans-Pritchard, E. E. 1940a *The Nuer*, Oxford: Clarendon.

1940b 'The Nuer of the southern Sudan', in M. Fortes and E. E. Evans-Pritchard (eds.), *African political systems*, pp 272–96.

1950a 'Kinship and the local community among the Nuer', in A. R. Radcliffe-Brown and D. Forde (eds.), *African systems of kinship and marriage*, pp. 360–91.

1950b 'Anthropology and history', *Man*, 1950: 118–24.

1951 *Kinship and marriage among the Nuer*, Oxford: Clarendon.

1976 *Witchcraft, oracles and magic among the Azande*, Oxford: Clarendon.

Feit, H. 1983 'Negotiating recognition of aboriginal rights: history, strategies and reactions to the James Bay and Northern Quebec agreement', in N. Peterson and M. Langton (eds.), *Aborigines, land and land rights*, Canberra: Australian Institute of Aboriginal Studies, pp. 416–38.

Fichter, J. H. 1957 *Sociology*, Chicago: University of Chicago Press.

Firth, R. 1929 *Primitive economics of the New Zealand Maori*, London: Routledge.

1936 *We, the Tikopea: a sociological study of kinship in primitive Polynesia*, London: Unwin.

1939 *Primitive Polynesian economy*, London: Routledge.

1954 'Social organisation and social change', *Journal of the Royal Anthropological Institute*, 84: 1–20.

1955 'Some principles of social organisation', *Journal of the Royal Anthropological Institute*, 85: 1–18.

Fortes, M. 1940 'The political system of the Tallensi of the northern territories of the Gold Coast', in M. Fortes and E. E. Evans-Pritchard (eds.), *African political systems*, pp. 239–71.

1945 *The dynamics of clanship among the Tallensi*, London: Oxford University Press for the International African Institute.

1949a 'Time and the social structure: an Ashanti case study', in M. Fortes (ed.), *Social structure: studies presented to A. R. Radcliffe-Brown*, Oxford: Clarendon, reprinted in M. Fortes, 1970, *Time and the social structure, and other essays*, London: Athlone, pp. 1–32.

1949b *The web of kinship among the Tallensi*, London: Oxford University Press for the International African Institute.

1950 'Kinship and marriage among the Ashanti', in A. R. Radcliffe-Brown and D. Forde (eds.), *African systems of kinship and marriage*, pp. 252–84.

Fortes, M. and E. E. Evans-Pritchard (eds.) 1940 *African political systems*, London: Oxford University Press for the International African Institute.

Foucault, M. 1972 *The archaeology of knowledge*, trans. A. M. Sheridan Smith, London: Tavistock.

Fox, R. G. 1971 *Kin, clan, raja and rule*, Berkeley: University of California Press.

Frake, C. O. 1961 'The diagnosis of disease among the Subanam of Mindanao', *American Anthropologist*, 63: 113–32.

Friedman, J. 1975 'Tribes, states and transformations', in M. Bloch (ed.), *Marxist Analyses and social anthropology*, London: Malaby, pp. 161–202.

Ganesh, K. 1993 'Breaching the wall of difference: fieldwork and a personal journey to Srivaikuntam, Tamil Nadu', in D. Bell, P. Caplan and W. J. Karim (eds.), *Gendered fields: women, men and ethnography*, London: Routledge, pp. 128–42.

Garfield, V. and Wingert, P. S. 1966 *The Tsimshian Indians and their arts*, Seattle: University of Washington Press.

Geertz, C. 1973a 'Thick description: towards an interpretive theory of culture', in C. Geertz, *The interpretation of culture*, London: Hutchinson, pp. 3–30.

1973b 'Deep play: notes on the Balinese cockfight', in C. Geertz, *The interpretation of culture*, London: Hutchinson, pp. 412–53.

1988 *Works and lives: the anthropologist as author*, Stanford, Calif.: Stanford University Press.

Gennep, A. van 1960 *The rites of passage*, trans. M. B. Vizedom and G. L. Caffee, London: Routledge.

Giddens, A. 1979 *Central problems in social theory: action, structure and contradiction in social analysis*, London: Macmillan.

Glickman, M. 1971 'Kinship and credit among the Nuer', *Africa*, 41: 306–19.

Gluckman, M. 1955 *The judicial process among the Barotze of northern Rhodesia*, Manchester: Manchester University Press for the Rhodes-Livingstone Institute.

1970 *Custom and conflict in Africa*, Oxford: Blackwell.

Godelier, M. 1972 *Rationality and irrationality in economics*, trans. Brian Pearce, New York: Monthly Review Press.

1974 'On the definition of a social formation: the example of the Incas', *Critique of Anthropology*, 1: 63–73.

1975 'Modes of production, kinship and demographic structures', in M. Bloch (ed.), *Marxist analyses and social anthropology*, London: Malaby, pp. 3–27.

1977 *Perspectives in Marxist anthropology*, Cambridge: Cambridge University Press.

Goldschmidt, W. 1979, 'A general model for pastoral social systems', in *Equipe Ecologique* (ed.), *Pastoral production and society*, Cambridge: Cambridge University Press, pp. 15–28.

Gombrich, E. 1960 *Art and illusion*, London: Phaidon.

Goodenough, W. H. 1965 'Rethinking "status" and "role": toward a general model of the cultural organisation of social relationships', in M. Banton (ed.), *The relevance of models for social anthropology*, London: Tavistock.

Goody, J. 1977 *The domestication of the savage mind*, Cambridge: Cambridge University Press.

1983 *The development of the family and marriage in Europe*, Cambridge: Cambridge University Press.

1987 *The interface between the oral and the written*, Cambridge: Cambridge University Press.

Gould, J. 1989 *Herodotus*, London: Weidenfeld and Nicolson.

Gower, B. 1997 *Scientific method: an historical and philosophical introduction*, London: Routledge.

Grillo, R. 1985 'Applied anthropology in the 1980s: retrospect and prospect', in R. Grillo and A. Rew (eds.), *Social anthropology and development policy*, London: Tavistock, pp. 1–36.

1991 'Paper presented at the 1991 conference of the Association of Social Anthropologists'. A revised version is published as Grillo 1993.

1993 'The construct of "Africa" in "African Socialism"', in C. Hann (ed.), *Socialism: ideals, ideologies and local practices*, London: Routledge, pp. 59–76.

Hames, R. B. and Vickers, W. 1982 'Optimal diet breadth theory as a model to explain variability in Amazonian hunting', *American Ethnologist*, 9: 359–78.

Hamilton, W. D. 1964 'The evolution of social behaviour', *Journal of Theoretical Biology*, 12: 1–52.

Harako, R. 1981 'The cultural ecology of hunting behaviour among Mbuti pygmies', in R. V. O. Harding and G. Teleki (eds.), *Omnivorous primates: gathering and hunting in human evolution*, New York: Columbia University Press, pp. 499–555.

Harris, M. 1979 *Cultural materialism: the struggle for a science of culture*, New York: Random House.

Hart, C. W. W. and Pilling, A. 1966 *The Tiwi of north Australia*, New York: Holt, Rinehart and Winston.

Hawkes, K., Hill, K. and O'Connell, J. F. 1982 'Why hunters gather: optimal foraging and the Ache of eastern Paraguay', *American Ethnologist*, 9: 379–98.

Hedeager, L. 1992 *Iron Age societies: from tribe to state in northern Europe, 500BC to AD700*, Oxford: Blackwell.

Herodotus 1954 *The Histories*, trans. A. de Selincourt, Harmondsworth: Penguin.

Hertz, R. 1960 *The pre-eminence of the right hand*, trans. R. and C. Needham, London: Cohen and West.

Hill, C. 1958 *Puritanism and revolution*, London: Secker and Warburg.

Hobbes, T. 1970 *Leviathan, or the matter, form, and power of a commonwealth, ecclesiastical and civil*, London: Dent.

Hobsbawm, E. J. 1964, 'Introduction', in K. Marx, *Pre-capitalist economic formations*, pp. 9–65.

Hymes, D. 1974 'The uses of anthropology: critical, political, personal', in D. Hymes (ed.), *Reinventing anthropology*, New York: Random House, pp. 3–79.

Irons, W. 1979 'Investment and primary social dyads', in N. Chagnon and W. Irons (eds.), *Evolutionary biology and human social behaviour*, North Scituate, Mass.: Duxbury, pp. 181–213.

Jakobson, R. and Halle, M. 1956 *Fundamentals of language*, 'S-Gravenhage: Mouton.

Jones, R. 1980 'Hunters in the Australian coastal savanna', in D. R. Harris (ed.), *Human ecology in Savanna environments*, London: Academic Press, pp. 107–46.

Jones, R. and Meehan, B. 1989 'Plant foods of the Gidjingali: ethnographic and archaeological perspectives from northern Australia on tuber and seed exploitation', in D. Harris and G. Hillman (eds.), *Foraging and farming: the evolution of plant exploitation*, London: Unwin, pp. 120–35.

Kaberry, P. 1957 'Myth and ritual: some recent theories', *Bulletin of the Institute of Classical Studies, University of London*, 4: 42–54.

Kaplan, H. and Hill, K. 1985 'Food sharing among Ache foragers: tests of explanatory hypotheses', *Current Anthropology*, 26: 223–46.

Keen, I. 1982 'How some Murngin men marry ten wives', *Man*, 17: 620–42.

1994 *Knowledge and secrecy in an Aboriginal religion*, Oxford: Clarendon.

Kenyatta, J. 1968 *Suffering without bitterness*, Nairobi: East African Publishing House.

Krebs, J. R. and Davis, N. B. 1984 *Behavioural ecology: an evolutionary approach*, second edition, Oxford: Blackwell.

Kuper, A. 1983 *Anthropology and anthropologists: the modern British School*, London: Routledge.

1988 *The invention of primitive society: transformations of an illusion*, second edition, London: Routledge.

Lawrence, W. E. and Murdock, G. P. 1949 'Murngin social organisation', *American Anthropologist*, 51: 58–65.

Layton, R. 1986 'Political and territorial structures among hunter-gatherers', *Man*, 21: 18–33.

1989a 'Are sociobiology and social anthropology compatible? The significance of sociocultural resources in human evolution', in V. Standen and R. Foley (eds.), *Comparative socioecology: the behavioural ecology of mammals and man*, Oxford: Blackwell, pp. 433–55.

1989b 'Introduction', in R. Layton (ed.), *Conflict in the archaeology of living traditions*, London: Unwin, pp. 1–21.

Layton, R., Foley, R. and Williams, E. 1991 'The transition between hunting and gathering and the specialized husbandry of resources', *Current Anthropology*, 32: 255–74.

Leach, E. R. 1954 *Political systems of highland Burma*, London: Athlone.

1961a 'Rethinking anthropology', in E. R. Leach, *Rethinking anthropology*, London: Athlone, pp. 1–27.

1961b 'The structural implications of cross-cousin marriage', in E. R. Leach, *Rethinking anthropology*, London: Athlone, pp. 54–104.

1976 *Culture and communication: the logic by which symbols are connected. An introduction to the use of structuralist analysis in social anthropology*, Cambridge: Cambridge University Press.

Lee, R.B. 1968 'What hunters do for a living, or How to make out on scarce resources', in R. B. Lee and I. DeVore (eds.), *Man the hunter*, Chicago: Aldine, pp. 30–48.

1979 *The !Kung San: men, women and work in a foraging society*, Cambridge: Cambridge University Press.

Lefébure, C. 1979 'Introduction', in Equipe écologie et anthropologie des sociétés pastorales (eds.), *Pastoral production and society*, Cambridge: Cambridge University Press, pp. 1–14.

Lévi-Strauss, C. 1952 'Social structure', in A. L. Kroeber (ed.), *Anthropology today*, Chicago: Chicago University Press, pp. 524–53.

1960 *Entretiens avec Claude Lévi-Strauss*, ed. G. Charbonnier, Paris: Plon.

1963 *Structural anthropology*, trans. C. Jacobson and B. G. Schoepf, New York: Basic Books (since republished as *Structural anthropology I*).

1966 *The savage mind*, trans. anon., London: Weidenfeld and Nicolson.

1969 *The elementary structures of kinship*, trans. J. H. Bell and J. R. von Sturmer, London: Eyre and Spottiswoode.

1970 *The raw and the cooked: introduction to a science of mythology*, London: Cape.

1973 *From honey to ashes*, trans J. and D. Weightman, London: Cape.

Linton, R. 1936 *The study of man*, New York: Appleton-Century-Crofts.

Lounsbury, F. G. 1964 'A formal account of the Crow- and Omaha-type kinship terminologies', in W. H. Goodenough (ed.), *Explorations in cultural anthropology*, New York: McGraw-Hill, pp. 351–93.

Lukes, S. 1973 *Emile Durkheim, his life and work: a historical and critical study*, Harmondsworth: Penguin.

MacDougall, H. A. 1982 *Racial myth in English history*, London: University Press of New England.

Malinowski, B. 1922 *Argonauts of the Western Pacific: an account of native enterprise and adventure in the archipelagoes of Melanesian New Guinea*, London: Routledge.

1929 *The sexual life of savages*, London: Routledge.

1947 *Freedom and civilisation*, London: Unwin.

1954 *Magic, science and religion*, New York: Doubleday.

1967 *A diary in the strict sense of the term*, London: Routledge.

Marshall, L. 1976 'Sharing, talking and giving: relief of social tensions among the !Kung', in R. B. Lee and I. DeVore (eds.), *Kalahari hunter-gatherers: studies of the !Kung San and their neighbours*, Cambridge, Mass.: Harvard University Press, pp. 350–71.

Marx, K. 1930 *Capital (volume 1)*, trans. E. and C. Paul, London: Dent.

1964 *Pre-capitalist economic formations*, trans. J. Cohen, New York: International Publishers.

1971 *A contribution to the critique of political economy*, trans. S. W. Ryazanskaya, New York: International Publishers.

1973 *Grundrisse*, trans. M. Nickolaus, Harmondsworth: Penguin.

Marx, K. and Engels, F. 1967 *The communist manifesto*, trans. S. Moore, Harmondsworth: Penguin.

1970 *The German ideology (part one)*, trans. W. Lough, C. Dutt and C. P. Magill, London: Lawrence and Wishart.

Mauss, M. 1965 *The gift: forms and functions of exchange in archaic societies*, trans. I. Cunnison, London: Cohen and West.

Mayer, A. 1966 'The significance of quasi-groups in the study of complex societies', in M. Banton (ed.), *The social anthropology of complex societies*, London: Tavistock, pp. 97–122.

Maynard Smith, J. 1982 *Evolution and the theory of games*, Cambridge: Cambridge University Press.

McCarthy, F. and McArthur, M. 1960 'The food quest and the time factor in Aboriginal economic life', in C. P. Mountford (ed.), *Records of the Australian-American Scientific Expedition to Arnhem Land, vol. 2: anthropology and nutrition*, Melbourne: Melbourne University Press.

McLeod, M. 1981 'The Ashanti', London: British Museum Publications.

Mead, M. 1928 *Coming of age in Samoa*, London: Cape.

Meillassoux, C. 1964 *L'Anthropologie économique des Gouro de Côte d'Ivoire*, Paris: Mouton.

Moore, H. 1986 *Space, text and gender: an anthropological study of the Marakwet of Kenya*, Cambridge: Cambridge University Press.

Morphy, H. 1978 'Rights in paintings and rights in women: a consideration of the basic problems posed by the asymmetry of the Murngin system', *Mankind*, 11(3): 208–19.

1984 *Journey to the crocodile's nest*, Canberra: Aboriginal Studies Press.

1991 *Ancestral connections: art and an Aboriginal system of knowledge*, Chicago: Chicago University Press.

Murphy, R. F. 1977 'Introduction: the anthropological theories of Julian H. Steward', in J. C. Steward and R. F. Murphy (eds.), *Evolution and ecology: essays on social transformation*, Urbana: University of Illinois Press, pp. 1–39.

Myers, F. 1986 'Always ask: resource use and land ownership among Pintupi Aborigines of the Australian Western Desert', in N. Williams and E. Hunn (eds.), *Resource managers: North American and Australian hunter-gatherers*, Canberra: Aboriginal Studies Press, pp. 173–96.

1988 'Burning the truck and holding the country: time and the negotiation of identity among Pintupi Aborigines', in T. Ingold, D. Riches and J. Woodburn (eds.), *Hunters and gatherers: property, power and ideology*, Oxford: Berg, pp. 52–74.

Narayan, K. 1993 'On nose cutters, gurus and story tellers', in R. Rosaldo, S. Lavie and K. Narayan (eds.), *Creativity/Anthropology*, Ithaca: Cornell University Press, pp. 30–53.

Needham, R. 1963 'Introduction', in E. Durkheim and M. Mauss, *Primitive Classification*, pp. vii–xlvii.

1974 *Remarks and inventions: skeptical essays about kinship*, London: Tavistock.

Neumann, J. von and Morgenstern, O. 1953 *Theory of games and economic behaviour*, Princeton, N. J.: Princeton University Press.

O'Connell, J. and Hawkes, K. 1981 'Alyawara plant use and optimal foraging theory', in B. Winterhalder and E. A. Smith (eds.), *Hunter-gatherer foraging strategies: ethnographic and archaeological analyses*, Chicago: University of Chicago Press, pp. 99–125.

Odling-Smee, J. 1995 'Biological evolution and cultural change', in E. Jones and V. Reynolds (eds.), *Survival and religion: biological evolution and cultural change*, New York: Wiley, pp. 1–43.

O'Hanlon, M. 1989 *Reading the skin: adornment, display and society among the Wahgi*, London: British Museum Publications.

1995 'Modernity and the "graphicalization" of meaning: New Guinea Highland shield design in historical perspective', *Journal of the Royal Anthropological Institute*, NS, 1: 469–93.

Ong, W. 1982 *Orality and literacy: the technologising of the world*, London: Methuen.

Ostrom, E. 1990 *Governing the commons: the evolution of institutions for collective action*, Cambridge: Cambridge University Press.

Panter-Brick, C. 1993 'Seasonal organisation of work patterns', in S. J. Ulijaszek and S. S. Strickland (eds.), *Seasonality and human ecology*, Cambridge: Cambridge University Press, pp. 220–34.

Parry, J. P. 1979 *Caste and kinship in Kangra*, London: Routledge.

Pinker, S. 1994 *The language instinct*, New York: William Morrow.

Polanyi, K. 1945 *Origins of our time: the great transformation*, Gollancz (first edition 1944, New York: Holt, Rinehart and Winston; page references are to the British edition, Gollancz).

1957 'The economy as instituted process', in K. Polanyi, C. M. Arensberg and H. W. Pearson (eds.), *Trade and market in the early empires*, New York: Free Press, pp. 243–70.

Pospisil, L. 1963 *Kapauku Papuan economy*, Newhaven: Yale University Press.

Puttnam, H. 1995 *Pragmatism, an open question*, Oxford: Blackwell.

Quine, W. V. O. 1960 *Word and object*, Cambridge, Mass.: MIT Press.

Rabinow, P. 1977 *Reflections on fieldwork in Morocco*, Berkeley: University of California Press.

Radcliffe-Brown, A. R. 1930–1 'The social organisation of Australian tribes', *Oceania*, 1: 34–63, 206–46, 322–41, 426–56.

1940a 'On social structure', *Journal of the Royal Anthropological Institute*, 70; reprinted in Radcliffe-Brown 1952, pp. 188–204.

1940b 'Preface', in M. Fortes and E. E. Evans-Pritchard (eds.), *African political systems*, pp. xi–xxiii.

1950 'Introduction', in A. R. Radcliffe-Brown and D. Forde (eds.), *African systems of kinship and marriage*, pp. 1–85.

1951 'Murngin social organisation', *American Anthropologist*, 53: 37–55.

1952 *Structure and function in primitive society*, London: Cohen and West.

Radcliffe-Brown, A. R. and Forde, D. (eds.), 1950 *African systems of kinship and marriage*, London: Oxford University Press for the International African Institute.

Raharijoana, V. 1989 'Archaeology and oral traditions in the Mitongoa-Andrainjato area (Betsileo region of Madagascar)', in R. Layton (ed.), *Who needs the past: indigenous values and archaeology*, London: Unwin, pp. 189–94.

Reid, J., Kerle, J. and Norton, S. (eds.), 1993 *Uḻuru fauna: the distribution and abundance of vertebrate fauna of Uḻuru (Ayers Rock-Mount Olga) National Park*, Canberra: Australian National Parks Service.

Reynolds, H. 1982 *The other side of the frontier: Aboriginal resistance to the European invasion of Australia*, Melbourne: Penguin.

Richardson, A. 1986 'The control of productive resources on the Northwest coast of North America', in N. Williams and E. Hunn (eds.), *Resource managers: North American and Australian hunter-gatherers*, Canberra: Aboriginal Studies Press, pp. 93–112.

Ricoeur, P. 1979 'The model of the text: meaningful action considered as a text', in P. Rabinow and W. M. Sullivan (eds.), *Interpretive social science, a reader*, Berkeley: University of California Press, pp. 73–101.

Ridley, M. 1996 *The origins of virtue*, London: Viking.

Robertson, J. 1985 *Future work: jobs, self-employment and leisure after the industrial age*, Aldershot: Gower/Temple Smith.

Rogers, E. S. and Black, M. B. 1976 'Subsistence strategy in the fish and hare period, northern Ontario: the Weagamow Ojibwa, 1880–1920', *Journal of Anthropological Research*, 32: 1–43.

Rosaldo, R. 1986 'From the door of his tent: the fieldworker and the inquisitor', in J. Clifford and G. E. Marcus (eds.), *Writing culture: the poetics and politics of ethnography*, Berkeley: University of California Press, pp. 77–97.

Rosman, A. and Ruebel, P. 1971 *Feasting with mine enemy: rank and exchange among Northwest Coast societies*, New York: Columbia University Press.

Ross, E. B. 1980 'Patterns of diet and forces of production: an economic and ecological history of the ascendancy of beef in the United States', in E. B. Ross (ed.), *Beyond the myths of culture: essays in cultural materialism*, New York: Academic Press.

Rousseau, J. J. 1963 *The social contract and discourses*, ed. G. D. H. Cole, London: Dent.

Rowlands 1979 'Local and long distance trade and incipient state formation on the Bamenda plateau in the late 19th Century', *Paideuma*, 25: 1–19.

Safa, H. I. 1974 *The urban poor of Puerto Rico*, New York: Holt Rinehart.

Sahlins, M. 1963 'Poor man, big-man, rich man, chief: political types in Melanesia and Polynesia', *Comparative studies in society and history*, 5: 285–303.

1974 *Stone age economics*, London: Tavistock.

1976a *Culture and Practical Reason*, Chicago: University of Chicago Press.

1976b *The use and abuse of biology: an anthropological critique of socio-biology*, Ann Arbor, Michigan: University of Michigan Press.

1985 *Islands of History*, Chicago: Chicago University Press.

Said, E. 1978 *Orientalism*, London: Routledge.

Sanderson, S. K. 1990 *Social evolutionism, a critical history*, Oxford: Blackwell.

Sarup, M. 1989 *An introductory guide to post-structuralism and postmodernism*, Athens: University of Georgia Press.

Saussure, F. de 1959 *Course in general linguistics*, trans. C. Bally and A. Sechehaye, London: Owen.

Schutz, A. 1972 *The phenomenology of the social world*, trans. G. Walsh and F. Lehnert, London: Heinemann.

Scott, J. 1976 *The moral economy of the peasant: rebellion and subsistence in Southeast Asia*, New Haven: Yale University Press.

Searle, J. R. 1969 *Speech acts: an essay in the philosophy of language*, Cambridge: Cambridge University Press.

Seligman, C. G. 1910 *The Melanesians of British New Guinea*, Cambridge: Cambridge University Press.

Service, E. R. 1962 *Primitive social organisation: an evolutionary perspective*, New York: Random House.

Sherman, P. 1980 'The limits of ground squirrel nepotism', in G. B. Barlow and J. Silverberg (eds.), *Sociobiology: beyond nature/nurture*, Boulder, Colorado: Westview, pp. 505–44.

Smith, A. 1976 [1776] *An enquiry into the nature and causes of the wealth of nations*, Oxford: Clarendon.

Smith, E. A. 1983 'Anthropological applications of optimal foraging theory: a critical review', *Current Anthropology*, 24: 625–51.

1988 'Risk and uncertainty in the "original affluent society": evolutionary ecology of resource-sharing and land tenure', in T. Ingold, D. Riches and J. Woodburn (eds.), *Hunters and gatherers: history, evolution and social change*, London: Berg, pp. 222–51.

1991 *Inujjuamiut foraging strategies: evolutionary ecology of an arctic hunting economy*, New York: Aldine de Gruyter.

Spencer, B. and Gillen, F. J. 1899 *The native tribes of central Australia*, London: Macmillan.

Spencer, H. 1972 *Herbert Spencer on social evolution: selected writings*, ed. J. D. Y. Peel, Chicago: University of Chicago Press.

Spencer, P. 1965 *The Samburu: a study of gerontocracy in a nomadic tribe*, London: Routledge.

1973 *Nomads in alliance: symbiosis and growth among the Rendille and Samburu of Kenya*, London: Oxford University Press.

Steward, J. H. 1936 'The economic and social basis of primitive bands', in R. H. Lowie (ed.), *Essays on anthropology in honour of Alfred Louis Kroeber*, Berkeley: University of California Press, pp. 311–50.

1938 *Basin-Plateau Aboriginal sociopolitical groups*, Bureau of American Ethnology, Bulletin 120, Washington: Smithsonian Institution.

1977a 'Evolutionary principles and social types', in J. H. Steward, *Evolution and ecology: essays on social transformation*, ed. J. C. Steward and R. F. Murphy, Urbana: University of Illinois Press, pp. 68–86.

1977b 'The evolution of prefarming societies', in J. H. Steward, *Evolution and ecology: essays on social transformation*, ed. J. C. Steward and R. F. Murphy, Urbana: University of Illinois Press, pp. 103–27.

1977c 'The foundations of Basin-Plateau Shoshonean society', in J. H. Steward, *Evolution and ecology: essays on social transformation*, ed. J. C. Steward and R. F. Murphy, Urbana: University of Illinois Press, pp. 366–406.

Stocking, G. W. 1982 'Introduction: the basic assumptions of Boasian anthropology', in G. W. Stocking (ed.), *A Franz Boas reader*, Chicago: University of Chicago Press, pp. 1–20.

1986 'Essays on culture and personality', in G. W. Stocking (ed.), *Malinowski, Rivers, Benedict and others: essays on culture and personality*, Madison: University of Wisconsin Press, pp. 3–12.

Strehlow, C. 1907–20 *Die Aranda- und Loritja-stämme in zentral Australien*, published in five parts, Frankfurt: Veröffentlichungen des Frankfurter Museums für Volkerkunde.

Tacitus, C. 1985 *The Agricola and the Germania*, trans. H. Mattingly and S. A. Handford, Harmondsworth: Penguin.

Terray, E. 1972 *Marxism and 'primitive' societies*, trans. M. Klopper, New York: Monthly Review Press.

Tertre, J. B. du 1992 'Jean Baptiste du Tertre and the Noble Savages', in P. Hulme and N. Whitehead (eds.), *Wild majesty*, Oxford: Clarendon, pp. 128–37.

Trigger, B. 1989 *A history of archaeological thought*, Cambridge: Cambridge University Press.

Trivers, R. 1985 *Social evolution*, Menlo Park: Benjamin/Cummins.

Turnbull, C. 1965 *Wayward servants: the two worlds of the African pygmies*, Westport: Greenwood.

Turner, V. W. 1990 'Are there any universals of performance in myth, ritual and drama?' in R. Schechner and W. Appel (eds.), *By means of performance: intercultural studies of theatre and ritual*, Cambridge: Cambridge University Press, pp. 8–13.

Twagiramutara, P. 1989 'Archaeological and anthropological hypotheses concerning the origin of ethnic divisions in sub-Saharan Africa', in R. Layton (ed.), *Conflict in the archaeology of living traditions*, London: Unwin, pp. 88–96.

Tylor, S. 1986 'Post-modern ethnography: from the document of the occult to occult document', in J. Clifford and G. E. Marcus (eds.), *Writing culture: the poetics and politics of ethnography*, Berkeley: University of California Press, pp. 122–40.

Verdon, M. 1982 'Where have all the lineages gone? Cattle and descent among the Nuer', *American Anthropologist*, 84: 566–79.

Waal, A. de 1989 *Famine that kills*, Oxford: Clarendon.

1994 'Genocide in Rwanda', *Anthropology Today*, 10: 1–2.

Waal, F. de 1982 *Chimpanzee politics: power and sex among apes*, Baltimore: Johns Hopkins University Press.

Warner, W. L. 1958 [1937] *A black civilisation*, New York: Harper and Row.

Watson, R. A. 1991 'What the new archaeology has accomplished', *Current Anthropology*, 32: 275–592.

Watson, W. 1958 *Tribal cohesion in a money economy*, Manchester: Manchester University Press.

Weber, M. 1930 *The Protestant Ethic and the Spirit of Capitalism*, trans. Talcott Parsons, London: Unwin.

1947 *The theory of social and economic organisation*, trans. A. R. Henderson and T. Parsons, London: Hedge and Co.

Weiner, A. 1976 *Women of value, men of renown: new perspectives in Trobriand exchange*, Austin: University of Texas Press.

White, I. 1981 'Mrs. Bates and Mr. Brown: an examination of Rodney Needham's allegations', *Oceania*, 52: 193–210.

White, L. A. 1943 'Energy and the evolution of culture', *American Anthropologist*, 45: 335–56.

1949 *The science of culture: a study of man and civilisation*, New York: Farrar, Straus and Giroux.

Whitehead, N. L. 1995 'The historical anthropology of text: the interpretation of Raleigh's *Discoverie of Guiana*', *Current Anthropology*, 36: 53–74.

Whorf, B. L. 1956 *Language, thought and reality: selected writings of Benjamin Lee Whorf*, ed. J. B. Carroll, New York: Wiley.

Wiessner, P. 1982 'Risk, reciprocity and social influences on !Kung San economics', in E. Leacock and R. Lee (eds.), *Politics and history in band societies*, Cambridge: Cambridge University Press, pp. 61–84.

Wilder, W. 1971 'Purum descent groups: some vagaries of method', in R. Needham (ed.), *Rethinking kinship and marriage*, London: Tavistock, pp. 203–18.

Wilkinson, G. 1984 'Reciprocal food sharing in the vampire bat', *Nature*, 308: 181–4.

Williams, N. and Baines, G. (eds.) 1993 *Traditional ecological knowledge; wisdom for sustainable development*, Canberra: Aboriginal Studies Press.

Winterhalder, B. 1981 'Foraging strategies in the Boreal forest: an analysis of Cree hunting and gathering', in B. Winterhalder and E. Alden Smith (eds.), *Hunter-gatherer foraging strategies: ethnographic and archaeological analyses*, Chicago: Chicago University Press, pp. 66–98.

Winterhalder, B. and Goland, C. 1993 'On population, foraging efficiency and plant domestication', *Current Anthropology*, 34: 710–15.

Wolf, E. 1982 *Europe and the people without history*, Berkeley: University of California Press.

Woodburn, J. 1968 'An introduction to Hadza ecology', in R. B. Lee and I. de Vore (eds.), *Man the hunter*, Chicago: Aldine, pp. 49–55.

1982 'Egalitarian societies', *Man*, 17: 431–51.

Worseley, P. 1956 'The kinship system of the Tallensi: a revaluation', *Journal of the Royal Anthropological Institute*, 86: 37–73.

Worth, S. and Adair, J. 1972 *Through Navajo eyes: an exploration in film communication and anthropology*, Bloomington: Indiana University Press.

Wouden, F. A. E. van 1968 [1935] *Types of social structure in Eastern Indonesia*, trans R. Needham, The Hague: Nijhoff.

Index